WHERE WE STAND

ALSO BY MICHAEL WOLFF

White Kids

WHERE WE STAND

Can America Make It in the Global Race for Wealth, Health, and Happiness?

BY

Michael Wolff

Peter Rutten & Albert F. Bayers III

and the World Rank Research Team

A MICHAEL WOLFF BOOK

BANTAM BOOKS   NEW YORK   TORONTO   LONDON   SYDNEY   AUCKLAND

DESIGNED BY
Christiaan Kuypers

MACINTOSH BY
Carter Burden III

ILLUSTRATIONS BY
Michael Bartalos & Daniel Carter

This book has been written and produced by
Michael Wolff & Company, Inc.
It has been wholly designed and produced
by means of desktop-publishing technology.
The text is set in the typefaces Bell Gothic,
Billy Bold, Bureau Grotesk 15,
New Baskerville, and Toronto Belvedere.
Billy Bold designed by Christiaan Kuypers

Library of Congress Cataloging-in-Publication Data

Wolff, Michael
Where we stand: can America make it in the global race for
wealth, health, and happiness/Michael Wolff and Peter Rutten,
Albert F. Bayers III and the World Rank research team.
p. cm.
ISBN 0-553-08199-5
1. Statistics. 2. Social indicators. 3. Economic indicators.
4. Quality of life—Statistics. I. Where We Stand. II. Title
HA155.W62 1992   91-43831
310—dc20   CIP

Bantam Books are published by Bantam Books, a division of Bantam
Doubleday Dell Publishing Group, Inc. Its trademark, consisting of the words
"Bantam Books" and the portrayal of a rooster, is registered in U.S. Patent
and Trademark Office and in other countries. Marca Registrada.
Bantam Books, 666 Fifth Avenue, New York, New York 10103.

PRINTED IN THE UNITED STATES OF AMERICA
0 9 8 7 6 5 4 3 2 1

Acknowledgments

This book grew out of continuing plans to launch a magazine in multilanguage versions in the U.S., Europe, and Japan. Such a medium and such an audience will surely define the next communications era. Meanwhile, this is the demographic profile of that one world audience.

Thanks are owed to our network of advisers, contributors, and supporters abroad: Paolo Lanapoppi in Venice; Luigi Bernabo in Milan; Christopher Sylvester at *Private Eye* in London; François Siégel, editor in chief of *VSD* in Paris; Colin Bowring at the research firm Serendipity in London; Jim Smith, formerly of WCRS in London and Della Femina McNamee in New York; Luca Formenton and Angelo Galli at Mondadori in Milan; and Ulrich Glatzer at Gruner & Jahr in Hamburg.

Our job was made immeasurably easier by the helpfulness and support of many other people at organizations around the globe: Dr. J. B. Brunet and Dr. J. Alex, European Center of Epidemiological Monitoring of AIDS (St. Moritz, France); Dr. D. M. Parken, International Agency for Research on Cancer (Lyons, France); J. P. Poullier, OECD Directorate for Social Affairs (Paris); Margot Gonzales, Canadian Consulate (New York); Janet Beacon, British Information Services (New York); Shi Raishi, Japanese Consulate (New York); Dieter Schulenburg, German Consulate (New York); Eila Laakso, Central Statistical Office of Finland (Helsinki); Matthew E. Brosius, OECD (Washington); James McGill, International Savings Bank Institute (Geneva); Will Werhane, International Survey Research Corporation; Debbie Leonard, National Consumer Council (London); Donna McLain, Reader's Digest Association; Rebecca Crawford, Union Bank of Switzerland; Judd Eberhart, Xerox Corporation; Patricia M. Sears, Population Crisis Committee; Irene Fu, MTV; Monica Gliva, National Association of Manufacturers; J. M. Johnson, National Science Foundation; Mardi Schmieder, Cray Research, Inc.; Loren T. McDonald, Arthur Andersen & Co.; and G. van Zessen, Nederlands Instituut voor Sociaal Sexuologisch Onderzoek (Amsterdam).

Appropriately for a visual book, this endeavor should rightly have movie-length credits. It has truly been a collaborative effort involving many people each of whom has made a distinctive and vital contribution.

Certainly this book would not have been possible without the talents, perseverance, and good humor of my colleagues Peter Rutten and Chip Bayers.

Christiaan Kuypers and Carter Burden guided and implemented our vision for clear and elegant graphics. Carter Burden pushed us to the technological precipice and then pulled us back too many times to count.

Michael Bartalos, who rendered the illustrations for the openers and, Daniel Carter, who illustrated the charts, have both lent the book a bit of their distinctive styles.

Eric Gelman counseled us on all aspects of the project and edited the manuscript with patience and care; the book is fairer, clearer, and smarter because of his contributions.

Matt Weingarden copy-edited the manuscript with skill and incredible speed.

This book would surely never have gotten off the ground without the support of Roger Black. Likewise, we owe Peter Kaplan a debt of gratitude for his generosity during the final days of *Smart*.

Peter Ginsberg, our agent at Curtis Brown, "got it" immediately and ran with it; his advice shaped what the book became.

Leslie Meredith at Bantam gave us the carte blanche to put on screen what was in our heads.

Alison Anthoine, our lawyer (and more), toughed it out for us.

Bill Grant, Larry Engel, and the rest of the "Made in America?" project at WGBH nagged us with too many questions—all of which improved the book.

Kristin Miller went down into the stacks and returned with amazing treasures.

Along the way, we were aided by Claudine Murphy at Bantam; Russell McGlinchey, who interned for us; Laurel de Guire, who put in hours on the Mac; and the technical support staff at Delta Point.

Aggy Aed was always there when we needed her.

And, only because she is always the last one to leave, finally, my thanks to the redoubtable and amazing Kelly Maloni, who started as our intern and rose to all occasions.

All mistakes, misjudgments, omissions, and bad calls are my own.

Michael Wolff
New York
January 20, 1992

Contents

"Lies, damned lies, and statistics..."
MARK TWAIN QUOTING DISRAELI

Se non è vero, è ben trovato
(If it's not true, it might as well be)

WHERE WE STAND

Whose century is it, anyway?

Competition is as American as a Chevrolet. Proving what we're made of is rooted in all of our traditions—from the frontier, to free enterprise, to the credo of individualism, to the workings of democracy, to the Super Bowl. Winning isn't everything, it's the only thing. Better dead than second. We believe that the best will prevail, and that having the best, being the best, guarantees more of the best.

We are fanatical about being number one. It is central to our American pride and identity.

Remember grammar school in the 1950s and '60s? Social-studies class? How our teachers (and parents and politicians and presidents) urged us to compare our lives in America with life everywhere else, "And be thankful." The possibility of not having been born an American was an odd and in some ways terrifying thought. The whole notion of a life outside of the affluent society was, well, foreign; the very words *standard of living—having* a standard of living—somehow separated us from them.

Then, too, our grandparents or parents had come from the old world. That was the past, America the future. No one was looking back.

There really was no contest. America fed more people, educated more people, housed more people—and did it in considerable *style,* too, at least compared with "conditions in the rest of the world," as we used to say.

The first half of the twentieth century that devastated Europe and Japan made America the richest, strongest, luckiest nation the world had ever known. It all came together—massive military force, industrial muscle, corporate leadership,

> "As I look at the countries that are chipping in here now, I think we do have a chance at a new world order."
> —*George Bush at a news conference, August 30, 1990*

> "The Japanese plan 10 years in advance; the Americans, 10 minutes in advance."
> —*Akio Morita, Sony Corporation chairman*

> "Why should we subsidize intellectual curiosity?"
> —*Ronald Reagan*

> "Whether you like it or not, history is on our side. We will bury you."
> —*Nikita Khrushchev*

> "America has to take some responsibility for what Japan is today—a country without mental independence, able to think only of economic ➤

2

plenty of capital, a consumer society, and a fairly healthy political system to boot—into what Henry Luce called the American Century.

It lasted 30 years or so.

In hindsight, it seems to have ended the first time we—or even more startlingly, our parents—bought a foreign car. ("What if they gave a war and no one fought it?" was the question for the 1960s. "What if they made a car and no one bought it?" is the question for our time.) Or maybe it was the first time Germany's Bundesbank raised its rates and forced the U.S. Federal Reserve to follow; or the moment the U.S. balance of trade, positive for nearly a hundred years, went into the sewer. It ended on a day when someone noticed that much of the industrial world was richer, freer, happier, healthier, and more optimistic than we were.

For many of us, there exists the unnerving possibility that our lives might be richer and better if our immigrant grandparents had stayed where they were born.

Of course, the renewal of Europe and Japan was exactly the intention of U.S. postwar policy. Europe and Japan would be rebuilt in the U.S. economic and social image—market economies and egalitarian societies—and become acquisitive trading partners and stable global neighbors. But we seem to have been quite unprepared for the success of our own plans. And so while we, unmindful, exhausted a good deal of our resources fighting the Cold War, our allies hunkered down to win the economic struggles of the future, making cars, not war. While the U.S. was determined not to become a soak-the-rich welfare state, Europe and Japan were tolerating painful tax rates and creating a highly educated work force. While the U.S. middle class was shrinking, Europe's and Japan's were growing. While our standard of living stagnated, theirs advanced. While our productivity growth stalled, theirs leapt ahead.

Indeed, the most profound global event of our time, the one that is shaping us and will shape our children, quite likely will be not the collapse of the USSR and the Eastern bloc but the rise of Japan and a unified Europe (with its 380 million consumers, its educated and skilled work force, and a GNP that has surpassed America's) as economic superpowers to rival the U.S.

prosperity. Japan ultimately became exactly what America wanted it to be after the war."
—*Shintaro Ishihara, author of* Japan That Can Say No

"The Japanese should have no concern with business."
—*Rudyard Kipling*

"We must build a kind of United States of Europe."
—*Winston Churchill*

"In our century America begins to realize that she is just one part of the world and not a world to herself."
—*C. G. Jung*

"I for one am fed up hearing from the Japanese, and I might say some Americans, too, that all our problems in this industry, all our problems, are our own damn fault. We do not have idiots running General Motors, Ford, and Chrysler, or our suppliers. And our workers are not lazy and stupid."
—*Lee Iacocca, chairman, Chrysler Corporation*

"When I go to Asia or Europe, I feel like ➤→

I'm looking at tomorrow. When I go to many U.S. cities, I see decay and neglect and I feel like I'm looking at yesterday."
—*H. Ross Perot*

"As part of the globalization of technology, a research director must become a multidimensional Renaissance man. In other words, I have to learn to eat raw fish."
—*George Hilmeier, chief technical officer, Texas Instruments*

"The state dinner was the final event of a frenetic meeting of economic superpowers that bore earmarks of the vanished Moscow-Washington summits: tense all-night negotiations, carefully barbed remarks at news conferences, artery-clogging doses of diplomatic pomp and proclamations of success."
—*New York Times account of President Bush's 1992 trade mission to Japan*

"Perhaps while jogging in Tokyo's Palace Gardens, Mr. President, you noticed that an ➡

And yet, for all the glumness in America—stuck in what is perhaps its deepest identity crisis since it emerged from world isolation more than half a century ago—this is a remarkable moment in history.

Not since the First World War has the playing field of nations had so many countries with similar economies, political systems, capital markets, technologies, and national aspirations. It is truer to say that the world is getting richer than that America is getting poorer. What's more, even with the threats of trade fortresses and trade wars, the trend is clearly toward breaking down barriers. The international economy has created itself faster than national pride and self-interest can restrain it. Information—and money—travel ahead of politicians and bureaucrats. More and more, governments play catch-up, sanctioning the webs of cross-border relationships and transactions that would be impossible to undo, anyway.

Surely, the same old struggle for dominance can be found in this new order—one nation seeking to best another. But the quest is no longer for geopolitical power, nor for the spread of a particular ideology, nor even really for dominance of world markets, but for standard of living: the ability of a nation to provide its citizens security, comfort, opportunity, progress, and dreams. Not only jobs but health care, education, political freedom, consumer choices, business opportunities, up-to-the-minute technologies, and ample leisure time.

Nations no longer fight for glory or God or motherland but for quality of life, a much more difficult and complicated quest. On this score, the U.S. maintains a clear advantage: It has lived with the great conflicts inherent in the affluent experience longer than anyone else (after all the millennia of scarcity, people can't cope with such affluence, Saul Bellow says).

Japan may attain unquestioned world economic dominance by the turn of the century, but the Japanese people are already demanding the fruits of their work. Can Japan have growth and enjoyment too? Indeed, we watch the Japanese, arrogant and gadget-crazy in their iron conformity—like we were in the 1950s—and we think, *We know what's coming for you.* We see the Europeans with their remarkable social welfare system that has produced a middle class like ours in the 1960s, and we think,

You'll have taxpayer revolts, too (backlashes in the U.K. and Sweden have already begun). We wonder what will happen as Europeans learn the corollary to wealth: that it attracts poverty. How will Europe handle its new distinction as the destination of choice for the world's tired and poor?

But the most profound force at work is entirely new: Information—a powerful idea, a workable solution, a quarterly report; the cascade of data from which this book is made— travels cheaply and instantaneously. We cannot help but compare ourselves with others—our social experiments, our technology (indeed, we are all selling to the same customers), our medicine. We know what works and what doesn't work, what's sensible and what's ridiculous. We are only a fax or CNN moment apart. There are no more border guards.

In a way, this is a picture book, a kind of *Family of Man*, except the images are formed by bits of information. In some cases the data, like a haunting photograph, seem to say it all: The U.S. in 1990 had a murder rate for young men ten to twenty times higher than that of any other industrial nation. Other data—for instance, the 39,000 sex-discrimination suits filed to date in the U.S. versus the single sex-discrimination suit filed in Japan— create a picture more akin to *Life*'s famous elephant perched on a chair.

The portraits here are made up of just the facts. They are assembled from virtually every international source: the United Nations in New York; the Organization of Economic Cooperation and Development in Paris; the International Monetary Fund in Washington; UNESCO in Paris; the Food and Agriculture Organization in Rome; the World Health Organization in Geneva—as well as Interpol; the CIA; the World Bank; the Vatican; statistical offices in the U.S., Europe, and Japan; academic, industry, and government studies; newspaper and magazine reports; public-opinion surveys; marketing analyses; and data bases galore.

The information is as revealing and as limited as the plain facts usually are. But the sheer volume of data—the camera peering around every corner, through every statistical peephole—creates a picture of national direction, priorities,

"It's a point well taken."
—Dan Quayle, in response to Japanese criticism of the United States' economic record (specifically the savings rate and the federal deficit) during trip to Japan in his capacity as head of the President's Council on Competitiveness

"The traditional destiny of nation-states is coming to an end in these last years of the twentieth century, however vital the role they have played in the progress of the world."
—Giovanni Agnelli, chairman, Fiat

"Individual freedoms ...have created an atmosphere of openness and ➠

sharing that has enabled our economic competitors to acquire our most important technology—and they are using it to defeat us, to lower our own standard of living, and to threaten our national security."
—Japan 2000, *C.I.A. report*

"On the average, the United States is lower [in skills] because of a considerable number of blacks, Puerto Ricans, and Mexicans."
—*Yasuhiro Nakasone, prime minister of Japan*

"The majority of those men are homosexual—perhaps not the majority—but in the USA there are already 25 percent of them and in England and Germany it is much the same. You cannot imagine it in the history of France."
—*Edith Cresson, prime minister of France*

"The world can be divided into those who live in the era of economics and those who cling to noneconomic, atavistic forces: religion, national or tribal passions, ➡➡

passions, brilliance, and, of course, eccentricities. We aim to show not only a nation's successes and failures but its character.

This book is also a tout sheet. One of its messages ought to be very clear: The world is a horse race—and there are winners and losers. Indeed, the reason for limiting our worldview mostly to what are sometimes called the Country Club nations—members of the Organization of Economic Cooperation and Development (OECD)—is that these are the nations that can realistically and fairly compete against one another. It is, for instance, not very surprising that only 1.3 women per 100,000 die of malnutrition in the U.S. versus ten times that many in Third World countries. It is, however, no small indictment that significantly more women die of malnutrition every year in America than in any other nation with comparable wealth and resources.

Where it is noteworthy, we have included some of the developing nations in our comparisons—the South Korean work week, for instance, is the longest in the world. Where appropriate, and where we have some faith in the accuracy of the data, we have included figures from the former Soviet Union and from the nations of Eastern Europe. All currency relationships have been rendered in dollars, based on International Monetary Fund annual currency tables. In most instances, the base year is 1990. In every case, we have searched for the latest available information.

At the close of each part of the book, we offer our own index. Based on all the foregoing rankings, each weighted to reflect our judgment of the importance of the measure, we have provided a final tally that scores each nation on a scale of 2,000. While the tally relies on the subjective value we've placed on such questions as "How does the savings rate contribute to a nation's wealth?" and "How important is a teacher's salary to an educational system?" and "How does leisure time relate to productivity?," it still provides probably the most comprehensive quantitative answer to the question each nation asks more and more: *Wo befinden Wir uns? Où en sommes nous? Hoe staan we ervoor? Come stiamo? Where do we stand?*

While we worked on this book, the Soviet Union died. Any data used here, however, were reported from the old USSR, so we have not tried our hand at a new nomenclature. For the sake, however, of our new sensibility, we have decided to consign West Germany to the ash heap and use only "Germany" when the data reflect the former West Germany or the new, singular Germany. When the data reflect only the former German Democratic Republic, we've indicated that by using "East Germany."

It is worth noting that given the constantly changing nature and great amount of these data, this book would not have been possible without the Macintosh—from which it is fully born.

We are what we add up to. While this may be (for Americans, anyway) what economist Paul Krugman has called the Age of Diminished Expectations, where we stand today is not where we will be standing tomorrow. We are all traveling. Don't get comfortable.

militarism."
—*Henry Grunwald, former U.S. ambassador to Austria*

"Our own children or grandchildren may someday witness the disintegration of both the Soviet and American world systems. What new coalescings and coalitions may then emerge are beyond imagination."
—*George W. Ball, former undersecretary of State*

THE WEALTHIEST

Where has the affluent society gone?

The America of the 1950s still represents affluence in its most memorable form—a home of your own, money in the bank, a big car, appliances galore, all provided by a single wage earner.

In 1960, the U.S. standard of living was more than twice as great as that in most of the world's industrial democracies—the so-called Country Club nations. By the mid-1970s, the U.S. had begun to lose its lead. Some economists say American economic dominance ended with the 1973 OPEC oil embargo, which began the era of stagnation. Between 1972 and 1990, the U.S. had the slowest growth rate in standard of living—measured by wealth per citizen—of the major industrialized nations.

Myth:
The American standard of living is the highest in the world.

Reality:
The American standard of living is merely average.

The world has grown richer in virtually every measurable way, but no new standard of living—no quintessential standard of living—has emerged to rival that vision of the good life.

In many respects, Japan today emulates—and mimics—America of that time, with its devotion to social conformity, symbolized by the salaryman (Japan's version of the man in the gray flannel suit), nationalistic pride in its economic power and influence, and single-minded pursuit of material well-being. But government policies, old-fashioned marketing practices, and ever-rising demand for limited housing space combine to keep prices forbiddingly high in Japan—too high to allow many Japanese much taste of the idealized good life.

On the other hand, while Americans still appear to be living well, they have no savings. Indeed, they have gone grievously into debt and have had to send the entire household to work to keep up their payments on the American dream.

While no country may ever again economically dominate the world as America did in the 1950s, continental Europe now offers perhaps the closest equivalent to the fifties dream—rising prosperity, growing savings, and a shrinking work week. "*L'America sta qui,*" the Italians say. *America is here.* The dream sought by past generations of immigrants to the U.S. is now found in Europe.

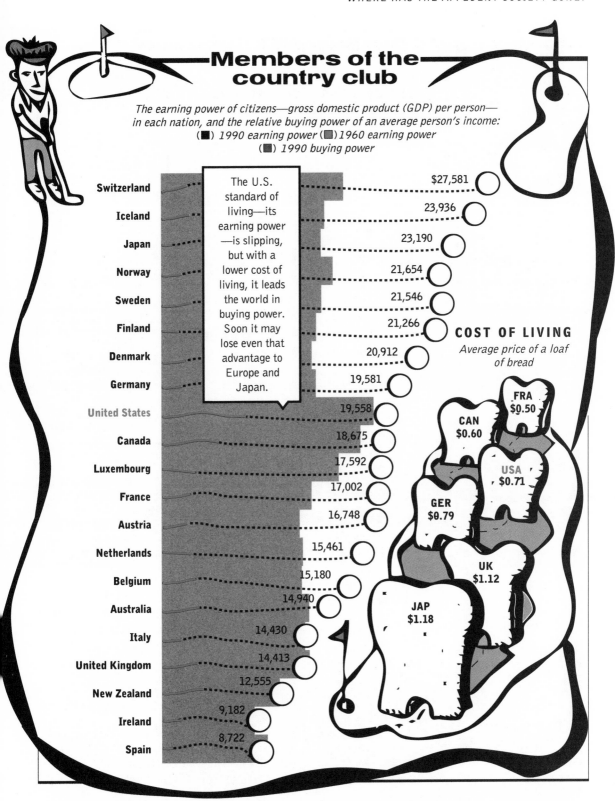

Members of the country club

The earning power of citizens—gross domestic product (GDP) per person— in each nation, and the relative buying power of an average person's income: (■) 1990 earning power (▨) 1960 earning power (▨) 1990 buying power

The U.S. standard of living—its earning power —is slipping, but with a lower cost of living, it leads the world in buying power. Soon it may lose even that advantage to Europe and Japan.

Country	GDP
Switzerland	$27,581
Iceland	23,936
Japan	23,190
Norway	21,654
Sweden	21,546
Finland	21,266
Denmark	20,912
Germany	19,581
United States	19,558
Canada	18,675
Luxembourg	17,592
France	17,002
Austria	16,748
Netherlands	15,461
Belgium	15,180
Australia	14,940
Italy	14,430
United Kingdom	14,413
New Zealand	12,555
Ireland	9,182
Spain	8,722

COST OF LIVING

Average price of a loaf of bread

FRA $0.50
CAN $0.60
USA $0.71
GER $0.79
UK $1.12
JAP $1.18

——Who gets the biggest paycheck?——

WHITE COLLARS AND SALARYMEN
Average income of a middle manager ($)

German businessmen get the world's top marks—with the average manager making the equivalent of $83,400 per year.

GER	SWI	DEN	JAP	BEL	USA	LUX	CAN	SWE	FIN	ÖST	IRE	NET	NOR	AUS	UK	TUR	FRA	ITA	SPA	POR
$83,400	81,100	77,100	73,000	64,600	58,200	55,200	53,300	48,600	47,200	46,700	44,400	44,000	39,300	39,000	37,600	32,400	29,100	28,200	11,800	7,600

BLUE COLLARS OF THE WORLD
Average income of a skilled factory worker ($)

Although they are among the least labor- or social-welfare-minded countries, the U.S., Japan, and Switzerland pay the highest worker wages.

SWI	JAP	USA	DEN	CAN	SWE	GER	BEL	NOR	ÖST	NET	LUX	ITA	FIN	UK	AUS	IRE	FRA	SPA	TUR	POR
$40,400	35,700	32,800	32,000	28,300	27,200	27,100	26,600	26,200	23,900	23,100	21,000	20,100	19,600	19,200	18,300	18,200	13,200	7,700	7,000	5,400

9-TO-5 OFFICE WORKERS
Average income of a secretary or clerical worker ($)

The "girls in the office" are among the lowest-paid workers.

SWI	DEN	GER	LUX	BEL	NOR	UK	CAN	JAP	USA	NET	ÖST	FIN	SWE	FRA	ITA	AUS	IRE	TUR	SPA	POR
$34,200	29,100	27,400	24,700	22,800	21,600	21,400	21,000	20,600	20,300	20,200	19,900	19,300	19,200	18,400	16,500	16,400	13,800	10,800	9,700	6,900

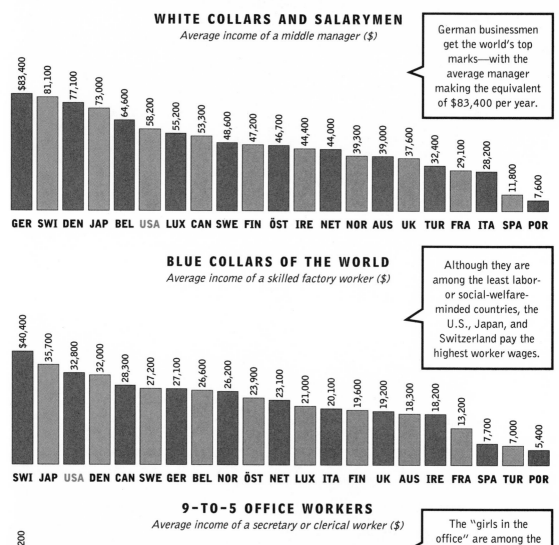

THE TWO-HEADED HOUSEHOLD
Families with double incomes

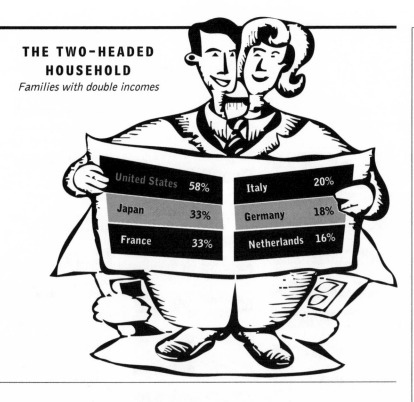

United States	58%	Italy	20%
Japan	33%	Germany	18%
France	33%	Netherlands	16%

THE MIDDLE-CLASS SOCIETY
Percent of population with incomes between 33 percent less than the national median and 50 percent more than the national median

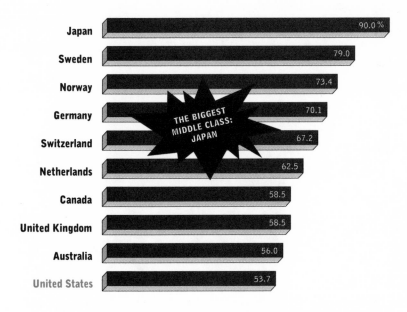

Japan	90.0%
Sweden	79.0
Norway	73.4
Germany	70.1
Switzerland	67.2
Netherlands	62.5
Canada	58.5
United Kingdom	58.5
Australia	56.0
United States	53.7

THE BIGGEST MIDDLE CLASS: JAPAN

If American earning power had risen at the same rate after 1973 as before, according to *The Economist*, U.S. incomes would be 50 percent higher than they are today. As it is, the U.S. has maintained its standard of living only because the majority of households contains two wage earners. Without those second incomes, the American standard of living would be the lowest among the major industrial nations.

"I think at times they wake up in the middle of the night and say, 'Goodness, we're terribly rich. How did this come about?'—and then they go back to sleep."
—*Franco Ferrarotti, professor of sociology, commenting on Europe's middle class*

Myth:
America is a middle-class society.

Reality:
Almost as many Americans are outside the middle class as in it.

What price glory?

YOU BETTER SHOP AROUND

The International Monetary Fund characterized the wealth of the nations of the world with a profile that showed 571 automobiles, 760 telephones, and 811 television sets for every 1,000 Americans—the highest ratios in the world.

Before reunification, Germany boasted 485 cars, 650 telephones, and 385 television sets for every 1,000 citizens. As for the Japanese, with 250 cars, 555 phones, and 377 TVs per 1,000, they hardly reach the first rank in consumer life-style.

To buy a car in Japan, you must not only be able to pay for it but also be able to park it. Proof of a space is required for purchase. In Tokyo, personal car elevators, which allow you to park your second car on top of your first, are all the rage.

The Mac
Price of a Big Mac ($)

Russia	$6.25
Denmark	3.99
Sweden	3.93
Italy	3.17
France	3.14
Belgium	2.80
Netherlands	2.79
Spain	2.78
Germany	2.56
Japan	2.33
United Kingdom	2.30
United States	2.20
Ireland	2.06
Canada	1.89
Australia	1.74

The rack
Cost of a moderately priced men's wardrobe ($)

Japan	$1,250
Denmark	940
Australia	890
Belgium	830
France	740
Italy	720
United States	690
Switzerland	680
United Kingdom	670
Germany	660
Spain	650
Finland	640
Norway	630
Ireland	590
Sweden	560
Netherlands	540
Canada	510

The compact
Cost of a mid-priced car ($)

Norway	$27,500
Finland	27,100
Ireland	21,700
Denmark	19,900
Spain	18,300
Italy	16,300
Sweden	16,100
United Kingdom	15,200
Switzerland	15,100
Australia	14,600
Japan	14,600
Netherlands	13,800
France	13,300
Belgium	12,100
Germany	11,100
United States	9,700
Canada	9,300

The sack
Monthly rent for a medium-priced four-room metropolitan apartment ($)

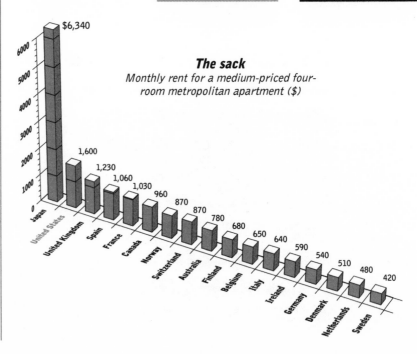

Japan $6,340; United States 1,600; United Kingdom 1,230; Spain 1,060; France 1,030; Canada 960; Norway 870; Switzerland 870; Australia 780; Finland 680; Belgium 650; Italy 640; Ireland 590; Germany 540; Denmark 510; Netherlands 480; Sweden 420

WE'VE GOTTA HAVE IT

Wheels...
Cars per 1,000 people

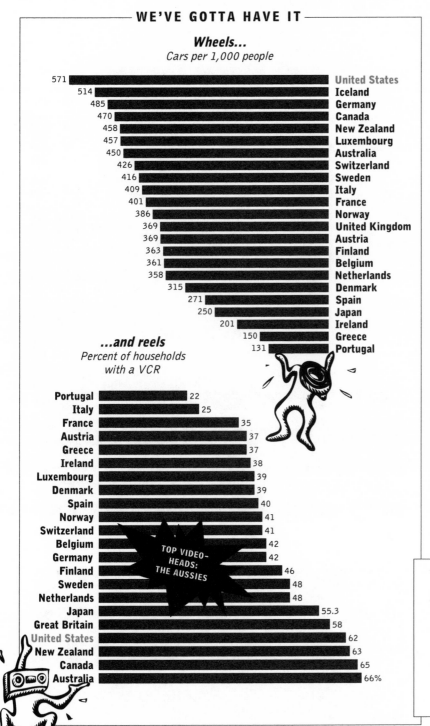

571	United States
514	Iceland
485	Germany
470	Canada
458	New Zealand
457	Luxembourg
450	Australia
426	Switzerland
416	Sweden
409	Italy
401	France
386	Norway
369	United Kingdom
369	Austria
363	Finland
361	Belgium
358	Netherlands
315	Denmark
271	Spain
250	Japan
201	Ireland
150	Greece
131	Portugal

...and reels
Percent of households with a VCR

Portugal	22
Italy	25
France	35
Austria	37
Greece	37
Ireland	38
Luxembourg	39
Denmark	39
Spain	40
Norway	41
Switzerland	41
Belgium	42
Germany	42
Finland	46
Sweden	48
Netherlands	48
Japan	55.3
Great Britain	58
United States	62
New Zealand	63
Canada	65
Australia	66%

TOP VIDEO-HEADS: THE AUSSIES

The U.S. is a shopper's paradise. Thanks to a remarkably competitive marketplace and an efficient distribution system, American consumers enjoy more choices and better prices than anyone else in the world.

Although consumer comforts serve as one measure of national wealth, in the U.S. they also point to the profligacy of a debt-driven society. He may not have as much, but a German or Japanese consumer is far more likely to own—rather than be paying off—his gadgets and goodies.

Myth:
Japan has become the world's greatest car culture.

Reality:
The Japanese build them, but they don't own them.

Do you own your own home?
(Is that the real test?)

In Japan, perpetually squeezed for space, the long economic boom has pushed real-estate prices up to unreal levels—by current property values, all of Japan is worth 25 times the entire U.S. One effect of this inflation has been to make home-ownership—an essential ingredient of the middle-class dream—tougher to achieve in Japan than anywhere else. To enable more young people to afford a house, Japanese banks have begun offering multigeneration mortgages that commit children to paying off their parents' debts.

Despite today's high prices, a greater portion of Japanese than American households own the homes they live in. The average Japanese house, however, hardly offers the amenities associated with the modern middle-class good life. Each has an average of 800 square feet, versus 1,773 in America. Children's bedrooms, almost always shared by two or more children, tend to be the size of an American walk-in ➻

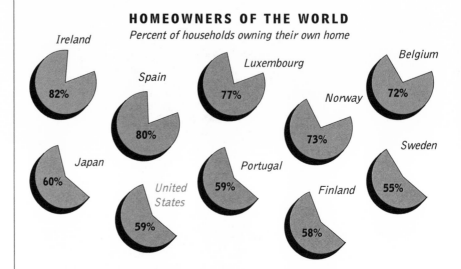

HOMEOWNERS OF THE WORLD
Percent of households owning their own home

Ireland 82%
Spain 80%
Japan 60%
United States 59%
Luxembourg 77%
Portugal 59%
Belgium 72%
Norway 73%
Finland 58%
Sweden 55%

THE MONEY PIT
Average cost of a home ($)

Japan	$346,400
Canada	200,000
Italy	180,000
United Kingdom	135,000
United States	118,100
Australia	110,000
Netherlands	99,500
Sweden	76,000

REAL COST
Average price of a home as a multiple of average annual salary

Japan	8.62
Italy	6.42
United Kingdom	6.13
Canada	4.87
Australia	3.36
United States	3.00
Sweden	2.99
Netherlands	1.80

Ireland and Spain have the highest level of home-ownership in the world.

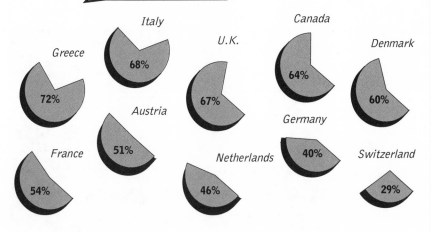

Greece 72%

Italy 68%

U.K. 67%

Canada 64%

Denmark 60%

Austria 51%

Germany 40%

Switzerland 29%

France 54%

Netherlands 46%

closet. Camp stoves are hot sellers each winter, because fewer than 20 percent of Japanese homes have central heating. With the nation's weak physical infrastructure, including a notoriously inadequate sewer system, little more than 40 percent of Japanese homes have flush toilets. Yet 80 percent of new homes are equipped with an early-1960s American invention: a remote-control toilet that automatically cleans and dries your bottom.

"Anyone who has spent more than a week in Japan understands that its real standard of living is still far below that of Western Europe or the United States."
—*James Fallows,* The Atlantic

LIVING ROOM
Average home size (square feet)

Australia
3,038

Netherlands
2,500

Canada
2,000

Italy
1,345

Japan
800

United States
1,773

United Kingdom
1,050

Sweden
1,250

Myth:
Widespread home-ownership is the mark of a middle-class life-style.

Reality:
The world's wealthiest countries have some of the lowest levels of home-ownership in the industrial world.

Who's worth the most?

America's savings rate—a prime indicator of both a family's and a nation's underlying economic stability and resources—is the lowest among the industrial nations. In less than a generation, it has fallen from a solid 9 percent to less than 3 percent, as both the people and the government have gone on a spending binge. In the long term, diminished savings not only undermine a family's security but also severely lessen the amount of money available for investment in a nation's future: scientific and industrial research and development, education, roads and communication, new factories and equipment.

Is America's self-indulgence unique? Or are its spendthrift ways just an unavoidable outgrowth of prosperity, and hence the inevitable fate of all rich nations?

"For a long time there was an attitude that you had to save 20 or 30 percent of your salary. Now, young people ➡→

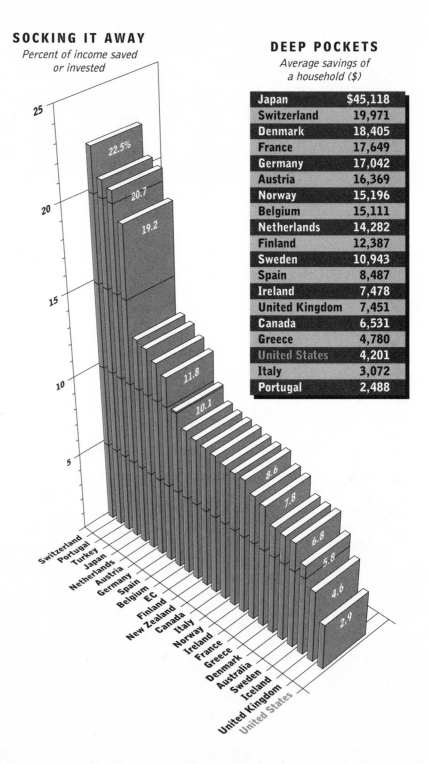

SOCKING IT AWAY
Percent of income saved or invested

DEEP POCKETS
Average savings of a household ($)

Japan	$45,118
Switzerland	19,971
Denmark	18,405
France	17,649
Germany	17,042
Austria	16,369
Norway	15,196
Belgium	15,111
Netherlands	14,282
Finland	12,387
Sweden	10,943
Spain	8,487
Ireland	7,478
United Kingdom	7,451
Canada	6,531
Greece	4,780
United States	4,201
Italy	3,072
Portugal	2,488

Who owes the most?

UP TO THEIR EYEBALLS
Average amount owed by a household ($)

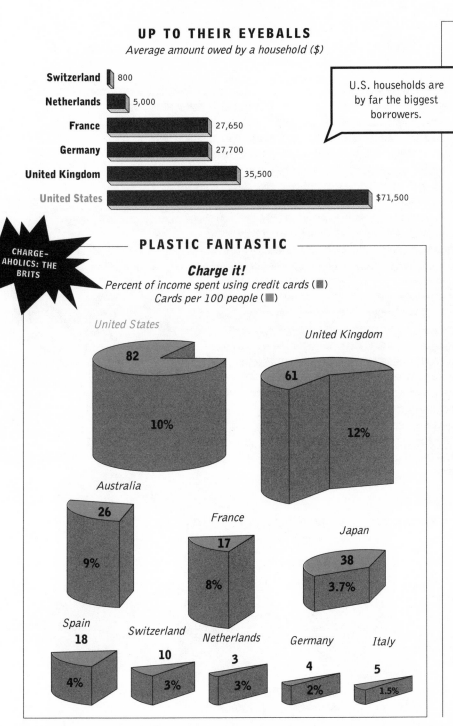

Switzerland — 800
Netherlands — 5,000
France — 27,650
Germany — 27,700
United Kingdom — 35,500
United States — $71,500

> U.S. households are by far the biggest borrowers.

PLASTIC FANTASTIC

CHARGE-AHOLICS: THE BRITS

Charge it!
Percent of income spent using credit cards (■)
Cards per 100 people (■)

United States
82
10%

United Kingdom
61
12%

Australia
26
9%

France
17
8%

Japan
38
3.7%

Spain
18
4%

Switzerland
10
3%

Netherlands
3
3%

Germany
4
2%

Italy
5
1.5%

spend everything they earn. They don't have any fear of the future."
—*Honda director Takashi Matsuda*

One result of abundant credit—it is easier to borrow money in the U.S. than anywhere else in the world—is that the average American household owes $71,500, including mortgage and consumer debt. Germany's experience with the destabilizing effects of hyper-inflation after World War I has led it to take a very hard line against government and consumer borrowing (which puts upward pressure on prices, as more money chases available goods). It was big news when in 1990 Deutsche Bank—Germany's largest commercial bank—reversed its long-held opposition to revolving-credit cards.

"When I buy something big, I don't want to carry cash like my parents did."
—*Yoko Yokohama, 21-year-old Tokyo office worker with three credit cards*

Who pays the most taxes?

THE BIGGEST BITE
Total taxes as a percent of gross domestic product

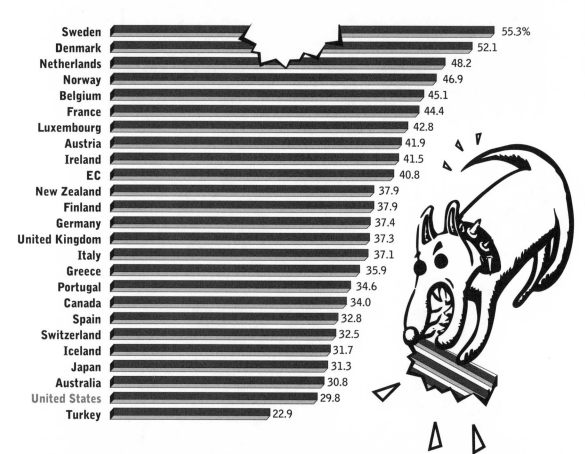

Sweden	55.3%
Denmark	52.1
Netherlands	48.2
Norway	46.9
Belgium	45.1
France	44.4
Luxembourg	42.8
Austria	41.9
Ireland	41.5
EC	40.8
New Zealand	37.9
Finland	37.9
Germany	37.4
United Kingdom	37.3
Italy	37.1
Greece	35.9
Portugal	34.6
Canada	34.0
Spain	32.8
Switzerland	32.5
Iceland	31.7
Japan	31.3
Australia	30.8
United States	29.8
Turkey	22.9

HOW THEY SPEND YOUR TAX DOLLAR
Government spending by category

Canada
3.5%
6.3%
1.8%
35.2%
45.9%
7.3%

France
6.1%
23.7%
2.5%
39.1%
20.8%
7.8%

Germany
8.7%
18.6%
0.3%
49.0%
14.6%
8.8%

Italy
39.7%
1.6%
9.6%
7.4%
3.7%
38.0%

■ *Housing*　■ *Health*　■ *Education*

SOAKING THE RICH
Top tax rate (percent of income)

In the Netherlands, the rich face the world's highest tax rate.

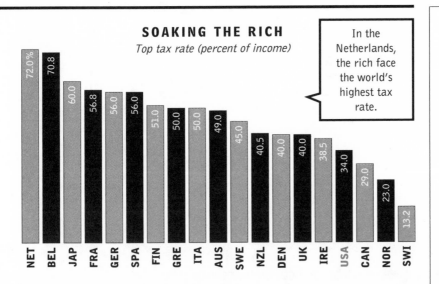

NET 72.0% · BEL 70.8 · JAP 60.0 · FRA 56.8 · GER 56.0 · SPA 56.0 · FIN 51.0 · GRE 50.0 · ITA 50.0 · AUS 49.0 · SWE 45.0 · NZL 40.5 · DEN 40.0 · UK 40.0 · IRE 38.5 · USA 34.0 · CAN 29.0 · NOR 23.0 · SWI 13.2

LEAVE SOME FOR ME
Average percent of median income left after all taxes

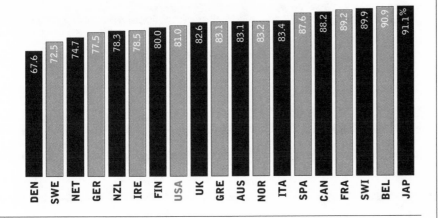

DEN 67.6 · SWE 72.5 · NET 74.7 · GER 77.5 · NZL 78.3 · IRE 78.5 · FIN 80.0 · USA 81.0 · UK 82.6 · GRE 83.1 · AUS 83.1 · NOR 83.2 · ITA 83.4 · SPA 87.6 · CAN 88.2 · FRA 89.2 · SWI 89.9 · BEL 90.9 · JAP 91.1%

If one looks at taxation levels around the globe, one fact stands out: Americans enjoy a lighter overall tax burden than citizens of any other major industrial nation. If the U.S. taxed itself at, say, average German rates, it could not only wipe out its deficit but alleviate its poverty.

For the international rich, the U.S. is one of the world's most popular tax havens. But the U.S. middle class—losing on average 19 percent of its paycheck to taxes, versus 9 percent in Japan—still bears a hefty burden.

"Just whispering the word 'taxes'...today is like quoting The Satanic Verses to the Ayatollah. You could get a contract put out on you."
—*Lee A. Iacocca, chairman, Chrysler Corporation*

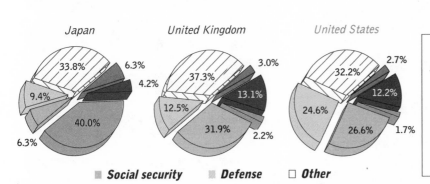

Japan United Kingdom United States

Japan: 33.8% · 6.3% · 4.2% · 9.4% · 40.0% · 6.3%

United Kingdom: 37.3% · 3.0% · 13.1% · 2.2% · 31.9% · 12.5%

United States: 32.2% · 2.7% · 12.2% · 1.7% · 26.6% · 24.6%

▩ *Social security* ▩ *Defense* ☐ *Other*

Myth:
Americans are overtaxed.

Reality:
The U.S. tax burden on the wealthy is among the lightest in the developed world.

Where are the filthy rich?

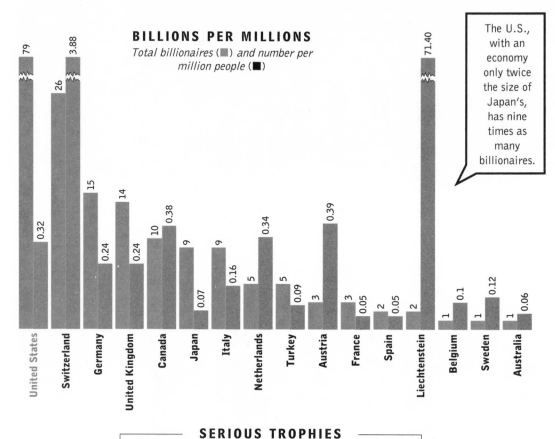

BILLIONS PER MILLIONS

Total billionaires (■) and number per million people (■)

The U.S., with an economy only twice the size of Japan's, has nine times as many billionaires.

	Total billionaires	Number per million
United States	79	0.32
Switzerland	26	3.88
Germany	15	0.24
United Kingdom	14	0.24
Canada	10	0.38
Japan	9	0.07
Italy	9	0.16
Netherlands	5	0.34
Turkey	5	0.09
Austria	3	0.39
France	3	0.05
Spain	2	0.05
Liechtenstein	2	71.40
Belgium	1	0.1
Sweden	1	0.12
Australia	1	0.06

SERIOUS TROPHIES

Luxury cars
As a percent of all cars

Germany	12.9 %
Switzerland	11.3
United States	9.2
Japan	7.8
European Community	6.9
United Kingdom	6.8
Netherlands	4.9
Italy	4.2
France	2.9
Spain	2.4

Private jets
Total number

United States	3,500
Canada	200
France	134
United Kingdom	117
Netherlands	26
Germany	19
Japan	18
Sweden	5
Denmark	2
Finland	1

Who's been left behind?

OFFICIALLY BELOW THE LINE
Percent of population earning less than half the median income

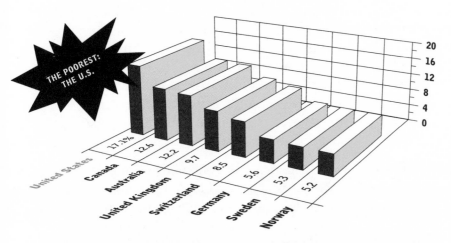

THE POOREST: THE U.S.

United States 17.1% · Canada 12.6 · Australia 12.2 · United Kingdom 9.7 · Switzerland 8.5 · Germany 5.6 · Sweden 5.3 · Norway 5.2

20 16 12 8 4 0

As poverty has declined in most developed nations, it has grown dramatically in the U.S., where more than 17 percent of the population earns less than half the median national income, up from 12.5 percent in 1970. Rich Americans have gotten notably richer thanks to higher wages, incentive compensation plans, the stock- and bond-market booms, real-estate appreciation, and disproportionate tax relief. Meanwhile, the poor have gotten strikingly poorer. From the late 1960s to the late 1980s, the share of all family income earned by the poorest 20 percent of families dropped to 4.7 percent from 7.4 percent.

The Atkinson Inequality Index, a gauge of income distribution, ranks countries on a scale of 0 to 100, with 0 representing the most equal distribution and 100 the most unequal. In a comparison of nine major industrial democracies, the U.S. was rated most unequal, with a score of 99, while Sweden and Norway, at 60, were most equal.

SUFFER THE CHILDREN
Percent of children below the poverty line

United States	22.4%
Australia	15.9
Canada	15.5
United Kingdom	9.3
Switzerland	7.8
Sweden	5.0
Germany	4.9
Norway	4.8

SOAKING THE POOR
Percent of income going to the poorest 20 percent of households

Japan	8.7%
Sweden	8.0
Germany	6.8
Norway	6.2
United Kingdom	5.8
Canada	5.7
Switzerland	5.2
United States	4.7

CAN THE CENTER HOLD?
Income distribution on a scale of 0 to 100 (0 represents the most equal society, 100 the least equal)

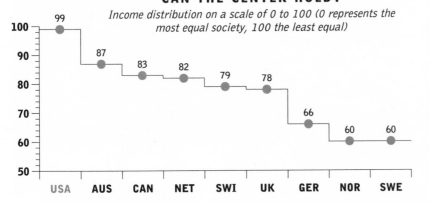

USA	AUS	CAN	NET	SWI	UK	GER	NOR	SWE
99	87	83	82	79	78	66	60	60

The balance sheet

In 1950, the U.S. accounted for more than 59 percent of the world's industrial output—from its lathes, cars, and backhoes, to its meat and potatoes, to the services of its banks and insurance companies. Physically and psychologically undamaged by war, with its vast natural resources and huge manufacturing base, it easily dominated the world economy.

Today, finance ministers, not armies, determine the fate of nations. Communism's collapse was fundamentally an economic defeat, not a military one. Japan's rise was masterminded by the farsighted mandarins of MITI (Ministry of International Trade and Industry), not Tojo. And most remarkably, after a decade of debate, bureaucrats in Brussels accomplished what 2,000 years of warfare could not—the unification of Europe. The twelve members of the European Community joined with the seven nations of the European Free Trade Association to create an economic behemoth stretching from the Arctic Circle to the Mediterranean Sea.

"The decade of the 1990s will be the decade of Europe, and not Japan."
—*Helmut Kohl, chancellor of Germany*

But contained in America's overwhelming economic advantage were the seeds of its decline. As the nation got fat, it got sloppy, losing its manufacturing edge in everything from steel and autos to televisions and baseballs. But as consumers, Americans went right on shopping—financed by debt—and as citizens, they kept demanding more from government without being willing to pay the price.

So voracious was the American appetite—for Armani suits as well as weapons systems—that the federal debt grew from $1 trillion to $3 trillion over the course of the 1980s.

As it transformed itself from the world's largest creditor into the world's largest debtor and reversed a trade balance that had been positive for nearly a century, America sent the economies of Europe and Asia into hypergrowth. In a sense, Ronald Reagan, whose unprecedented levels of deficit spending set off America's borrowing-and-buying binge, became the greatest Keynesian of all time.

One effect of the global boom was to heighten the contrast between capitalism and communism—indeed, to flaunt the immense wealth-building power of free markets—and help push the regimes of Eastern Europe and even any pretense of a Soviet Union into oblivion.

But another effect was to leave the U.S.—and the world—in a moment of vast economic uncertainty. What will happen when the U.S. finally exhausts its ability to buy?

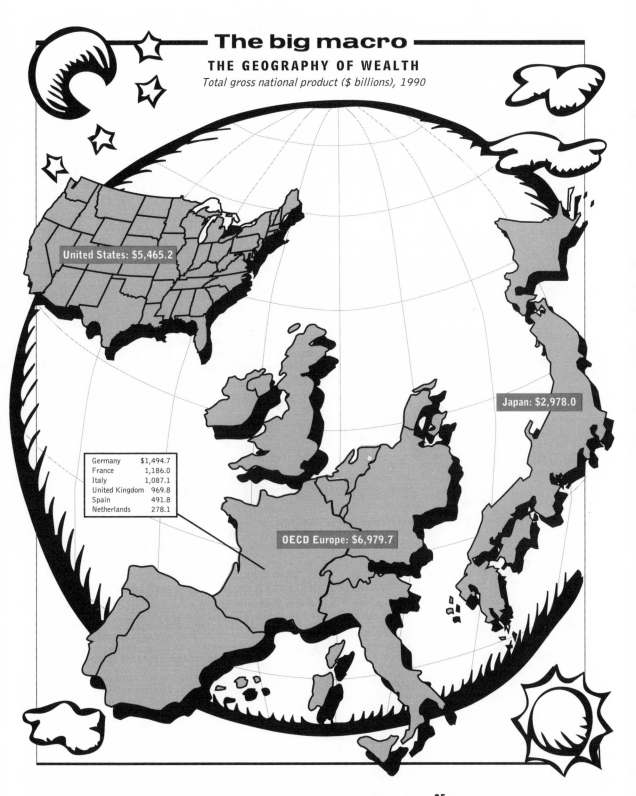

The big macro

THE GEOGRAPHY OF WEALTH

Total gross national product ($ billions), 1990

United States: $5,465.2

Japan: $2,978.0

Germany	$1,494.7
France	1,186.0
Italy	1,087.1
United Kingdom	969.8
Spain	491.8
Netherlands	278.1

OECD Europe: $6,979.7

Hey, big spender

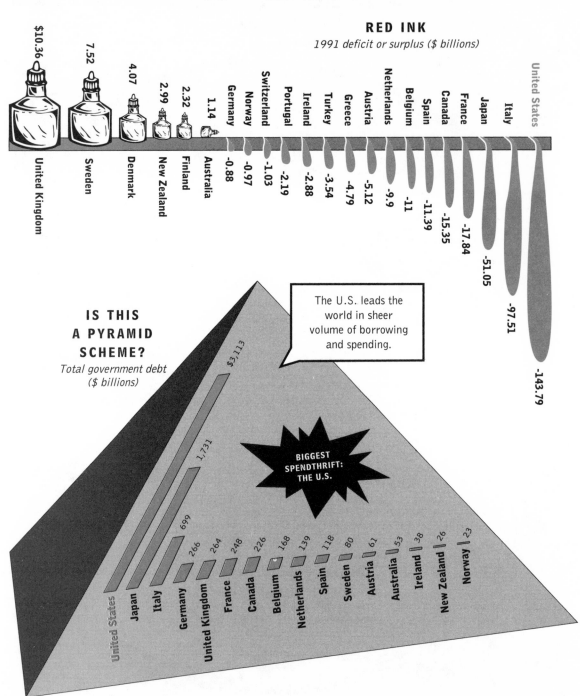

RED INK
1991 deficit or surplus ($ billions)

United States

$10.36	United Kingdom
7.52	Sweden
4.07	Denmark
2.99	New Zealand
2.32	Finland
1.14	Australia
-0.88	Germany
-0.97	Norway
-1.03	Switzerland
-2.19	Portugal
-2.88	Ireland
-3.54	Turkey
-4.79	Greece
-5.12	Austria
-9.9	Netherlands
-11	Belgium
-11.39	Spain
-15.35	Canada
-17.84	France
-51.05	Japan
-97.51	Italy
-143.79	

**IS THIS
A PYRAMID
SCHEME?**

*Total government debt
($ billions)*

The U.S. leads the
world in sheer
volume of borrowing
and spending.

BIGGEST
SPENDTHRIFT:
THE U.S.

$3,113 — United States
1,731 — Japan
699 — Italy
266 — Germany
264 — United Kingdom
248 — France
226 — Canada
168 — Belgium
139 — Netherlands
118 — Spain
80 — Sweden
61 — Austria
53 — Australia
38 — Ireland
26 — New Zealand
23 — Norway

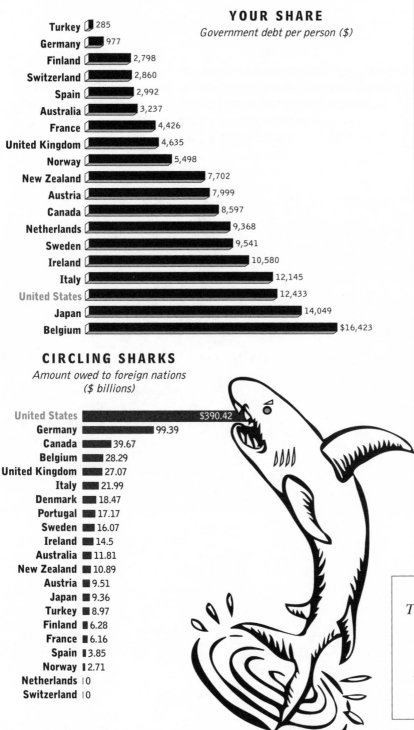

YOUR SHARE
Government debt per person ($)

Country	Amount
Turkey	285
Germany	977
Finland	2,798
Switzerland	2,860
Spain	2,992
Australia	3,237
France	4,426
United Kingdom	4,635
Norway	5,498
New Zealand	7,702
Austria	7,999
Canada	8,597
Netherlands	9,368
Sweden	9,541
Ireland	10,580
Italy	12,145
United States	12,433
Japan	14,049
Belgium	$16,423

CIRCLING SHARKS
Amount owed to foreign nations ($ billions)

Country	Amount
United States	$390.42
Germany	99.39
Canada	39.67
Belgium	28.29
United Kingdom	27.07
Italy	21.99
Denmark	18.47
Portugal	17.17
Sweden	16.07
Ireland	14.5
Australia	11.81
New Zealand	10.89
Austria	9.51
Japan	9.36
Turkey	8.97
Finland	6.28
France	6.16
Spain	3.85
Norway	2.71
Netherlands	0
Switzerland	0

The U.S. government's total debt, more than $3 trillion at the end of 1990 (now estimated to be more than $3.5 trillion), works out to $12,433 for every man, woman, and child in the country. This might not look so bad when compared with the per-person government debt in Japan ($14,049) or Italy ($12,145). But the Japanese and the Italians hold almost all of their public debt internally; in other words, they owe it to themselves. A large portion of the U.S. debt, $390 billion, is held by foreigners, burdening each American with an overseas liability of $1,572, compared with $75 for every Japanese citizen and $382 for every Italian.

As recently as 1979, the U.S. was the largest creditor nation, owed $141 billion. Now it's the largest debtor nation, owing almost $400 billion.

Myth:
The U.S. dominates the world's economy.

Reality:
Foreign bondholders dominate the U.S. economy.

27

How bad is our debt, really?

TOTAL DEBT vs. TOTAL INCOME
Deficit or surplus as a percent of GDP

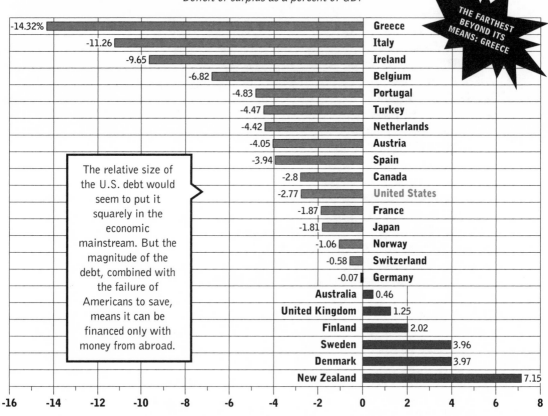

-14.32%	Greece
-11.26	Italy
-9.65	Ireland
-6.82	Belgium
-4.83	Portugal
-4.47	Turkey
-4.42	Netherlands
-4.05	Austria
-3.94	Spain
-2.8	Canada
-2.77	United States
-1.87	France
-1.81	Japan
-1.06	Norway
-0.58	Switzerland
-0.07	Germany
Australia	0.46
United Kingdom	1.25
Finland	2.02
Sweden	3.96
Denmark	3.97
New Zealand	7.15

-16 -14 -12 -10 -8 -6 -4 -2 0 2 4 6 8

> The relative size of the U.S. debt would seem to put it squarely in the economic mainstream. But the magnitude of the debt, combined with the failure of Americans to save, means it can be financed only with money from abroad.

THE FARTHEST BEYOND ITS MEANS: GREECE

WAS IT BETTER IN THE OLD DAYS?
Deficit as a percent of GNP: 1975–1990

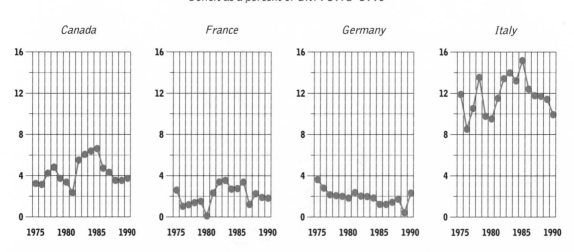

Canada   France   Germany   Italy

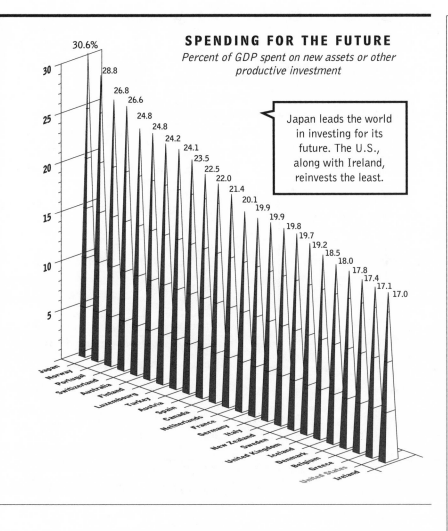

SPENDING FOR THE FUTURE

Percent of GDP spent on new assets or other productive investment

Japan leads the world in investing for its future. The U.S., along with Ireland, reinvests the least.

30.6%
28.8
26.8
26.6
24.8
24.8
24.2
24.1
23.5
22.5
22.0
21.4
20.1
19.9
19.9
19.8
19.7
19.2
18.5
18.0
17.8
17.4
17.1
17.0

Japan · Norway · Portugal · Switzerland · Australia · Finland · Luxembourg · Turkey · Austria · Spain · Canada · Netherlands · France · Germany · Italy · New Zealand · Sweden · United Kingdom · Iceland · Denmark · Belgium · Greece · United States · Ireland

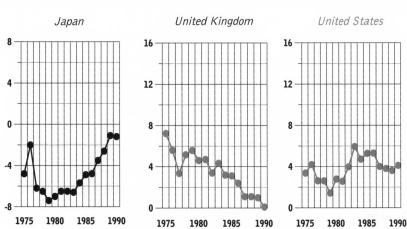

Japan

United Kingdom

United States

The optimists say our debt as a percentage of our national income is not much higher than it was in the past.

But there's good debt and there's bad debt, the pessimists say. You can borrow money for productive purposes— like research and new, more efficient factories—and chances are you will create enough wealth to pay back your debts and still have money left to invest in future growth. Or you can borrow to support an inflated consumer life-style, and be paying for it for the rest of your life— and your children's lives as well.

While America has wasted its borrowed billions on military junk and foreign luxuries, the pessimists argue, the Japanese and Germans have plowed money back into their economies. In 1990, the United States reinvested only 17.1 percent of its wealth in new factories, machinery, and other productive assets, while Japan reinvested 30.6 percent of its wealth.

29

A precarious balancing act

In 1895, the U.S. had its first trade surplus. America continued to sell to the world more than it bought from it, becoming the world's greatest manufacturing, agricultural, and trading nation, until the Reagan administration, when more goods came in— from fusilli to Mazdas—than went out. Even with the dollar down to its lowest postwar level, the trade deficit runs at nearly $10 billion a month.

"Sure, the trade deficit symbolizes a profligate America, consuming more than it produces and spending more than it has. But it also represents the biggest gravy train ever for U.S. trading partners, who have been selling America all that stuff and lending the money to pay for it."
—The Wall Street Journal

"We have all, in Europe and Japan and Asia, expanded on the shoulders of U.S. consumers."
—*Carlo De Benedetti, chairman, Olivetti*

THE OLD IN-AND-OUT
Trade balance ($ millions)

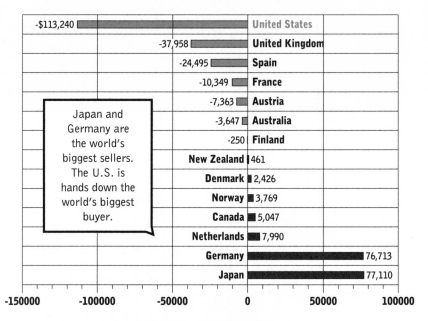

Japan and Germany are the world's biggest sellers. The U.S. is hands down the world's biggest buyer.

	Trade balance
United States	-$113,240
United Kingdom	-37,958
Spain	-24,495
France	-10,349
Austria	-7,363
Australia	-3,647
Finland	-250
New Zealand	461
Denmark	2,426
Norway	3,769
Canada	5,047
Netherlands	7,990
Germany	76,713
Japan	77,110

FOLLOW THE MONEY
Current account balance ($ millions)

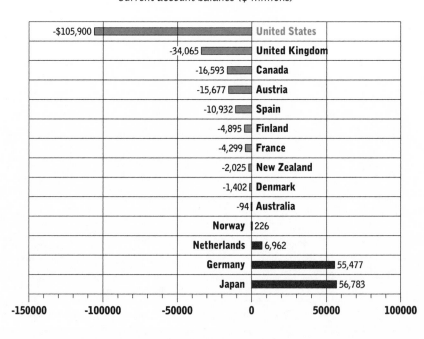

	Current account balance
United States	-$105,900
United Kingdom	-34,065
Canada	-16,593
Austria	-15,677
Spain	-10,932
Finland	-4,895
France	-4,299
New Zealand	-2,025
Denmark	-1,402
Australia	-94
Norway	226
Netherlands	6,962
Germany	55,477
Japan	56,783

Panic in the streets! Inflation

LOWEST INFLATION: THE NETHERLANDS

STABILITY INDEX
Five-year total inflation rate (1985–1990)

Country	Rate	Country	Rate
Netherlands	3.7%	Finland	27.3
Japan	6.9	Italy	31.7
Germany	7.0	United Kingdom	33.4
Luxembourg	9.0	Sweden	35.2
Belgium	11.0	Norway	35.4
Austria	11.4	Spain	36.8
Switzerland	13.2	Australia	46.4
France	16.5	New Zealand	56.4
Ireland	17.6	Portugal	71.1
Denmark	21.2	Greece	122.6
United States	21.5	Iceland	153.0
Canada	24.4	Turkey	758.0

UNDER CONTROL
1991 inflation rate (%)

Sweden	8.1%
Italy	6.2
Canada	5.9
Spain	5.7
Switzerland	5.7
Netherlands	4.4
United Kingdom	4.1
Germany	3.9
United States	3.8
Australia	3.4
Japan	3.3
France	2.6
Belgium	2.5

Nothing has a more demoralizing effect on an economy than runaway inflation. Since World War II, Germany and Japan have been obsessed with keeping inflation low—which they have done by keeping interest rates relatively high. This has forced the U.S. to hike its rates to persuade foreigners to keep buying Treasury bonds.

The Germans now have a new reason for raising their rates: the threat of inflation as the government spends billions of marks to absorb the impoverished Easterners.

U.S. inflation during the 1980s averaged about 5 percent per year—a level almost everyone considers acceptable. But in 1973, panicked by an inflation of just over 4 percent, Richard Nixon imposed wage and price controls.

Myth:
Inflation has been kept quite low.

Reality:
The definition of "low" has gotten much higher.

Big business

Between 1945 and 1960, the label MADE IN AMERICA appeared on more than half of the products manufactured in the world. By 1990, less than one-third of the world's goods bore that legend. In a survey of chief executives by *Industry Week* magazine, 46 percent of those surveyed said they felt that American industry was lagging behind its foreign rivals. But only 16 percent put their own companies in that category.

In the 1960s, Japan's powerful MITI declared that Japan would concentrate on steel production and shipbuilding; the 1970s were proclaimed the era of cars and consumer electronics; in the 1980s, chips and information technology would be king. In the 1990s, according to MITI, Japanese industry will concentrate on aircraft building and leisure-time products.

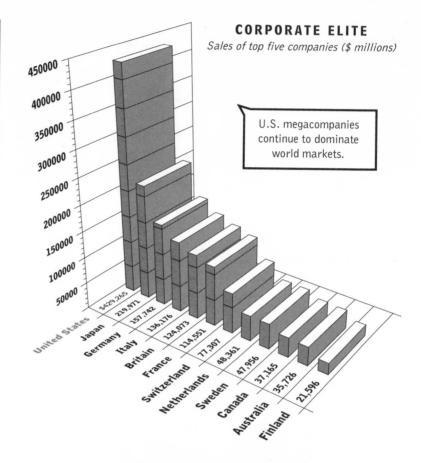

CORPORATE ELITE
Sales of top five companies ($ millions)

U.S. megacompanies continue to dominate world markets.

United States $429,265
Japan 239,971
Germany 219,971
Italy 157,742
Britain 136,176
France 124,073
Switzerland 114,551
Netherlands 77,307
Sweden 48,361
Canada 47,956
Australia 37,165
Finland 35,726
21,596

FORTUNE 500 BIG BOYS
Number of companies in Fortune's *"Global 500"*

United States	164		Italy	7
Japan	111		Netherlands	7
United Kingdom	43		Spain	4
Germany	30		Belgium	4
France	30		Norway	2
Sweden	17		Turkey	1
Canada	12		Austria	1
Switzerland	11		Portugal	1
Australia	9		Luxembourg	1
Finland	8		New Zealand	1

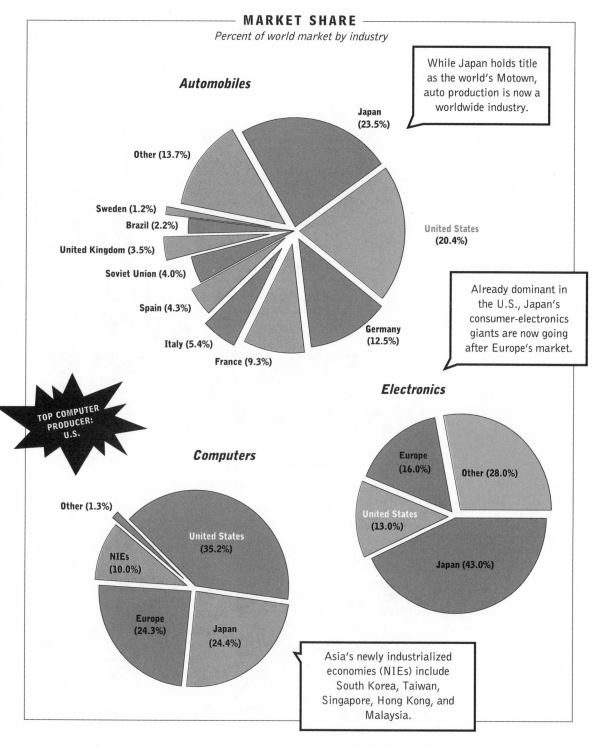

MARKET SHARE

Percent of world market by industry

Automobiles

Japan (23.5%)

Other (13.7%)

Sweden (1.2%)

Brazil (2.2%)

United Kingdom (3.5%)

Soviet Union (4.0%)

Spain (4.3%)

Italy (5.4%)

France (9.3%)

United States (20.4%)

Germany (12.5%)

> While Japan holds title as the world's Motown, auto production is now a worldwide industry.

> Already dominant in the U.S., Japan's consumer-electronics giants are now going after Europe's market.

Electronics

Europe (16.0%)

Other (28.0%)

United States (13.0%)

Japan (43.0%)

TOP COMPUTER PRODUCER: U.S.

Computers

Other (1.3%)

United States (35.2%)

NIEs (10.0%)

Europe (24.3%)

Japan (24.4%)

> Asia's newly industrialized economies (NIEs) include South Korea, Taiwan, Singapore, Hong Kong, and Malaysia.

The market

U.S. stock markets trade 37 percent of the total value of all world stock markets, while Japanese markets trade 32.6 percent. Since 1980, Japanese markets have almost doubled in size. The phenomenal growth of Japan's stock markets throughout the 1980s created a fountain of cash that financed not only Japan's corporate growth but vast amounts of U.S. debt. Fabled money manager George Soros says that the Japanese markets' 50 percent rise in 1987 despite the worldwide crash marked "the transfer of economic and financial power from the United States to Japan." But in 1991, Japan's go-go years came to a sudden stop, with the Nikkei index taking a fast nosedive. Many believe the era of cheap capital—one of Japan's major economic advantages— is over.

WORLD MARKETS

Share of total world stock markets' capitalization

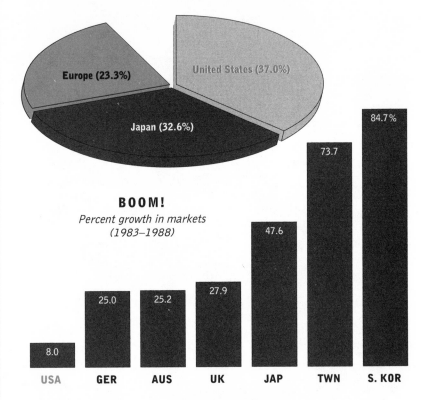

Europe (23.3%)

United States (37.0%)

Japan (32.6%)

BOOM!

Percent growth in markets (1983–1988)

USA	8.0	
GER	25.0	
AUS	25.2	
UK	27.9	
JAP	47.6	
TWN	73.7	
S. KOR	84.7%	

SHEER SIZE

Market value of domestic companies ($ millions)

United States	$2,539,241	Netherlands	96,818
Japan	2,235,840	Spain	79,785
Europe	1,599,315	Belgium	45,899
United Kingdom	661,534	Denmark	27,562
Germany	232,661	Sweden	26,726
France	197,561	Austria	12,000
Canada	148,168	Ireland	8,377
Switzerland	100,943	New Zealand	7,878
Italy	99,788	Norway	7,793
Australia	97,577	Finland	1,870

Credit report

THE BEST
CREDIT RISK:
JAPAN

INSTITUTIONAL INVESTOR RATING
Credit worthiness of national governments (100-point scale)

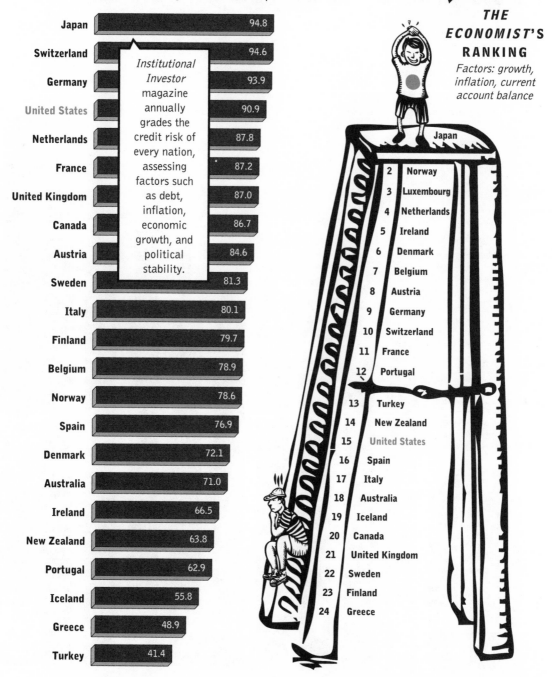

Country	Rating
Japan	94.8
Switzerland	94.6
Germany	93.9
United States	90.9
Netherlands	87.8
France	87.2
United Kingdom	87.0
Canada	86.7
Austria	84.6
Sweden	81.3
Italy	80.1
Finland	79.7
Belgium	78.9
Norway	78.6
Spain	76.9
Denmark	72.1
Australia	71.0
Ireland	66.5
New Zealand	63.8
Portugal	62.9
Iceland	55.8
Greece	48.9
Turkey	41.4

Institutional Investor magazine annually grades the credit risk of every nation, assessing factors such as debt, inflation, economic growth, and political stability.

THE ECONOMIST'S RANKING
Factors: growth, inflation, current account balance

1	Japan
2	Norway
3	Luxembourg
4	Netherlands
5	Ireland
6	Denmark
7	Belgium
8	Austria
9	Germany
10	Switzerland
11	France
12	Portugal
13	Turkey
14	New Zealand
15	United States
16	Spain
17	Italy
18	Australia
19	Iceland
20	Canada
21	United Kingdom
22	Sweden
23	Finland
24	Greece

And the winner is...

WHERE-WE-STAND INDEX
(0=least affluent; 2,000=extremely affluent)

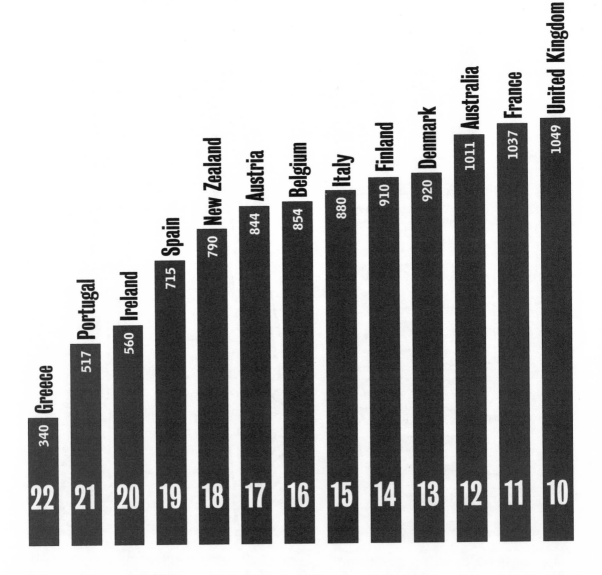

Greece	Portugal	Ireland	Spain	New Zealand	Austria	Belgium	Italy	Finland	Denmark	Australia	France	United Kingdom
340	517	560	715	790	844	854	880	910	920	1011	1037	1049
22	21	20	19	18	17	16	15	14	13	12	11	10

Germany

Out of all the world's industrial nations, Germany, as in *West* Germany, ranks most consistently near the top in salaries, equitable wealth distribution, luxury-goods consumption, trading strength, low levels of poverty, limited personal and national indebtedness, inflation control, business strength, and credit-worthiness. Japan has had greater economic growth, but it has not been able economically to enfranchise its citizens. German citizens (in the West)—from workers to executives—have benefited from their country's economic bounty and are now the world's most affluent people. Germany's economy is so strong that it may well succeed in quickly absorbing an impoverished East Germany.

Rank	Country	Value
9	Norway	1061
8	Sweden	1079
7	Netherlands	1087
6	Luxembourg	1178
5	United States	1178
4	Canada	1216
3	Switzerland	1332
2	Japan	1363
1	Germany	1382

THE SMARTEST

The best schools

The United States educational system, once seen as the engine of the world's mightiest economy, is now viewed as one of America's biggest handicaps in the global competitiveness race.

The U.S. ranks third among the G7 nations and seventh among all major industrial countries in overall spending on education. Even though the U.S. has almost twice as many college students as any other country, it ranks ninth in total public spending for higher education. Per-pupil expenditures average $3,232, putting the U.S. fifth among wealthy nations.

"Dollar bills don't educate students." So says George Bush, the self-anointed "Education President," who proposes to make America first in the world rank of math and science performance—from its current place at the bottom of the lists—without spending an extra dime. In addition, many critics say the Republican Party is loath to increase educational spending—and the size of the educational bureaucracy—because teachers tend to vote for Democrats.

The decline of America's schools—which, some observers say, began with the postwar urban flight—was fast and complete. Where the U.S. once had the best public school system in the world, it now has the worst among affluent nations.

This crisis was agonizingly memorialized in the 1983 government report "A Nation at Risk," which focused explicitly on the contrast between U.S. schools and those of its industrial competitors. In the U.S., schools are hitched to the economic fortunes of their neighborhoods, while schools in Europe and Japan offer students similar opportunities regardless of family income. In Europe and Japan, governments set precise standards of achievement, enforcing and monitoring them through various national tests; in the U.S., even a high-school diploma does not guarantee literacy. In Europe and Japan, teachers are well paid and accorded high levels of professional respect; in the U.S., teaching is among the least desired professional jobs.

But the most pernicious aspect of schooling in America is not the failure rate but the disparity rate: the atmosphere of wonder and achievement that marks a well-financed school versus the sense of deprivation and futility that pervades a poor one; the wealth of opportunities offered by educational success versus the bleak prospects that await those who fail.

Can you buy quality?

CUT OF THE PUBLIC PIE
Education spending as a percent of all public expenditures

18% — FRA
17.7 — JAP
17.5 — USA
15.4 — CAN
11.3 — UK
9.2 — GER
8.6 — ITA

THE COMMITMENT
Education expenditures as a percent of GDP

4.0 — ITA
4.4 — GER
5.0 — UK
5.0 — JAP
5.6 — USA
5.7 — FRA
7.2% — CAN

WHAT'S YOUR KID'S SHARE?
Per-pupil expenditure ($)

SWE $4,181
SWI 4,026
CAN 3,665
JAP 1,922
NOR 3,307
USA 3,232
DEN 3,060
OST 2,825
ITA 1,212
GER 1,941
AUS 2,050
NET 2,059
FRA 2,084
BEL 2,273
UK 2,502
FIN 2,605

Where does it all go?

In the U.S., where public schools are financed through property taxes, a poor school district might spend as little as $7,000 per student while a neighboring one spends as much as $18,000, as is the case in New York City and its surrounding, affluent suburbs.

Despite all the fretting over the decline of America's schools, the U.S. still treats its teachers like members of an underclass profession and pays them accordingly. In fact, the U.S. is the only industrialized nation to pay its teachers less than its blue-collar workers. In Japan, where teachers earn 2.4 times the nation's per capita income (versus 1.7 times in the U.S.), teachers are considered to be on the same professional plane as engineers. In Japan and Switzerland, a teacher with ten to ➡

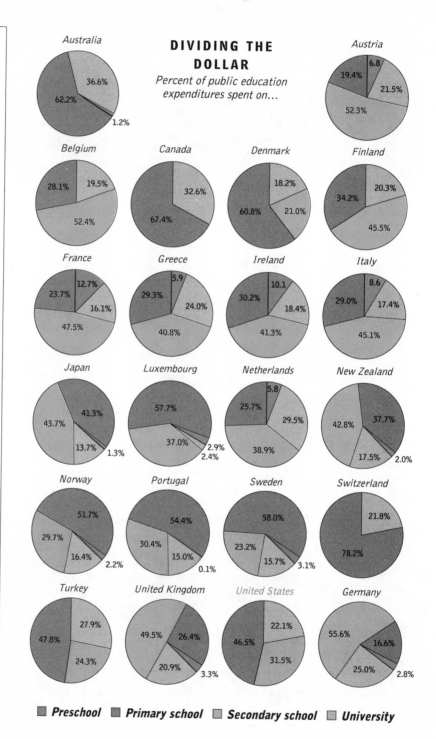

DIVIDING THE DOLLAR
Percent of public education expenditures spent on...

Australia — 36.6%, 62.2%, 1.2%

Austria — 6.8, 19.4%, 21.5%, 52.3%

Belgium — 28.1%, 19.5%, 52.4%

Canada — 32.6%, 67.4%

Denmark — 18.2%, 60.8%, 21.0%

Finland — 34.2%, 20.3%, 45.5%

France — 23.7%, 12.7%, 16.1%, 47.5%

Greece — 5.9, 29.3%, 24.0%, 40.8%

Ireland — 10.1, 30.2%, 18.4%, 41.3%

Italy — 8.6, 29.0%, 17.4%, 45.1%

Japan — 41.3%, 43.7%, 13.7%, 1.3%

Luxembourg — 57.7%, 37.0%, 2.9%, 2.4%

Netherlands — 5.8, 25.7%, 29.5%, 38.9%

New Zealand — 37.7%, 42.8%, 17.5%, 2.0%

Norway — 51.7%, 29.7%, 16.4%, 2.2%

Portugal — 54.4%, 30.4%, 15.0%, 0.1%

Sweden — 58.0%, 23.2%, 15.7%, 3.1%

Switzerland — 21.8%, 78.2%

Turkey — 27.9%, 47.8%, 24.3%

United Kingdom — 49.5%, 26.4%, 20.9%, 3.3%

United States — 22.1%, 46.5%, 31.5%

Germany — 55.6%, 16.6%, 25.0%, 2.8%

■ **Preschool** ■ **Primary school** ■ **Secondary school** ■ **University**

WHAT DOES A TOP TEACHER MAKE?

Average salary for a teacher with ten years' experience ($)

HIGHEST-PAID TEACHERS: SWITZERLAND

twelve years' experience will earn almost twice the salary of his counterpart in the U.S.

The U.S. does lead the world in at least one educational category: private secondary-school and college tuition. Average annual tuition at a private university is now almost $14,000. The full tab (tuition, room, and board) at an Ivy League college is approaching $25,000. The Japanese pay too, with many parents sending their children to private tutoring schools—the famous *juku*—which can cost up to $10,000 a year. More than 47 percent of Japanese students have attended a *juku* by the ninth grade.

WHAT DOES COLLEGE COST?

Average annual tuition at leading private universities ($)

United States	**$13,960**
Japan	2,633
United Kingdom	0
Germany	0

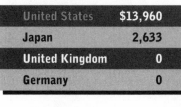

$53,900

44,200

35,900
34,000

29,900
28,300
26,000
26,000
25,700
22,900
22,800
22,700
22,500
21,300
20,900
18,800
17,300
17,300
17,000

7,900

2,700

Switzerland
Japan
Luxembourg
Germany
Canada
Denmark
Finland
United States
Netherlands
Ireland
Sweden
Australia
Norway
Belgium
United Kingdom
Austria
France
Italy
Spain
Portugal
Turkey

Myth:
Teachers get no respect.

Reality:
In most nations, they're among the highest-paid and most respected members of their communities.

43

What are you getting?

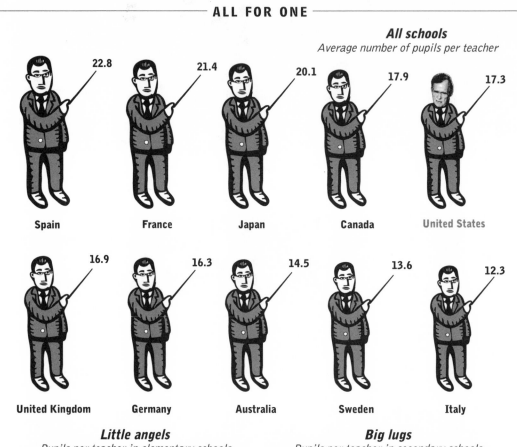

ALL FOR ONE

All schools
Average number of pupils per teacher

22.8	21.4	20.1	17.9	17.3
Spain	France	Japan	Canada	United States

16.9	16.3	14.5	13.6	12.3
United Kingdom	Germany	Australia	Sweden	Italy

Little angels
Pupils per teacher in elementary schools

Spain	25.5
Japan	23.3
France	20.5
United Kingdom	20.3
United States	18.3
Germany	17.4
Australia	16.6
Sweden	16.3
Italy	14.1
Canada	7.5

Big lugs
Pupils per teacher in secondary schools

Spain	21.2
France	19.6
Japan	17.8
Canada	17.2
United States	15.7
United Kingdom	15.3
Germany	14.4
Australia	12.6
Italy	10.2
Sweden	10.1

44

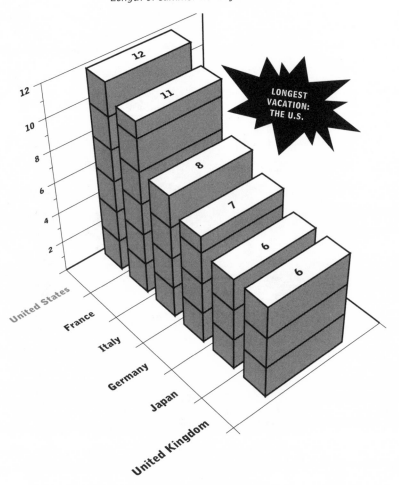

SEE YOU IN SEPTEMBER
Length of summer holiday (weeks)

LONGEST VACATION: THE U.S.

SCHOOL DAZE
Length of school year (days)

The Japanese classroom, which produces some of the world's highest test scores, is also one of the world's most crowded—a conundrum that confounds and annoys educational reformers everywhere.

By the time an American reaches the twelfth grade, his counterparts in Japan and Germany have spent four more years in school. In his essay "The Case for More School Days," Michael J. Barrett calls the American affection for a long, idle summer an example of Huck Finn's law: "The authentic American flourishes in spite of schooling, not because of it."

"Americans think that they can learn in 180 days what the rest of the world takes 220 to 240 days to learn."
—*Lester Thurow, Massachusetts Institute of Technology*

Country	Days
Japan	243
Germany	240
Luxembourg	216
Netherlands	200
United Kingdom	192
Finland	190
New Zealand	190
Canada	185
France	185
Ireland	184
Spain	180
Sweden	180
United States	180
Belgium	175

Myth: *Summer vacation is an important part of growing up.*

Reality: *Summer vacation stunts academic growth.*

What are you getting?

In a survey of students and families in the U.S., Taiwan, and Japan, 40 percent of American mothers said they were "very satisfied" with the performance of their children in school. Fewer than 5 percent of the mothers in Japan and Taiwan said they were "very satisfied." Of the American mothers, 91 percent said they believed their children's schools were doing an "excellent" or a "good" job. Only 39 percent of Japanese mothers could express similar enthusiasm. The study's author, Harold Stevenson of the University of Michigan, points to this as a central paradox in American educational life: "low measures of student performance and high measures of parental satisfaction."

Myth:
America has a head-start program.

Reality:
America has among the lowest preschool enrollments in the industrial world.

HEAD START

Percent of age group enrolled in preschool

Two-year-olds

In the U.S., a statistically insignificant number of two-year-olds are in school programs.

USA	SWI	ÖST	UK	SPA	NZL	GER	FIN	BEL	NOR	FRA
0.0	0.6	1.0	1.3	4.5	8.8	9.1	20.2	21.6	22.8	35.7%

Three-year-olds

IRE	SWI	GRE	JAP	FIN	SPA	UK	ÖST	USA	NOR	GER	NZL	BEL	FRA
0.7	5.4	9.1	15.6	16	17.8	25.9	28.5	28.9	31.6	32.3	42.6	94.1	96.3%

Four-year-olds

SWI	FIN	CAN	GRE	NOR	USA	IRE	JAP	ÖST	UK	GER	NZL	SPA	NET	BEL	FRA
18.7	19.6	41.4	43.2	44.1	49.0	52.1	54.6	63.4	69.2	71.6	72.8	90.6	97.9	98.1	100%

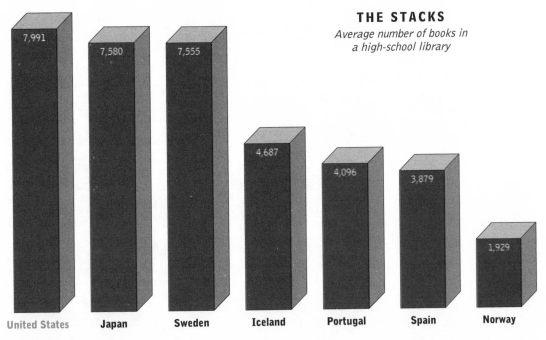

THE STACKS

*Average number of books in
a high-school library*

7,991 — United States
7,580 — Japan
7,555 — Sweden
4,687 — Iceland
4,096 — Portugal
3,879 — Spain
1,929 — Norway

SHOP TALK

*Percent of high-school students on
vocational track*

Germany	79%
Sweden	78
Italy	76
Denmark	69
Luxembourg	55
Norway	53
Finland	52
France	52
Spain	45
Turkey	42
Belgium	41
Austria	39
Netherlands	35
Greece	30
Japan	27
United States	27
Ireland	16
Switzerland	11
United Kingdom	10
New Zealand	2

HARD–DRIVING KIDS

*Percent of elementary schools with
two or more computers*

Canada	98%
United States	96
France	91
New Zealand	78
Netherlands	53
Belgium	36
Portugal	33
Japan	28

0   20   40   60   80   100

Who studies hardest?

The nerd is a Hollywood update of the bookworm, both uniquely American outsiders. In a nation that has traditionally, or mythically, relied on brawn, stamina, motors, glamour, and commercial instincts to clear its frontiers and build its economy, bookishness has been seen as somehow antithetical to the common good—a lifestyle that costs money rather than one that makes money.

Educators argue that America's disdain for intellectuals has made resistance to school—to teachers, classroom time, and homework—an admirable attribute, regularly endorsed on television and in movies, where students who enjoy school and who do well are often portrayed as the misfits. In Japan, by contrast, excelling in school is an almost sacred goal (with Japanese mothers devoting much of their time to helping their children succeed in the classroom).

"American parents believe their kids will get ahead if they're smart; Japanese parents believe ➛

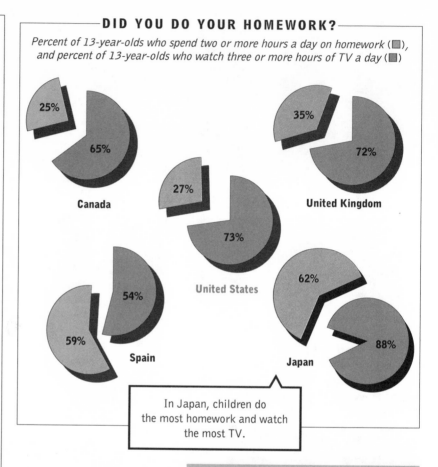

DID YOU DO YOUR HOMEWORK?

Percent of 13-year-olds who spend two or more hours a day on homework (■), and percent of 13-year-olds who watch three or more hours of TV a day (■)

Canada 25% 65%

United Kingdom 35% 72%

United States 27% 73%

Spain 54% 59%

Japan 62% 88%

> In Japan, children do the most homework and watch the most TV.

HAPPY KIDS

Percent of 13-year-olds who like school

United Kingdom	72%
Canada	66
United States	64
Ireland	61
Spain	48

GRINDS

Hours per week spent on academic subjects in primary school

Japan	38
Belgium	29
Greece	28
Norway	26
United States	22
France	20

MR. WIZARDS

Quantum leap
Percent of high-school seniors taking advanced physics

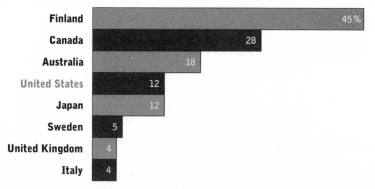

Finland	45%
Canada	28
Australia	18
United States	12
Japan	12
Sweden	5
United Kingdom	4
Italy	4

Test-tube babies
Percent of high-school seniors taking advanced chemistry

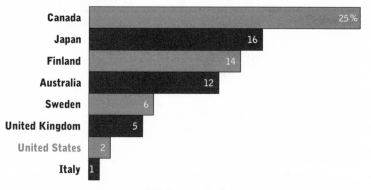

Canada	25%
Japan	16
Finland	14
Australia	12
Sweden	6
United Kingdom	5
United States	2
Italy	1

Slicing and dicing
Percent of high-school seniors taking advanced biology

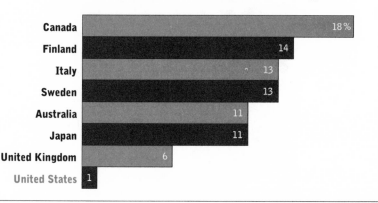

Canada	18%
Finland	14
Italy	13
Sweden	13
Australia	11
Japan	11
United Kingdom	6
United States	1

kids will get ahead if they work hard."
—*Diane Ravitch, author of* Schools We Deserve

"Success in formal education is considered largely synonymous with success in life and is, for most students, almost the only path to social and economic status."
—Japanese Education Today*, a U.S. Department of Education report*

By the end of high school, American students have spent 2,000 more hours in front of the television set than in school. Japanese students, however, are now outwatching Americans.

Myth:
American kids watch the most TV.

Reality:
Japanese kids do.

What the tests show

The International Association for the Evaluation of Educational Achievement (I.E.A.) first began to assess educational quality in mathematics and science in the early 1960s. Since then, the U.S. test results have steadily declined while those of Asia and Europe have been on the rise.

Defenders of American students, however, say it is unfair to compare the achievements of vastly different educational systems. They point out that on most international tests, scores from the entire pool of students in the U.S. are compared with scores from the academic elite of other nations.

Sample question from the test taken by Japanese students wishing to attend a public or private university:

A series of incidents involving Cuba, such as the Cuban revolution of 1959 and the Cuban crisis of 1962, were the most notable events in modern Latin American history and drew world ➤→

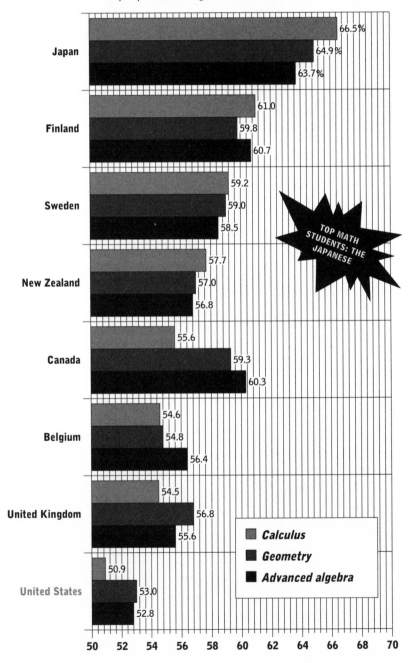

SUPER CRUNCHERS

Percent of correct answers on I.E.A. test for top 5 percent of high-school seniors

Japan: 66.5%, 64.9%, 63.7%

Finland: 61.0, 59.8, 60.7

Sweden: 59.2, 59.0, 58.5

New Zealand: 57.7, 57.0, 56.8

Canada: 55.6, 59.3, 60.3

Belgium: 54.6, 54.8, 56.4

United Kingdom: 54.5, 56.8, 55.6

United States: 50.9, 53.0, 52.8

TOP MATH STUDENTS: THE JAPANESE

Legend:
- Calculus
- Geometry
- Advanced algebra

BEST SCIENCE SCORES

Percent of correct answers on I.E.A. test for high-school seniors

Chemistry

United Kingdom	69.5%
Japan	51.9
Australia	46.6
Norway	41.9
Sweden	40.0
Italy	38.0
United States	37.7
Canada	36.9
Finland	33.3

Physics

United Kingdom	58.3%
Japan	56.1
Norway	52.8
Australia	48.5
United States	45.5
Sweden	44.8
Canada	39.6
Finland	37.9
Italy	28.0

KNOW YOUR PLACE

Of 16 spots on a world map, number identified correctly by 18-year-olds

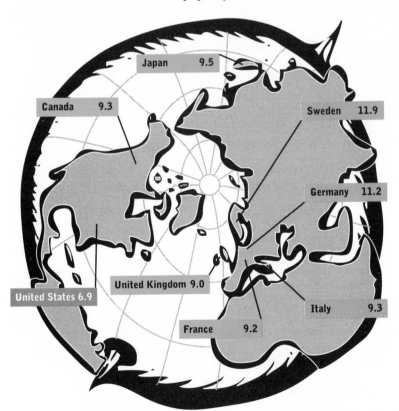

Japan 9.5
Canada 9.3
Sweden 11.9
Germany 11.2
United Kingdom 9.0
United States 6.9
Italy 9.3
France 9.2

attention. They affected the political situation not only in Latin America but also the world at large.

Choose the TWO correct sentences from the following:

a) As a result of the Cuban revolution, a socialist regime was established for the first time in the Americas, North and South.

b) In response to the Cuban revolution, the Organization of American States was established and the containment of Cuba pursued.

c) Nixon and Khrushchev were the leaders of the United States and the Soviet Union during the Cuban crisis.

d) At the time of the crisis, China and the Soviet Union united in countering the United States.

e) The Cuban crisis excited fear of nuclear war throughout the world.

Answers:
ə puɐ ɐ

How much is enough?

> The U.S. system encourages a continuing general education while most other countries emphasize early specialization.

In Japan, as *Atlantic* magazine correspondent James Fallows points out, a good education is much more precisely defined than in the U.S.: It is a degree from Todai— "an institution with the power and prestige and all-around intimidation value of the entire Ivy League, plus Stanford, Berkeley, West Point and the next dozen most famous American universities thrown in." Fallows goes on to note that while John F. Kennedy and George Bush attended Ivy League schools (Harvard and Yale, respectively), you find between them graduates of Southwest Texas State, Whittier, the University of Michigan, the Naval Academy, and Eureka College. In Japan, only two postwar prime ministers have not attended Todai.

Myth:
In America, only the rich can afford higher education.

Reality:
More people go to college in America than anywhere else.

LOCKED UP
Mean number of years spent in school

United States	12.2
Canada	11.4
U.K.	10.8
Japan	10.4
Denmark	9.7
Austria	9.6
Norway	9.6
France	9.4

Sweden	9.4
Australia	9.3
Finland	9.2
New Zealand	8.9
Germany	8.8
Switzerland	8.3
Belgium	7.9
Netherlands	7.9

Ireland	7.7
Luxembourg	7.7
Soviet Union	7.6
Iceland	7.5
Greece	6.5
Italy	6.4
Spain	5.9

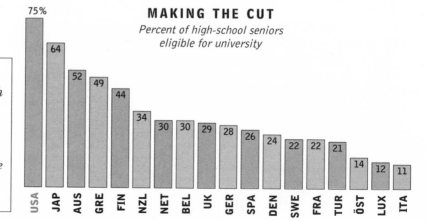

THE HIGHER YOU GO
Percent of students who go beyond high school

USA	CAN	FIN	NZL	BEL	NOR	NET	FRA	SWE	JAP	SPA	GER	DEN	ÖST	GRE	IRE	ITA	SWI	UK	TUR
60%	53	36	36	32	32	31	30	30	30	30	29	28	27	27	26	24	22	22	10

MAKING THE CUT
Percent of high-school seniors eligible for university

USA	JAP	AUS	GRE	FIN	NZL	NET	BEL	UK	GER	SPA	DEN	SWE	FRA	TUR	ÖST	LUX	ITA
75%	64	52	49	44	34	30	30	29	28	26	24	22	22	21	14	12	11

Who's been left behind?

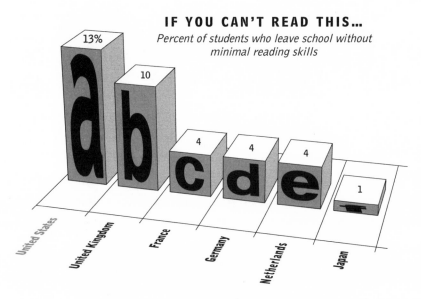

IF YOU CAN'T READ THIS...

Percent of students who leave school without minimal reading skills

- United States — 13%
- United Kingdom — 10
- France — 4
- Germany — 4
- Netherlands — 4
- Japan — 1

One measure of a school system is the number of people it fails. Ninety percent of Japanese students finish high school. Twenty-five percent of American high-school students—nearly 1 million teenagers a year—drop out. America's problem might well be a lot worse except that many teenagers hang on in school so that they can take driver's education and thereby get a better deal on their auto insurance. Moreover, many Americans graduate from high school without being able to read, write, or do simple arithmetic.

DROPOUTS

Percent of students who fail to complete curriculum

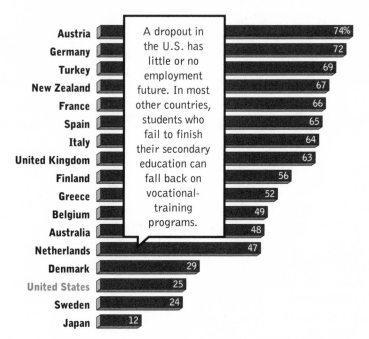

Country	Percent
Austria	74%
Germany	72
Turkey	69
New Zealand	67
France	66
Spain	65
Italy	64
United Kingdom	63
Finland	56
Greece	52
Belgium	49
Australia	48
Netherlands	47
Denmark	29
United States	25
Sweden	24
Japan	12

A dropout in the U.S. has little or no employment future. In most other countries, students who fail to finish their secondary education can fall back on vocational-training programs.

Myth:
The U.S., with its high number of college graduates, is the most educated country.

Reality:
It also has the highest number of uneducated citizens.

Stepping into the knowledge society

The story of how America began to lose its lead in technology development and production has a lot to do with its self-proclaimed postwar role as defender of the free world.

Although the U.S. has twice the population of Japan, and a significantly greater network of advanced technical-training programs, it produces 10 percent fewer engineers—the professionals at the forefront of technological development and innovation. This is partly explained by the imbalances in American salaries (starting lawyers can earn twice as much as rookie engineers), the high cost of an advanced degree, and the willingness of American companies to hire undertrained (read: cheaper) personnel in the engineering area. Many believe the engineer dearth is also a function of national priorities and emphasis, that the glamorous jobs are in selling products, not making them.

America concentrated its scientific prowess on military-related R&D, and Japan focused its talents on consumer markets. While the U.S. built the Stealth bomber, Japan turned the VCR into a mass-market money-maker.

Consumer electronics is a vivid cautionary tale.

In 1948, American scientists invented the transistor at Bell Labs. Throughout the 1950s and 1960s, the Japanese used this American technology to manufacture small, cheap radios. While ridiculed by U.S. consumers, the Japanese were learning from, and improving upon, both U.S. technology and U.S. marketing methods. In 1956, an American company, Ampex, developed the video recorder. In 1963, it went on sale at Neiman Marcus for $30,000. Ampex saw that it would be costly to pursue the home market, so it sold only to professional users. By the early 1970s, the U.S. still owned nearly 100 percent of its consumer-electronics market. Its brand names were the world's leaders: RCA, Motorola, Zenith, GE. But in 1976, Japan's Sony and JVC staked their corporate coffers on the battle between the home video systems Betamax and VHS to ensure their market share of the next generation of consumer electronics. American manufacturers, risking nothing, stood fat and happy on the sidelines. Sony lost, but came roaring back with the Walkman—one of the all-time most successful consumer-electronics products—and there were no American companies in the business anymore.

Brainpower

GEEKS

Scientists and engineers per 1,000 people

Japan	5.0	Germany	2.7	France	2.0
United States	3.3	Netherlands	2.5	Denmark	1.9
Norway	2.9	Switzerland	2.3	Italy	1.2
Sweden	2.7	Canada	2.2	Ireland	1.1
		Australia	2.2	Austria	1.0
				Spain	0.5
				Greece	0.1

STATE OF THE ART

Nobel prizes in the sciences 1950–1990

United States	138
United Kingdom	40
Germany	25
Sweden	9
France	7
Italy	5
Switzerland	5
Japan	4
Australia	3
Belgium	3
Denmark	3
Norway	3
Austria	2
Canada	2
Ireland	1
Netherlands	1
Finland	0
Greece	0
New Zealand	0
Portugal	0
Spain	0
Turkey	0

$e = mc^2$

Inventing the new world

One indicator of future wealth is the value of the patents a nation holds. It had long been assumed that the U.S. had nearly an insurmountable lead in basic scientific research, and therefore an ultimate advantage in the world's industrial competition. Recent studies have shown, however, that while the U.S. is strong in a variety of academic fields like environmental studies, agricultural sciences, and clinical medicine and life sciences, it is behind in areas necessary for supporting industrial advances: engineering, computer science, electronics, communications, robotics, and instrumentation. Several studies have attempted to ➠

PATENT PENDING
Patent applications

GIZMO DENSITY
Patents per 100,000 people

Switzerland	486	Australia	123
Japan	334	France	118
Sweden	296	United States	112
Germany	261	Norway	92
Finland	176	Belgium	69
Denmark	172	Ireland	47
Netherlands	156	Canada	46
Austria	133	New Zealand	46
United Kingdom	133	Greece	16
		Iceland	15
		Spain	12
		Portugal	2

Country	Patent applications
Japan	345,239
United States	146,904
Germany	84,806
United Kingdom	79,916
France	66,095
Italy	52,939
Netherlands	40,115
Sweden	37,410
Switzerland	36,940
Belgium	33,867
Austria	31,872
Canada	31,641
Spain	26,251
Luxembourg	23,041
Australia	22,096
Greece	13,764
Denmark	11,080
Finland	9,986
Norway	9,435
New Zealand	4,425
Ireland	3,901
Portugal	2,464
Turkey	900
Iceland	126

OUT-OF-TOWN TALENT
Patents held by foreign nationals (%)

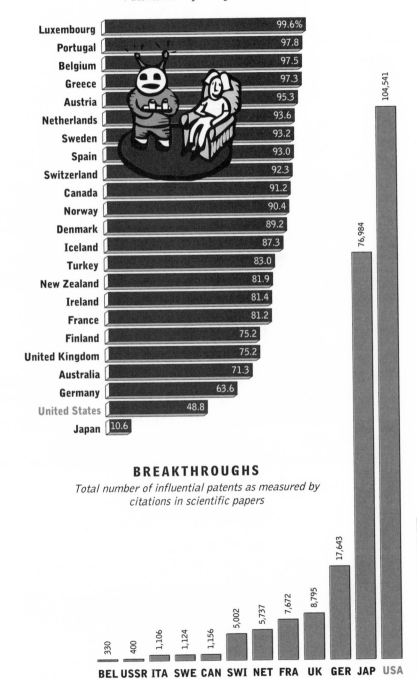

Luxembourg	99.6%
Portugal	97.8
Belgium	97.5
Greece	97.3
Austria	95.3
Netherlands	93.6
Sweden	93.2
Spain	93.0
Switzerland	92.3
Canada	91.2
Norway	90.4
Denmark	89.2
Iceland	87.3
Turkey	83.0
New Zealand	81.9
Ireland	81.4
France	81.2
Finland	75.2
United Kingdom	75.2
Australia	71.3
Germany	63.6
United States	48.8
Japan	10.6

BREAKTHROUGHS
Total number of influential patents as measured by citations in scientific papers

BEL	USSR	ITA	SWE	CAN	SWI	NET	FRA	UK	GER	JAP	USA
330	400	1,106	1,124	1,156	5,002	5,737	7,672	8,795	17,643	76,984	104,541

measure not just the overall number of patents, but the number of important and influential ones—those that will most likely generate wealth and growth for a nation. These studies show a new world in which Japan is rapidly overtaking the United States.

U.S. spending on R&D has only nominally increased over the past ten years, holding between 1.5 and 2 percent of GNP. In Japan, R&D spending has reached 3 percent of GNP.

"We're losing our creative edge. American industry is on the decline because U.S. managers are too concerned about protecting short-term earnings to innovate."
—*James Clark, founder of Silicon Graphics.*

Myth:
The Japanese merely imitate Western technology.

Reality:
The Japanese lead the world in technological creativity.

Computers

The U.S. is far and away the most computer-literate, computer-eager society. And in America, computers are not the exclusive province of college-educated white-collar workers, as they are in Europe and Japan. According to a study by the Roper Organization, 25 percent of adults with only a high-school education regularly use personal computers.

The Japanese have strongly resisted the computer. JAL executive Shinzo Suto, 54, says, "Most people our age, except for the technical departments, are allergic to machines." Another problem: Often there isn't enough room on a Japanese salaryman's tiny desk for a standard-size PC.

PC UNIVERSE
Computers per 1,000 people

Country	Computers per 1,000
United States	202
United Kingdom	114
Canada	112
Norway	103
Ireland	99
Switzerland	92
Denmark	89
Sweden	87
Germany	82
Japan	75
New Zealand	72
Belgium	70
Netherlands	70
Finland	68
France	68
Australia	66
Austria	47
Italy	43
Portugal	24
Greece	22
Spain	17

MOST DIGITIZED: THE U.S.

A CLONE AT HOME
Percent of households with a personal computer

United States	26%	Belgium	15	Sweden	12
U.K.	22	Denmark	14	Austria	11
Netherlands	20	France	14	Spain	8
Finland	16	Switzerland	14	Japan	8
Norway	16	Ireland	12	Portugal	7
Germany	16	Italy	12	Greece	6

Myth:
The Japanese have all the latest gizmos.

Reality:
But few computers.

POWER UP
MIPS—millions of (computer) instructions per second (thousands)

MOST MIPS: THE U.S.

50,372

SOUPED UP
Amount spent on work stations ($ billions)

United States	$4.20
France	1.96
Japan	0.58
Italy	0.52
Germany	0.51
United Kingdom	0.48

MIPS

7,048
5,138
4,071
3,115
2,384
2,080
901 864 608 581 509 490 383 360 297

United States · Japan · United Kingdom · Germany · France · Canada · Italy · Australia · Netherlands · Sweden · Belgium · Switzerland · Spain · Denmark · Norway · Austria

"In Japan, people will buy expensive cars because they look attractive. You need to make computers that are more attractive, more automatic and easier to use. It's still difficult to enjoy using a PC and they don't look nice."
—Kiyoshi Hayamizu, general manager in NEC's PC sales promotion division

Will the United States blow its seemingly insurmountable lead in computers? So far, the U.S. has lost its advantage in semiconductor manufacturing, dropping almost half of its market share during the 1980s. This same period saw Japan's piece of the chip market more than double. If the U.S. semiconductor industry dies, many observers say, so will the PC industry. Sun Microsystems president Scott McNealy says that U.S. computer-makers will be "history" unless the Japanese computer-chip headlock is broken with a "baseball bat."

Computers

In 1989, the U.S. became a net importer of computers—running a deficit of $6 million with Japan.

"The most profound advantages will go to companies that have access to patient capital, that maintain close links with component and equipment developers, and that can afford huge, continuing expenditures for R&D and capital investment. These facts play directly into the strategic and technical strengths of Japanese companies."
—*Charles H. Ferguson,* Harvard Business Review

Myth:
Illegal software copying in the U.S. has gotten out of hand.

Reality:
In Europe, it's standard practice.

THE CRAYS
Supercomputers in use

Once the exclusive province of American companies, foremost among them Cray Research, the supercomputer monopoly has recently been broken by Japanese newcomers such as Hitachi and NEC.

United States 156
Europe 84
France 25
Japan 24
Germany 20
United Kingdom 17
Italy 5

BOOT UP!
Share of world software market (%)

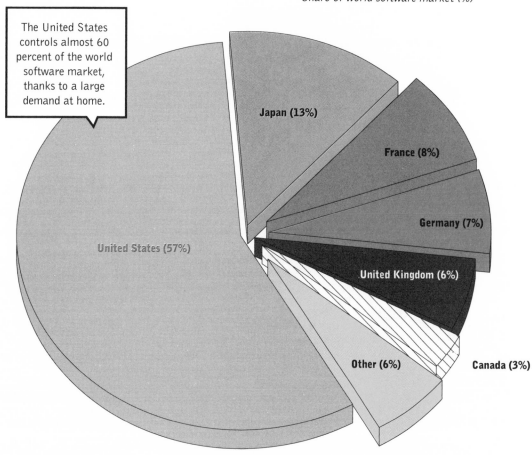

The United States controls almost 60 percent of the world software market, thanks to a large demand at home.

United States (57%)

Japan (13%)

France (8%)

Germany (7%)

United Kingdom (6%)

Other (6%)

Canada (3%)

WORD CRUNCHERS
Annual sales of word processing programs ($ millions)

United States	$6,154
France	1,420
Italy	1,243
United Kingdom	1,185
Germany	824
Japan	83

NUMBER CRUNCHERS
Annual sales of spreadsheet programs ($ millions)

United States	$4,913
France	1,136
Italy	994
Germany	824
United Kingdom	404
Japan	51

COPYRIGHT CRUNCHERS
Percent of software in use that is bootlegged

Portugal	90%
Italy	81
Spain	78
Germany	71
France	65
United Kingdom	51
United States	45

Telecommunications

ROAD CALL
Percent of population owning a mobile phone

Finland 2.83%

Canada 1.79

United States 1.42

Australia 0.72

New Zealand 0.40

Germany 0.29

Japan 0.20

Italy 0.11

Portugal 0.002

THE TELEMARKET
Total spending on telephone-network expansion, 1990 ($ millions)

Although the U.S. continues to outspend other nations on its telecommunications systems, most moneys are spent on maintaining older equipment, while in Europe and Japan, investment is in new technologies.

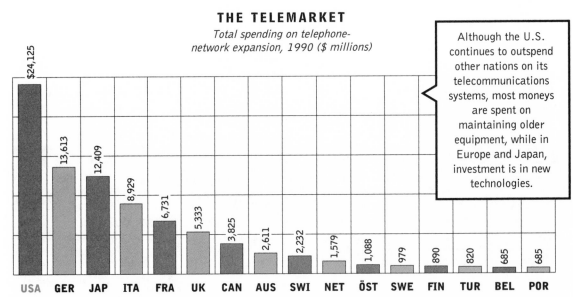

USA	GER	JAP	ITA	FRA	UK	CAN	AUS	SWI	NET	ÖST	SWE	FIN	TUR	BEL	POR
$24,125	13,613	12,409	8,929	6,731	5,333	3,825	2,611	2,232	1,579	1,088	979	890	820	685	685

AFTER THE BEEP

Percent of households owning an answering machine

Greece	1
Portugal	1
Luxembourg	2
Italy	2
Ireland	2
Spain	2
Austria	3
Germany	4
Netherlands	4
Denmark	4
Belgium	5
Switzerland	5
United Kingdom	6
Finland	6
Norway	6
France	7
Sweden	9
United States	42%

JUST THE FAXES

Fax machines per 10,000 people

Netherlands	198	United Kingdom	30
Germany	84	Italy	26
Switzerland	71	Finland	23
Japan	65	Denmark	23
Sweden	61	Spain	17
United States	50	Austria	14
Australia	45	Portugal	12
New Zealand	42	France	11
Belgium	41	Greece	11
Canada	40	Ireland	10

American phone companies spend heavily just to maintain the still-adequate system that was put in place over the past twenty years. Europe and Japan, however, are now scrapping their antiquated systems and replacing them with advanced systems that will catapult them beyond the U.S.

By some estimates, AT&T and the seven regional Bell companies will have to double their capital spending to match the sophistication of the telecommunications networks being installed in other countries around the world.

Myth:
The U.S. phone system is the world's best.

Reality:
It will soon be the best old system, surpassed by many newer ones.

Telecommunications

Telecommunications and related industries account for almost 9 percent of Japanese GNP and are projected to reach 20 percent by the year 2000. In the U.S., these industries will remain at little more than 4 percent of GNP.

The biggest investment, however, is taking place in Europe—where spending reached almost $50 billion in 1990. With major upgrades in every country—a digital trunk network in the U.K., a broadband network in Denmark, and full ISDN capability in Spain, for instance—post-1992 Europe will have the world's most advanced telecommunications system. France, the world's leader in telecom development, is trying to put a video phone—the fantasy promised to Americans (in the near future) as long ago as the 1964 New York World's Fair—into every French home by early next century.

By the year 2000, the telecommunications-equipment industry will be dominated by three manufacturers—not one of them American.

THE PHONE BILL

Government telecommunications investment as a percent of GNP

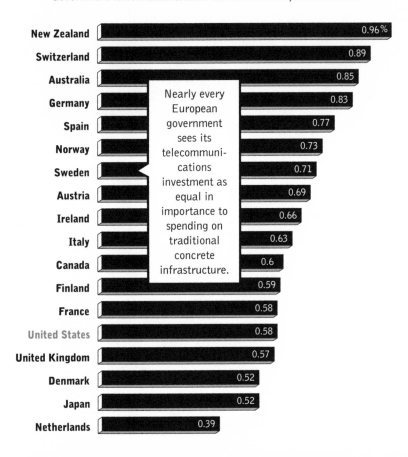

New Zealand	0.96%
Switzerland	0.89
Australia	0.85
Germany	0.83
Spain	0.77
Norway	0.73
Sweden	0.71
Austria	0.69
Ireland	0.66
Italy	0.63
Canada	0.6
Finland	0.59
France	0.58
United States	0.58
United Kingdom	0.57
Denmark	0.52
Japan	0.52
Netherlands	0.39

Nearly every European government sees its telecommunications investment as equal in importance to spending on traditional concrete infrastructure.

FIBER-OPTIC SPAGHETTI

Miles of cabling per 1,000 square miles

France	161.80
United Kingdom	100.82
Germany	75.43
Japan	55.89
United States	34.47
Canada	7.33

TOUCH-TONES

Digital lines (%)

France	70.7%
Canada	51.4
United States	42.5
United Kingdom	38.0
Japan	31.0
Italy	16.1
Germany	2.6

REACH FAR OUT AND TOUCH SOMEONE
Peak cost of a three-minute international call ($)

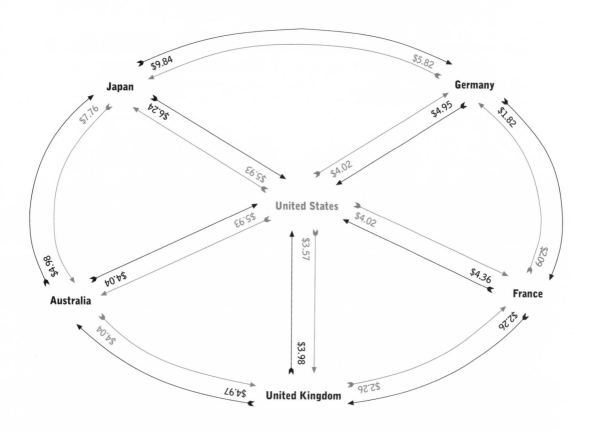

OFFICE PHONE
Monthly costs per business phone line ($)

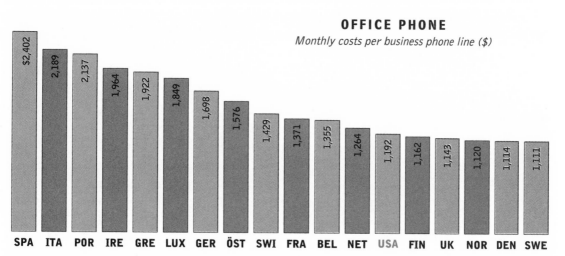

Culture—high and low

American popular culture dominates the world. No other nation even comes close to matching the U.S. genius for manufacturing and selling myths and fantasies, icons and attitudes.

"What will remain of our cultural identity if audiovisual Europe consists of European consumers sitting in front of Japanese TV sets showing American programs?"
—Edith Cresson, prime minister of France

Despite the horror with which the European cultural establishment views the American pop invasion, cultural imperialism has begun to cut both ways. Foreign sales have become so important to Hollywood that the foreign market now strongly influences which films and TV shows get made. Some people are describing the demands of the foreign market as a whole new cultural influence: universalism. The goal is to create programming that will appeal to the widest possible markets.

"Car goes down the street, car makes the wrong turn, car blows up," is how Group W Productions president Dirk Simmerman describes the formula.

With an annual trade surplus of $8 billion, entertainment rivals computers, aircraft, and food as America's most lucrative export.

The common culture of Europe may well be American—from logos and brand names (Ralph Lauren, Coca Cola, Timberland, American Express—all "badges of Americana," according to a study of foreign buying habits by the international advertising agency Ogilvy & Mather); to movies and television shows; to jazz, rock, and hip-hop; to enduring archetypes (Humphrey Bogart, James Dean, and the Marlboro Man).

"Have we the right to exist?" demanded EC president Jacques Delors about the fate of European cultural identity in the face of the popularity of *I Love Lucy, Who's the Boss, Santa Barbara, Dallas,* and *Wheel of Fortune* (*La Roue de la Fortune* in France), to name just a few of the American shows that saturate European airtime. After considerable gnashing of teeth, the EC finally approved a set of protectionist rules meant to ward off the total dominance of American game shows, sitcoms, and soap operas. But with the advent of satellite technologies and with increasing demand for American "product," almost no one expects these measures to change much of anything.

The Japanese have taken their characteristic approach to the problem: If you can't beat 'em, buy 'em. To gain control over the software that plays on their TVs, VCRs, and stereos, Japanese companies like Sony and Matsushita have bought heavily into Hollywood, acquiring Columbia Pictures, MCA, and CBS Records. German, English, and Italian companies are also gobbling up pieces of America's pop pantheon.

Audiovisual imperialism

REMOTE, COLOR, CABLE-READY

Percent of households with...

MOST COUCH *JAGAIMOS:* THE JAPANESE

Cable

Netherlands	87%
Switzerland	71
Canada	69
United States	55
Sweden	32
Germany	29
Spain	22
Austria	20
Japan	12
France	9
United Kingdom	3
Italy	0

Remote

Japan	100%
Germany	84
Switzerland	83
Italy	81
Luxembourg	79
United States	72
Sweden	70
Belgium	68
Netherlands	66
France	63
United Kingdom	60

Color

Japan	100%	Belgium	93
Australia	97	Spain	93
United States	97	Ireland	92
Luxembourg	96	Switzerland	91
Netherlands	96	Austria	90
Denmark	95	France	88
Norway	95	Italy	88
United Kingdom	94	Canada	69
Germany	94	Greece	64

Audiovisual imperialism

Europe is now the world's hottest TV market. One hundred thirty-four million television homes watched 573,000 hours of programing in 1990—a 20 percent increase over 1989 and a 76 percent rise from 1988.

"If we have a TV movie based on some very American theme, some social issue or what we call 'disease of the week,' we will try not to produce it. Soft pictures, cute romantic comedies, are very hard to sell outside the United States. But if you have a suspense drama, an action-adventure-type drama, that sells abroad. That's the type of program we want. It's got to have that universal theme."
—*Michael J. Solomon, president, International Television, Time Warner*

WHOSE SHOW IS IT ANYWAY?
Percent of programming created in another country

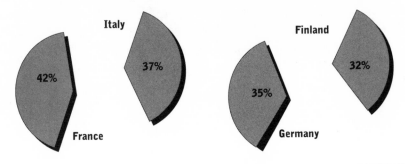

Italy 37%
France 42%
Finland 32%
Germany 35%

THE NIGHTLY NEWS
News shows as a percent of all programming

United States 2%
Japan 6%
France 17%
United Kingdom 17%
Germany 20%
Italy 18%

"WE'LL BE RIGHT BACK"
Average advertising minutes per hour

| United States | Ireland | Netherlands | Germany | Turkey |
| 13:30 | 04:41 | 03:00 | 02:45 | 02:38 |

| Spain | Switzerland | Finland | France | Japan |
| 02:13 | 01:41 | 01:34 | 00:50 | 00:22 |

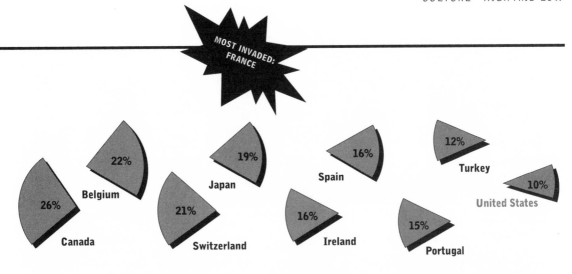

MOST INVADED: FRANCE

Canada 26%
Belgium 22%
Switzerland 21%
Japan 19%
Ireland 16%
Spain 16%
Portugal 15%
Turkey 12%
United States 10%

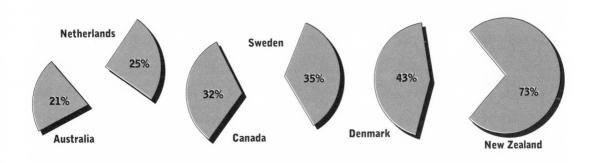

Australia 21%
Netherlands 25%
Canada 32%
Sweden 35%
Denmark 43%
New Zealand 73%

GLUED TO THE TUBE

Average number of hours per day spent watching television

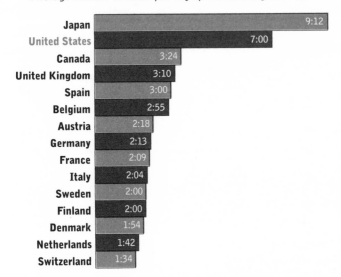

Japan	9:12
United States	7:00
Canada	3:24
United Kingdom	3:10
Spain	3:00
Belgium	2:55
Austria	2:18
Germany	2:13
France	2:09
Italy	2:04
Sweden	2:00
Finland	2:00
Denmark	1:54
Netherlands	1:42
Switzerland	1:34

"LIGHTS! CAMCORDERS!"

Percent of households with a video camera

United States	18%
Japan	12
Norway	9
Austria	7
Netherlands	7
Sweden	7
Switzerland	7
Belgium	6
Finland	6
France	6
Germany	6
Denmark	5
Italy	4
Spain	4
United Kingdom	4

Audiovisual imperialism

"Many Europeans
have an almost
colonialist attitude
toward us. We
provide them with
wonderful
distractions, the
feeling of diversion.
Perhaps Europeans
will eventually view
us as a wonderfully
advanced Third World
country with a lot of
rhythm—a kind of
pleasure country, so
cheap with the dollar
down and all that
singing and dancing
and TV."
—*Susan Sontag*

Some U.S. critics say
America's strength in
pop exports is a
symptom of industrial
decline eerily
reminiscent of the
period of the 1960s
when England, which
had begun its long
economic slide, was
supplying the world
with films and pop
stars.

Myth:
*Hollywood is the movie
capital of the world.*

Reality:
*Perhaps one day
Moscow will be.*

WRAP PARTY
Number of movies produced annually

United States	578
Japan	286
Soviet Union	156
France	133
Italy	116
Turkey	96
Spain	69
Germany	65
United Kingdom	51
Australia	34
Switzerland	32
Canada	26
Sweden	26
Greece	22
Netherlands	18
Finland	15
Austria	12
Belgium	12
Denmark	12
Norway	7
New Zealand	5
Portugal	5
Iceland	1
Ireland	1

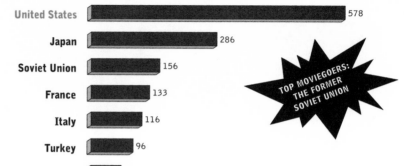

TOP MOVIEGOERS:
THE FORMER
SOVIET UNION

B.O. BOFFO!
*Average number of movies a
person sees each year*

Soviet Union	13.6
United States	4.5
Ireland	3.3
Canada	3.0
Norway	3.0
France	2.5
Switzerland	2.5
Denmark	2.2
Sweden	2.2
Spain	2.2
Italy	1.9
Germany	1.8
Portugal	1.7
Belgium	1.6
Austria	1.5
United Kingdom	1.3
Finland	1.3
Japan	1.2
Netherlands	1.1
Turkey	0.5

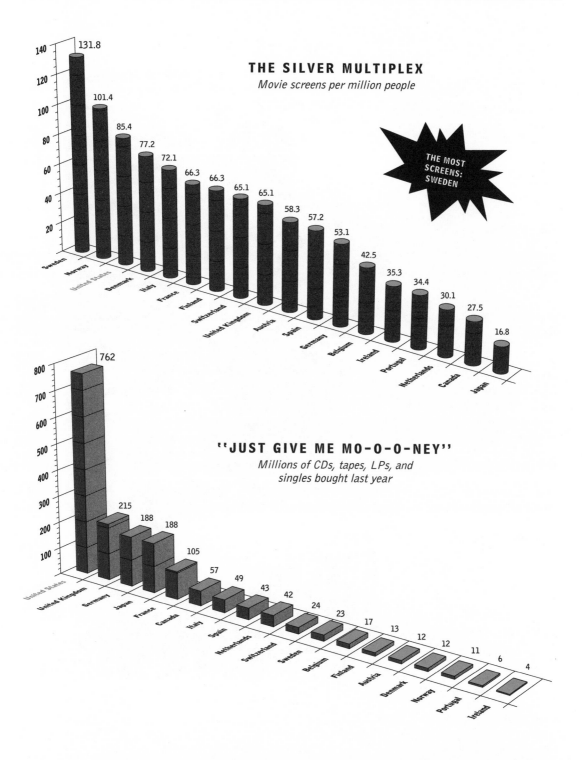

THE SILVER MULTIPLEX
Movie screens per million people

THE MOST SCREENS: SWEDEN

131.8 — Sweden
101.4 — Norway
85.4 — United States
77.2 — Denmark
72.1 — Italy
66.3 — France
66.3 — Finland
65.1 — Switzerland
65.1 — United Kingdom
58.3 — Austria
57.2 — Spain
53.1 — Germany
42.5 — Belgium
35.3 — Ireland
34.4 — Portugal
30.1 — Netherlands
27.5 — Canada
16.8 — Japan

"JUST GIVE ME MO-O-O-NEY"
Millions of CDs, tapes, LPs, and singles bought last year

762 — United States
215 — United Kingdom
188 — Germany
188 — Japan
105 — France
57 — Canada
49 — Italy
43 — Spain
42 — Netherlands
24 — Switzerland
23 — Sweden
17 — Belgium
13 — Finland
12 — Austria
12 — Denmark
11 — Norway
6 — Portugal
4 — Ireland

71

The word

While not the most read, the U.S. press is arguably the freest in the world. Most European and Japanese newspapers openly ally themselves with political parties, often receiving financial support from them. The British government regularly uses the Official Secrets Act to censor stories it finds embarrassing. In Italy, a significant portion of the news media is controlled by Gianni Agnelli, whose family-run company, Fiat, is also the nation's largest company. Japanese newspapers are famous both for their lack of controversial reporting and for their dullness. And almost every major newspaper in Japan maintains a close relationship with the ruling Liberal Democratic Party.

Myth:
New York is the world's publishing mecca.

Reality:
It trails Moscow and London.

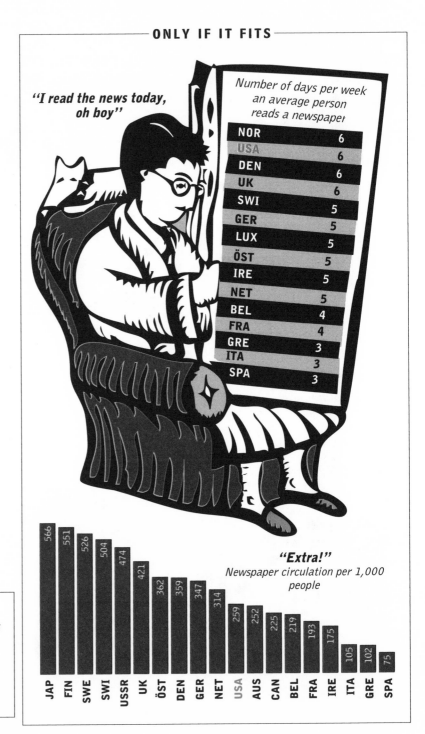

ONLY IF IT FITS

"I read the news today, oh boy"

Number of days per week an average person reads a newspaper

NOR	6
USA	6
DEN	6
UK	6
SWI	5
GER	5
LUX	5
ÖST	5
IRE	5
NET	5
BEL	4
FRA	4
GRE	3
ITA	3
SPA	3

"Extra!"
Newspaper circulation per 1,000 people

JAP	FIN	SWE	SWI	USSR	UK	ÖST	DEN	GER	NET	USA	AUS	CAN	BEL	FRA	IRE	ITA	GRE	SPA
566	551	526	504	474	421	362	359	347	314	259	252	225	219	193	175	105	102	75

BOOK 'EM

Bonfire of the vanities
Total books published per year

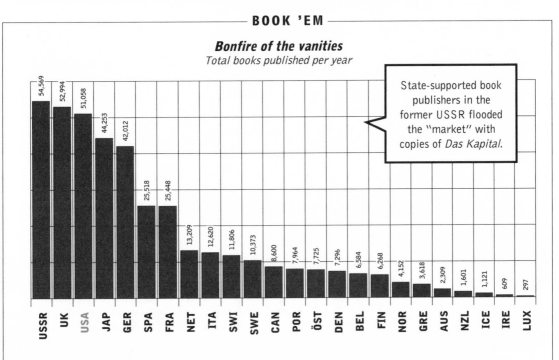

> State-supported book publishers in the former USSR flooded the "market" with copies of *Das Kapital*.

USSR 54,569 · UK 52,994 · USA 51,058 · JAP 44,253 · GER 42,012 · SPA 25,518 · FRA 25,448 · NET 13,209 · ITA 12,620 · SWI 11,806 · SWE 10,373 · CAN 8,600 · POR 7,964 · ÖST 7,725 · DEN 7,296 · BEL 6,584 · FIN 6,268 · NOR 4,152 · GRE 3,618 · AUS 2,309 · NZL 1,601 · ICE 1,121 · IRE 609 · LUX 297

Bucks for books
Annual per capita spending on books ($)

Norway	$119.61
Finland	113.63
Germany	84.62
Denmark	83.52
Belgium	75.42
Sweden	58.65
Switzerland	57.44
Japan	46.09
Austria	38.82
France	36.20
United Kingdom	31.19
United States	30.85
Ireland	22.51
Spain	20.28
Netherlands	19.49
Luxembourg	19.44
Italy	14.51
Greece	11.71
Portugal	5.05

"Shhh!"
Total public libraries

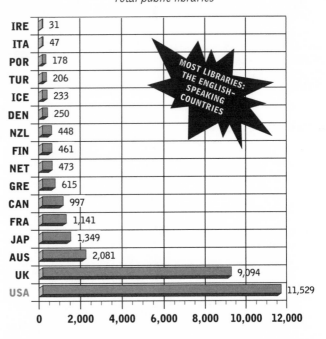

MOST LIBRARIES: THE ENGLISH-SPEAKING COUNTRIES

IRE	31
ITA	47
POR	178
TUR	206
ICE	233
DEN	250
NZL	448
FIN	461
NET	473
GRE	615
CAN	997
FRA	1,141
JAP	1,349
AUS	2,081
UK	9,094
USA	11,529

0   2,000   4,000   6,000   8,000   10,000   12,000

Arts for art's sake

More public money is available for cultural activities in Tokyo than in the entire U.S. Critics point out that penny-pinching the arts is shortsighted not only because they can play a vital part in a nation's sense of self, but also because culture can be a big money-maker. Employing half a million people in the U.K., and generating revenues of $25 billion, the arts are as big a force in the British economy, for instance, as the auto industry. Over the course of little more than a generation, the number of arts festivals in Europe has grown from a few dozen to more than 2,000 in 1990, providing a big boost to local and regional economies.

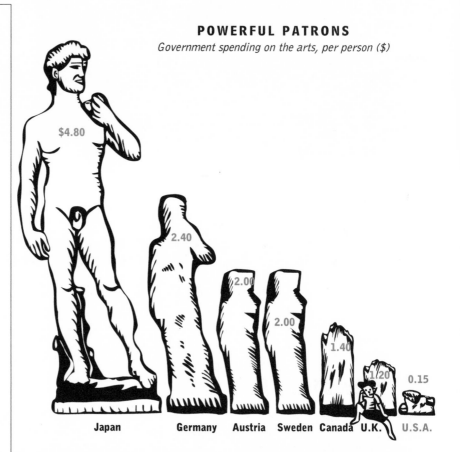

POWERFUL PATRONS
Government spending on the arts, per person ($)

$4.80 — Japan
2.40 — Germany
2.00 — Austria
2.00 — Sweden
1.40 — Canada
1.20 — U.K.
0.15 — U.S.A.

"ARE YOU REAL, ARE YOU REAL, MONA LISA?"
Annual museum visits per 1,000 people

Country	Visits		Country	Visits
Sweden	1,900		Soviet Union	630
Denmark	1,530		Finland	590
United States	1,500		Japan	480
Austria	1,200		Iceland	462
Norway	1,150		Italy	410
Netherlands	1,096		Australia	360
Germany	930		Belgium	350
United Kingdom	920		Spain	320
Canada	640		France	210

Myth:
The biggest problem for the arts in the U.S. is government censorship.

Reality:
The biggest problem is lack of funding.

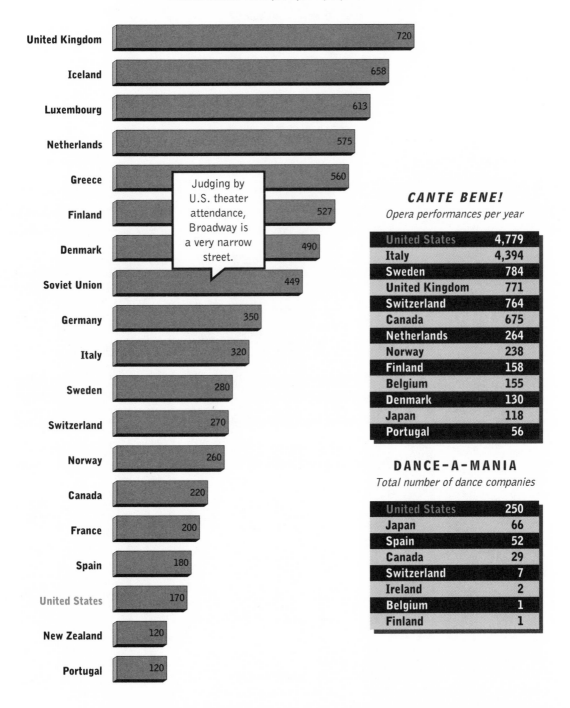

"WELCOME, *MEIN LIEBER HERR*"
Annual theater visits per 1,000 people

United Kingdom	720
Iceland	658
Luxembourg	613
Netherlands	575
Greece	560
Finland	527
Denmark	490
Soviet Union	449
Germany	350
Italy	320
Sweden	280
Switzerland	270
Norway	260
Canada	220
France	200
Spain	180
United States	170
New Zealand	120
Portugal	120

Judging by U.S. theater attendance, Broadway is a very narrow street.

CANTE BENE!
Opera performances per year

United States	4,779
Italy	4,394
Sweden	784
United Kingdom	771
Switzerland	764
Canada	675
Netherlands	264
Norway	238
Finland	158
Belgium	155
Denmark	130
Japan	118
Portugal	56

DANCE-A-MANIA
Total number of dance companies

United States	250
Japan	66
Spain	52
Canada	29
Switzerland	7
Ireland	2
Belgium	1
Finland	1

And the winner is...

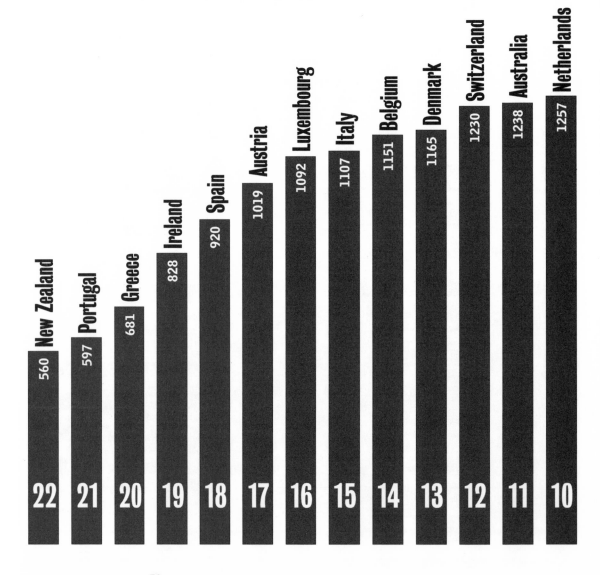

WHERE–WE–STAND INDEX
(0=least educated; 2,000=exceptionally educated)

New Zealand	Portugal	Greece	Ireland	Spain	Austria	Luxembourg	Italy	Belgium	Denmark	Switzerland	Australia	Netherlands
560	597	681	828	920	1019	1092	1107	1151	1165	1230	1238	1257
22	21	20	19	18	17	16	15	14	13	12	11	10

Germany

Germany most consistently tops the charts for educational accomplishments, technological advances, and communications sophistication. In fact, Germany spends the least on its educational system but—with its comprehensive trade-school programs, its long school year, and its rigorous standards—manages to produce some of the best overall results. As with its economic foundation, its overall educational, technological, and cultural infrastructure seems great enough to embrace the new German citizens in the East.

1259 Finland	1312 Norway	1333 France	1377 United Kingdom	1383 Canada	1427 Sweden	1492 United States	1510 Japan	1518
9	8	7	6	5	4	3	2	1

THE HEALTHIEST

What kills you?

Advanced nations are defined almost as well by their diseases as by their wealth. The overwhelming likelihood is that we will die as a result of our plentiful diets, our overdeveloped environments, our sedentary, stress-producing life-styles, and the very longevity that modern life and modern medicine have made possible.

Kidney stones and gallstones; breast, ovary, and prostate cancer; and, of course, myocardial infarctions—heart attacks by any other name—are our postmodern diseases, whereas appendicitis and ulcers are already dated, and chronic bronchitis and rheumatic heart disease are merely remnants of our past lower living standards.

Among the advanced nations, "Western disease" is a unifying malady, a group of afflictions common to most of the industrialized world and uncommon everywhere else. An eerie question that's emerging is whether Japan, along with the developing Asian nations, will join the West not only economically and culturally but epidemiologically. Indeed, the incidence of lung cancer in Japan climbed 85 percent between 1975 and 1985; breast cancer rose by 105 percent.

We are what kills us.

But each nation adds its special, perhaps characteristic, twist. In Japan, it's suicide and stomach cancer. In the U.S., heart attacks and murder. You stand the least chance of getting cancer in what used to be the Soviet Union. But that's because virtually everything else kills you first.

The good news is that because of preventive care, safer living conditions, and better drugs, it's unlikely you'll die of an infectious or parasitic ailment. The bad news is that you have more than an 80 percent chance of dying of cancer, heart disease, strokes, smoking-related respiratory illnesses, or injuries and car crashes. The Japanese, being among the world's greatest smokers, are more likely than anyone else to die of respiratory disease. For the Russians (with their salty diet), strokes are a good bet. The U.S. vies with Sweden and the former USSR for top heart-attack nation. But France, land of butterfat, is where your heart is least likely to kill you. According to a recent, although probably not final, study, red wine, especially tannic red wine, protects the heart—as do foie gras and goose fat.

What are your chances?

YOUR CHANCE OF DYING OF...
Heart disease (%)

Sweden	38.3%
United States	37.2
Soviet Union	37.1
Australia	35.2
Germany	33.2
Canada	33.0
Denmark	33.0
Switzerland	31.5
United Kingdom	31.2
Netherlands	29.2
Spain	25.3
Italy	25.0
East Germany	24.4
Japan	22.0
France	21.8

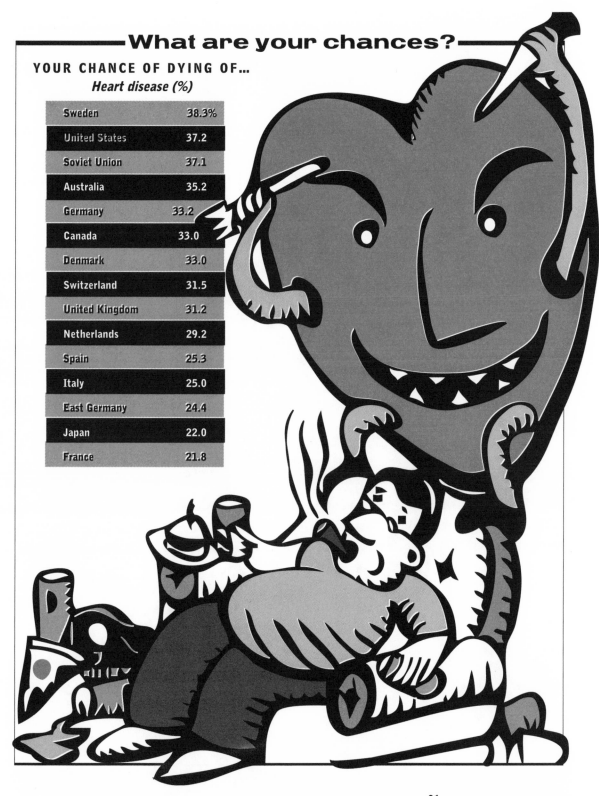

What are your chances?

YOUR CHANCE OF DYING OF...

The U.S. ranks 11th out of 16 in cancer deaths in the industrial world. Americans are 22 percent less likely to die of cancer than the high-risk Dutch.

Cancer
(%)

NET	SWI	DEN	FRA	UK	CAN	GER	ITA	AUS	JAP	USA	SWE	SPA	USSR
26.8%	24.8	24.4	24.0	24.0	23.7	23.7	22.2	21.8	21.2	21.1	19.9	18.8	14.9

Stroke
(%)

USSR	JAP	SPA	ITA	GER	UK	FRA	SWE	SWI	NET	DEN	CAN	USA	AUS
21.5%	17.9	16.8	15.4	12.8	12.5	11.3	10.8	10.7	10.4	9.4	8.8	8.0	7.6

TOP STROKE RISK: THE LATE USSR AND JAPAN

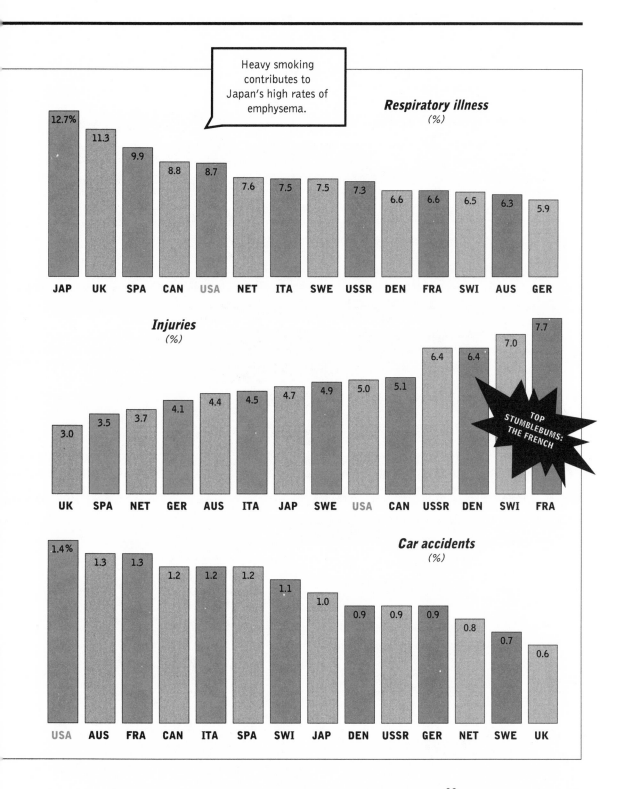

The heart of the matter

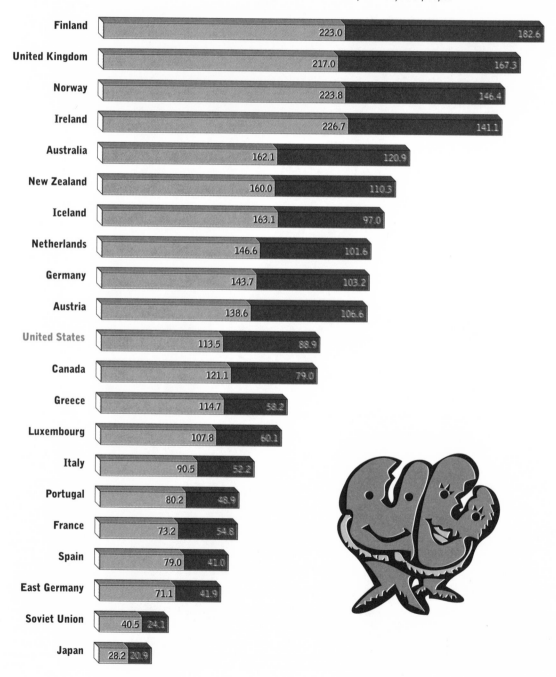

THE HARDEST-HIT COUNTRIES

Heart-attack death rate for men (▢) and women (■) per 100,000 people

Country	Men	Women
Finland	223.0	182.6
United Kingdom	217.0	167.3
Norway	223.8	146.4
Ireland	226.7	141.1
Australia	162.1	120.9
New Zealand	160.0	110.3
Iceland	163.1	97.0
Netherlands	146.6	101.6
Germany	143.7	103.2
Austria	138.6	106.6
United States	113.5	88.9
Canada	121.1	79.0
Greece	114.7	58.2
Luxembourg	107.8	60.1
Italy	90.5	52.2
Portugal	80.2	48.9
France	73.2	54.8
Spain	79.0	41.0
East Germany	71.1	41.9
Soviet Union	40.5	24.1
Japan	28.2	20.9

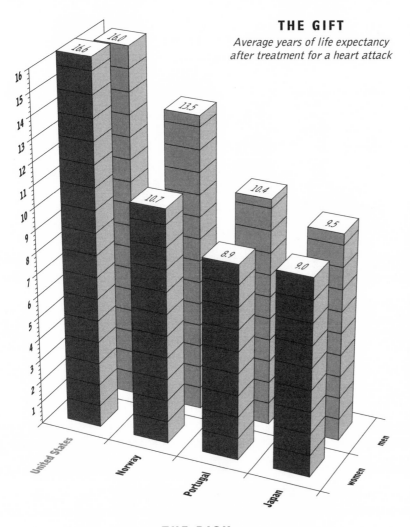

THE GIFT

*Average years of life expectancy
after treatment for a heart attack*

16.6   16.0   13.5   10.7   10.4   8.9   9.0   9.5

United States   Norway   Portugal   Japan   men   women

THE RISK

*Percent of men with at least two out of four risk factors (smoking, high body mass,
high blood pressure, and high cholesterol) for heart disease*

United Kingdom	42.6%		Northern Ireland	27.8
Finland	41.5		Switzerland	27.3
Denmark	32.9		Soviet Union	25.1
Luxembourg	31.4		Italy	24.8
Belgium	30.8		Australia	21.1
Germany	28.9		United States	18.7
France	28.2		New Zealand	16.8

The Japanese smoke and drink too much and exercise too little. Yet every health indicator, from life expectancy to infant mortality, is on their side, including the fact that they have four times fewer heart attacks than Europeans or Americans. But there are warning signals for the Japanese: The heart-attack rate has doubled since 1960. During that time, the daily consumption of meat has quadrupled.

Since mid-century, heart disease has killed more Americans than anything else. They smoked excessively; they were overweight and sedentary, and had high blood pressure and high cholesterol levels—all of which are risk factors for heart disease. Habits have changed, however, and now Americans fall near the bottom of the risk list. Another result of America's heart-attack era is that it has the best high-tech cardiac care, which means that on average, you'll live longer if you have a heart attack in the U.S. than in any other country.

The geography of cancer

According to figures released by the European Community's "Europe Against Cancer" project, one in four Europeans has, has had, or will have cancer. If the present rate of increase continues, that number will rise to one in three by the end of the century. One out of ten women in America will get breast cancer, the highest ratio in the world. For one out of four who get it, it will be fatal. When women from countries with low rates of breast cancer—Japan and Italy, for instance—move to the U.S., they are as likely to get breast cancer as native Americans. Stomach cancer, Japan's historic killer, is on the wane—while colon, ovary, and prostate cancer soars—as the Japanese shift from their traditional salty diet to fatty and caloric Western foods.

Myth:
America is cancer country.

Reality:
Europe is the cancer capital.

INTERNATIONAL METASTASES

Incidence of cancer for men (■) and women (□) per 100,000 people

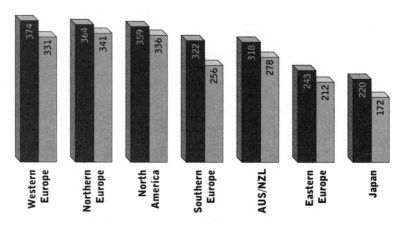

	Men	Women
Western Europe	374	331
Northern Europe	364	341
North America	359	336
Southern Europe	322	256
AUS/NZL	318	278
Eastern Europe	243	212
Japan	220	172

VULNERABLE SITES

Incidence per 100,000 people

Lung cancer

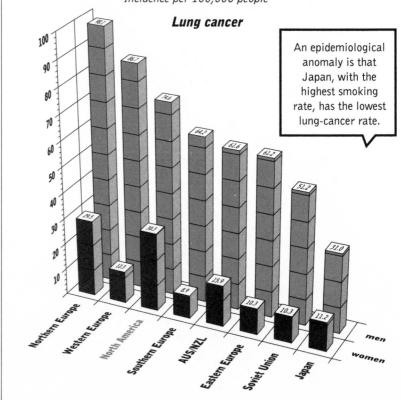

> An epidemiological anomaly is that Japan, with the highest smoking rate, has the lowest lung-cancer rate.

	men	women
Northern Europe	29.5	90.1
Western Europe	12.3	86.7
North America	30.7	74.6
Southern Europe	8.9	64.2
AUS/NZL	15.9	61.6
Eastern Europe	10.3	63.2
Soviet Union	10.3	51.2
Japan	11.2	31.0

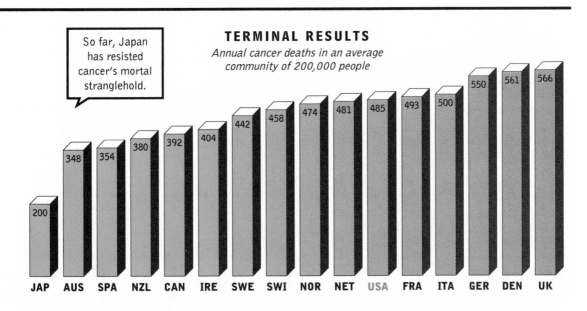

TERMINAL RESULTS
Annual cancer deaths in an average community of 200,000 people

So far, Japan has resisted cancer's mortal stranglehold.

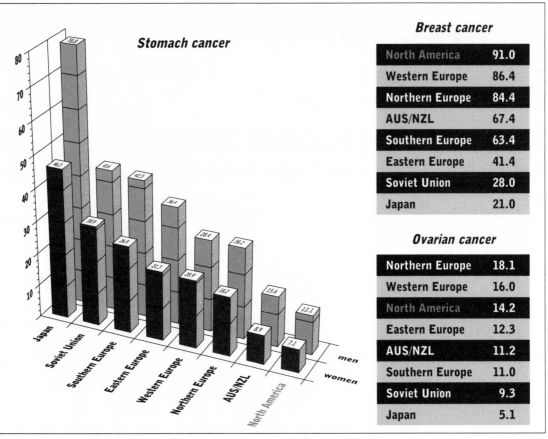

Stomach cancer

Breast cancer

North America	91.0
Western Europe	86.4
Northern Europe	84.4
AUS/NZL	67.4
Southern Europe	63.4
Eastern Europe	41.4
Soviet Union	28.0
Japan	21.0

Ovarian cancer

Northern Europe	18.1
Western Europe	16.0
North America	14.2
Eastern Europe	12.3
AUS/NZL	11.2
Southern Europe	11.0
Soviet Union	9.3
Japan	5.1

Aids toll

"In 1987 the World Health Organization (WHO) estimated that worldwide, from 5 to 10 million adults had become infected with HIV. As of late 1990, the WHO's global estimate of the number of adults infected with HIV was revised upward to 8–10 million.... Dramatic increases have been recorded among injecting drug users and female prostitutes in Southeast Asia, especially in Thailand and India, where up to half a million cases of HIV infection may have occurred since 1987.... As of late 1990, a cumulative global total of over 3 million HIV-infected women are estimated to have collectively given birth to about 3 million infants, of whom over 700,000 are estimated to have become infected with HIV."
—James Chin, from the Surveillance, Forecasting and Impact Assessment Unit, Global Programme on AIDS, World Health Organization

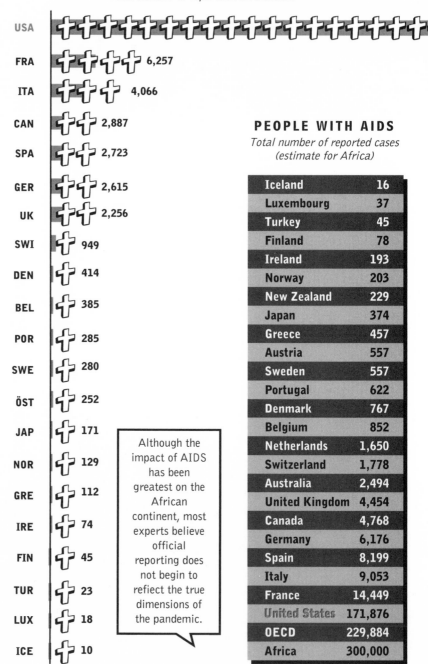

HOW MANY HAVE DIED?
Total number of reported AIDS deaths

USA	(cross symbols)
FRA	6,257
ITA	4,066
CAN	2,887
SPA	2,723
GER	2,615
UK	2,256
SWI	949
DEN	414
BEL	385
POR	285
SWE	280
ÖST	252
JAP	171
NOR	129
GRE	112
IRE	74
FIN	45
TUR	23
LUX	18
ICE	10

Although the impact of AIDS has been greatest on the African continent, most experts believe official reporting does not begin to reflect the true dimensions of the pandemic.

PEOPLE WITH AIDS
Total number of reported cases (estimate for Africa)

Iceland	16
Luxembourg	37
Turkey	45
Finland	78
Ireland	193
Norway	203
New Zealand	229
Japan	374
Greece	457
Austria	557
Sweden	557
Portugal	622
Denmark	767
Belgium	852
Netherlands	1,650
Switzerland	1,778
Australia	2,494
United Kingdom	4,454
Canada	4,768
Germany	6,176
Spain	8,199
Italy	9,053
France	14,449
United States	171,876
OECD	229,884
Africa	300,000

By the late 1990s, according to some estimates, AIDS will have killed over 1 million Americans—more than the total of all U.S. war deaths.

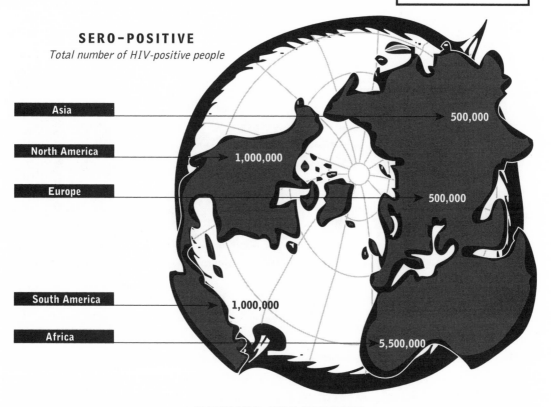

113,426

SERO-POSITIVE
Total number of HIV-positive people

Asia — 500,000

North America — 1,000,000

Europe — 500,000

South America — 1,000,000

Africa — 5,500,000

MAPPING THE DISEASE
Percent of world's reported cases

OECD	63.99%	**Australia**	0.69	**Greece**	0.13
United States	47.84	**Switzerland**	0.49	**Japan**	0.10
France	4.02	**Netherlands**	0.46	**New Zealand**	0.06
Italy	2.52	**Belgium**	0.24	**Norway**	0.06
Spain	2.28	**Denmark**	0.21	**Ireland**	0.05
Germany	1.72	**Portugal**	0.17	**Finland**	0.02
Canada	1.33	**Sweden**	0.16	**Turkey**	0.01
United Kingdom	1.24	**Austria**	0.16	**Luxembourg**	0.01

Aids toll

THE DEMOGRAPHICS

GAY MEN
Percent of all AIDS cases

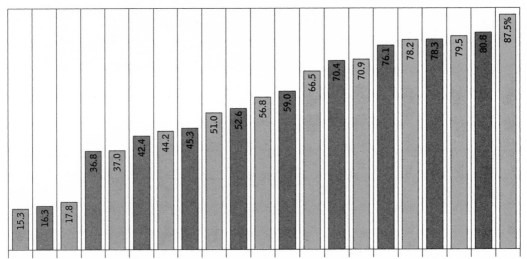

ITA	SPA	TUR	IRE	BEL	ÖST	SWI	POR	GRE	FRA	LUX	USA	NOR	GER	SWE	DEN	CAN	UK	NET	FIN	ICE
15.3	16.3	17.8	36.8	37.0	42.4	44.2	45.3	51.0	52.6	56.8	59.0	66.5	70.4	70.9	76.1	78.2	78.3	79.5	80.8	87.5%

HETEROSEXUALS
Percent of all AIDS cases

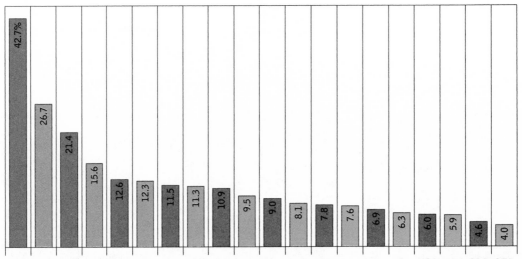

BEL	POR	GRE	TUR	SWE	SWI	FIN	NOR	FRA	AUS	DEN	LUX	IRE	CAN	UK	ITA	USA	NET	SPA	GER
42.7%	26.7	21.4	15.6	12.6	12.3	11.5	11.3	10.9	9.5	9.0	8.1	7.8	7.6	6.9	6.3	6.0	5.9	4.6	4.0

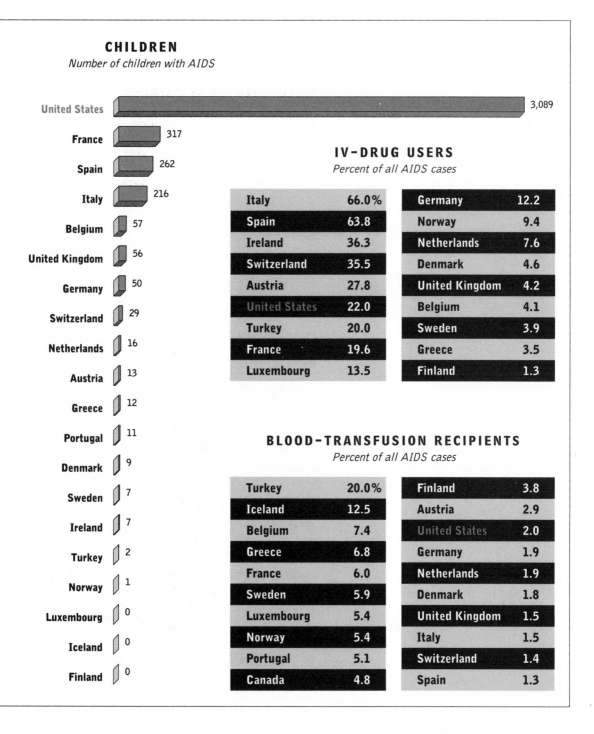

CHILDREN
Number of children with AIDS

United States	3,089
France	317
Spain	262
Italy	216
Belgium	57
United Kingdom	56
Germany	50
Switzerland	29
Netherlands	16
Austria	13
Greece	12
Portugal	11
Denmark	9
Sweden	7
Ireland	7
Turkey	2
Norway	1
Luxembourg	0
Iceland	0
Finland	0

IV-DRUG USERS
Percent of all AIDS cases

Italy	66.0%	Germany	12.2
Spain	63.8	Norway	9.4
Ireland	36.3	Netherlands	7.6
Switzerland	35.5	Denmark	4.6
Austria	27.8	United Kingdom	4.2
United States	22.0	Belgium	4.1
Turkey	20.0	Sweden	3.9
France	19.6	Greece	3.5
Luxembourg	13.5	Finland	1.3

BLOOD-TRANSFUSION RECIPIENTS
Percent of all AIDS cases

Turkey	20.0%	Finland	3.8
Iceland	12.5	Austria	2.9
Belgium	7.4	United States	2.0
Greece	6.8	Germany	1.9
France	6.0	Netherlands	1.9
Sweden	5.9	Denmark	1.8
Luxembourg	5.4	United Kingdom	1.5
Norway	5.4	Italy	1.5
Portugal	5.1	Switzerland	1.4
Canada	4.8	Spain	1.3

91

Final exit

One of the most popular measures of a nation's character is its suicide rate. It was emblematic of the 1960s that the Swedes, among the most liberated of peoples, were also the most likely to kill themselves. They haven't held that distinction for a while. In a fitting commentary on the 1980s and '90s, young Japanese men are at the highest risk for death by suicide. One out of three deaths among Japanese men between the ages of 24 and 34 is self-inflicted. Hanging is one of the most popular methods.

Myth:
Suicide is a particularly Scandinavian alternative.

Reality:
Young Japanese men and women are the people most likely to turn to suicide.

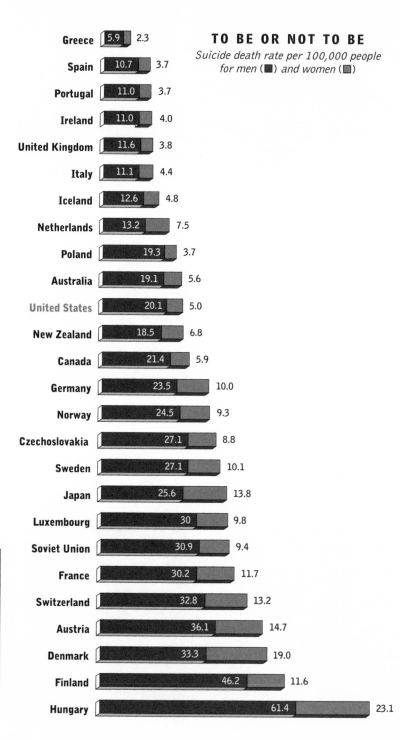

TO BE OR NOT TO BE
Suicide death rate per 100,000 people for men (■) and women (■)

Country	Men	Women
Greece	5.9	2.3
Spain	10.7	3.7
Portugal	11.0	3.7
Ireland	11.0	4.0
United Kingdom	11.6	3.8
Italy	11.1	4.4
Iceland	12.6	4.8
Netherlands	13.2	7.5
Poland	19.3	3.7
Australia	19.1	5.6
United States	20.1	5.0
New Zealand	18.5	6.8
Canada	21.4	5.9
Germany	23.5	10.0
Norway	24.5	9.3
Czechoslovakia	27.1	8.8
Sweden	27.1	10.1
Japan	25.6	13.8
Luxembourg	30	9.8
Soviet Union	30.9	9.4
France	30.2	11.7
Switzerland	32.8	13.2
Austria	36.1	14.7
Denmark	33.3	19.0
Finland	46.2	11.6
Hungary	61.4	23.1

TEENAGERS

Suicide as a percent of all deaths for 15-to-19-year-old boys (■) and girls (■)

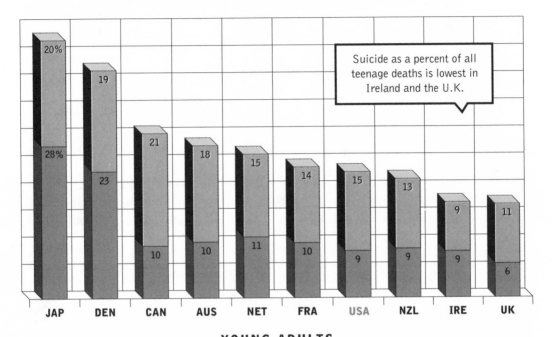

Suicide as a percent of all teenage deaths is lowest in Ireland and the U.K.

	JAP	DEN	CAN	AUS	NET	FRA	USA	NZL	IRE	UK
boys	20%	19	21	18	15	14	15	13	9	11
girls	28%	23	10	10	11	10	9	9	9	6

YOUNG ADULTS

Suicide as a percent of all deaths for 25-to-34-year-old men (■) and women (■)

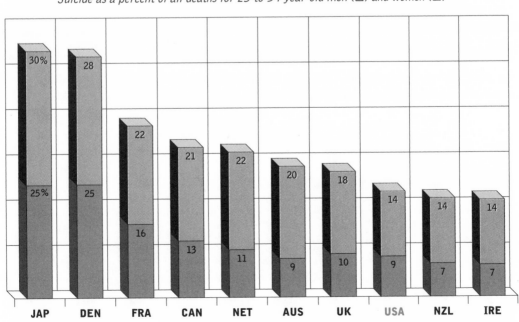

	JAP	DEN	FRA	CAN	NET	AUS	UK	USA	NZL	IRE
men	30%	28	22	21	22	20	18	14	14	14
women	25%	25	16	13	11	9	10	9	7	7

Final exit

THE METHODS

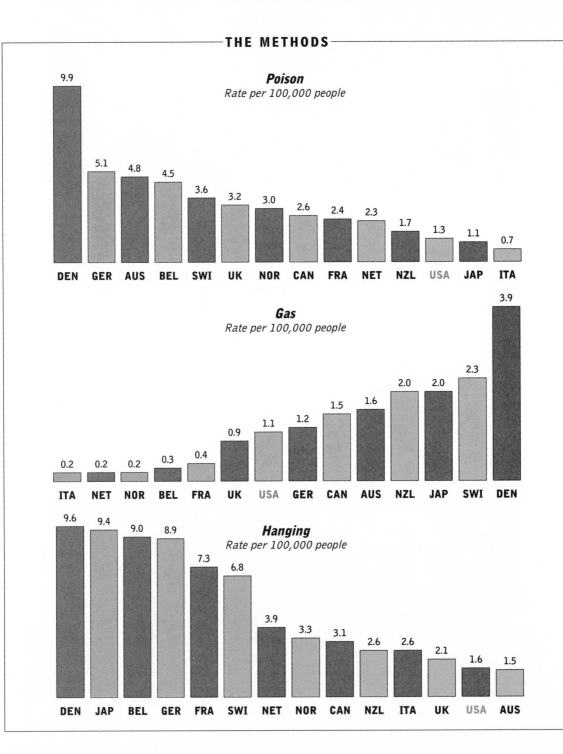

Poison
Rate per 100,000 people

DEN	GER	AUS	BEL	SWI	UK	NOR	CAN	FRA	NET	NZL	USA	JAP	ITA
9.9	5.1	4.8	4.5	3.6	3.2	3.0	2.6	2.4	2.3	1.7	1.3	1.1	0.7

Gas
Rate per 100,000 people

ITA	NET	NOR	BEL	FRA	UK	USA	GER	CAN	AUS	NZL	JAP	SWI	DEN
0.2	0.2	0.2	0.3	0.4	0.9	1.1	1.2	1.5	1.6	2.0	2.0	2.3	3.9

Hanging
Rate per 100,000 people

DEN	JAP	BEL	GER	FRA	SWI	NET	NOR	CAN	NZL	ITA	UK	USA	AUS
9.6	9.4	9.0	8.9	7.3	6.8	3.9	3.3	3.1	2.6	2.6	2.1	1.6	1.5

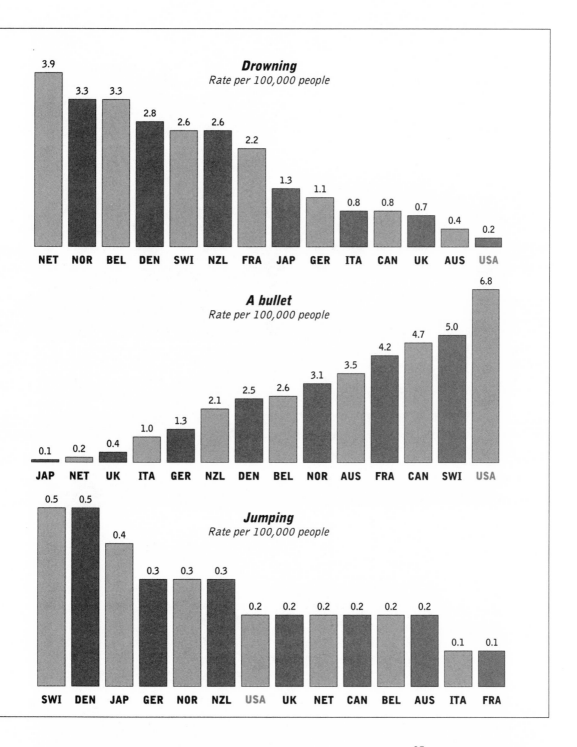

Drowning
Rate per 100,000 people

3.9 NET · 3.3 NOR · 3.3 BEL · 2.8 DEN · 2.6 SWI · 2.6 NZL · 2.2 FRA · 1.3 JAP · 1.1 GER · 0.8 ITA · 0.8 CAN · 0.7 UK · 0.4 AUS · 0.2 USA

A bullet
Rate per 100,000 people

0.1 JAP · 0.2 NET · 0.4 UK · 1.0 ITA · 1.3 GER · 2.1 NZL · 2.5 DEN · 2.6 BEL · 3.1 NOR · 3.5 AUS · 4.2 FRA · 4.7 CAN · 5.0 SWI · 6.8 USA

Jumping
Rate per 100,000 people

0.5 SWI · 0.5 DEN · 0.4 JAP · 0.3 GER · 0.3 NOR · 0.3 NZL · 0.2 USA · 0.2 UK · 0.2 NET · 0.2 CAN · 0.2 BEL · 0.2 AUS · 0.1 ITA · 0.1 FRA

Who's wasted?

The price of marijuana has shot up to between five and ten times what it was ten years ago, while the price of heroin has dropped by almost 50 percent. Once thought to be on the wane, heroin has returned as a drug of choice in the U.S. and Europe. The city of Milan says it picks up 3,000 to 4,000 used syringes every day off the streets and in the parks. One factor behind heroin's resurgence, U.S. officials say, is that the most plentiful poppy fields are in nations— Burma, Laos, Iran, Lebanon, and Afghanistan—resistant to the kind of policing and diplomatic pressure that might stop the flow. Drug-treatment experts report an increasing number of polydrug addictions, with the favorite being a combination crack-and-heroin habit. Although heroin is an increasing problem in Europe, drug use is far more prevalent in the U.S. than anywhere else.

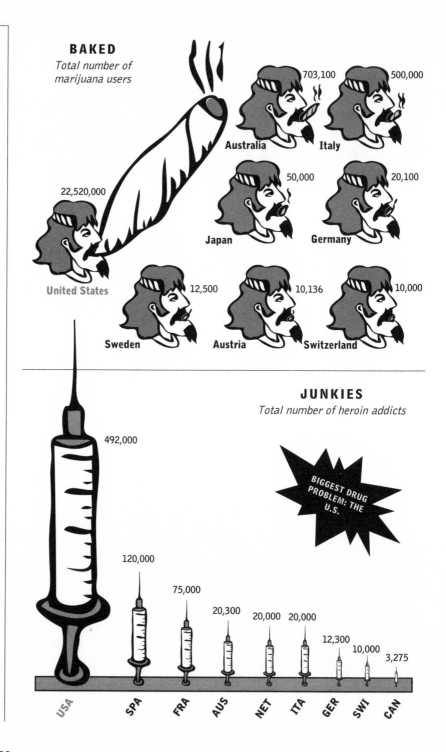

BAKED
Total number of marijuana users

United States 22,520,000

Australia 703,100

Italy 500,000

Japan 50,000

Germany 20,100

Sweden 12,500

Austria 10,136

Switzerland 10,000

JUNKIES
Total number of heroin addicts

BIGGEST DRUG PROBLEM: THE U.S.

USA 492,000

SPA 120,000

FRA 75,000

AUS 20,300

NET 20,000

ITA 20,000

GER 12,300

SWI 10,000

CAN 3,275

REHAB
Number of people under treatment for drug abuse

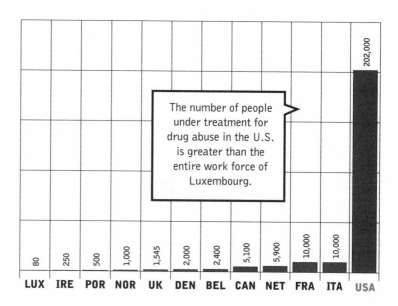

The number of people under treatment for drug abuse in the U.S. is greater than the entire work force of Luxembourg.

LUX	IRE	POR	NOR	UK	DEN	BEL	CAN	NET	FRA	ITA	USA
80	250	500	1,000	1,545	2,000	2,400	5,100	5,900	10,000	10,000	202,000

MAINTENANCE
Annual methadone consumption (pounds)

Per capita methadone consumption is highest in the Netherlands, where tolerance and effective treatment go hand in hand.

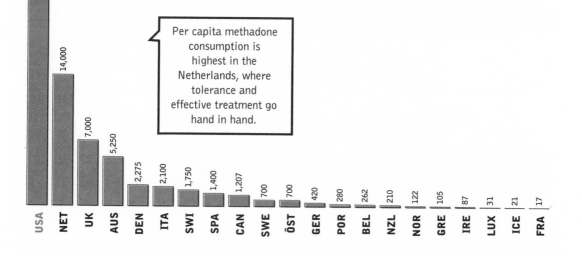

USA	NET	UK	AUS	DEN	ITA	SWI	SPA	CAN	SWE	ÖST	GER	POR	BEL	NZL	NOR	GRE	IRE	LUX	ICE	FRA
66,115	14,000	7,000	5,250	2,275	2,100	1,750	1,400	1,207	700	700	420	280	262	210	122	105	87	31	21	17

Who's smoking?

"Almost 800,000 lives are lost each year in the developed countries at ages 35–64 due to cigarette smoking. This represents about one-third of all deaths at these ages and is about eight times the mortality from either motor-vehicle accidents, other accidents, or suicide and homicide. Cigarette smoking is thus by far the leading cause of premature mortality in developed countries."
—*World Health Organization, 1990*

Myth:
Americans have quit smoking.

Reality:
They're still among the world's leading smokers.

THE SMOKING HEAP
Total cigarette consumption per year (millions)

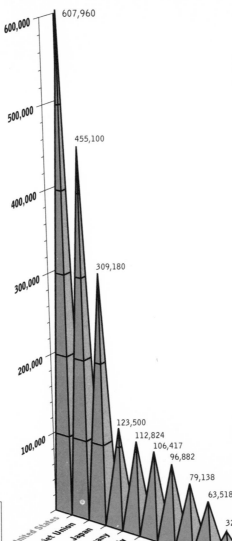

YOUR (UN)WANTED SHARE
Per capita cigarette consumption per year

Japan	3,280
United States	3,270
Canada	3,180
Iceland	3,100
Switzerland	2,960
Spain	2,740
Australia	2,720
Austria	2,560
Ireland	2,560
Italy	2,560
New Zealand	2,510
France	2,400
Germany	2,380
East Germany	2,340
Soviet Union	2,170
United Kingdom	2,120
Denmark	2,110
Belgium	1,990
Turkey	1,970
Norway	1,920
Portugal	1,730
Finland	1,720
Netherlands	1,690
Sweden	1,660

The Smoking Heap values (by country):
United States 607,960; Soviet Union 455,100; Japan 309,180; Germany 123,500; Italy 112,824; France 106,417; United Kingdom 96,882; Spain 79,138; Canada 63,518; Australia 32,675; Greece 28,651; Netherlands 19,606; Switzerland 16,470; Belgium 16,469; Austria 15,640; Sweden 11,320; Denmark 8,781; Finland 6,800

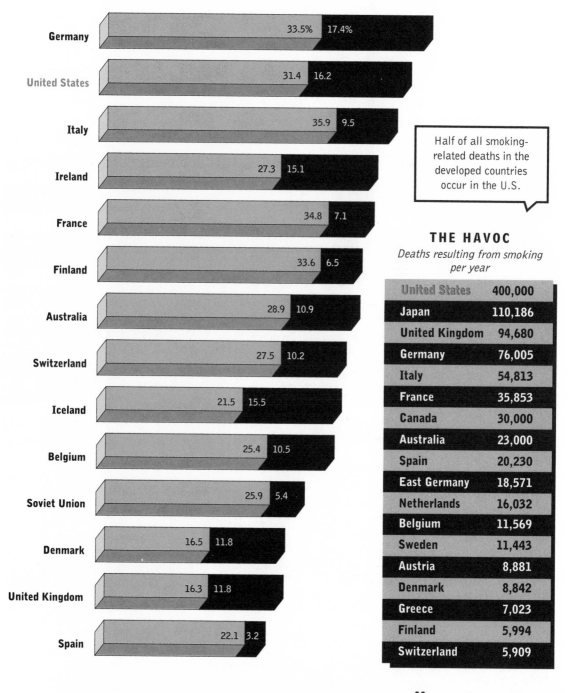

WHO'S QUITTING?
Percent of men (▣) and women (■) who have quit smoking since 1980

Country	Men	Women
Germany	33.5%	17.4%
United States	31.4	16.2
Italy	35.9	9.5
Ireland	27.3	15.1
France	34.8	7.1
Finland	33.6	6.5
Australia	28.9	10.9
Switzerland	27.5	10.2
Iceland	21.5	15.5
Belgium	25.4	10.5
Soviet Union	25.9	5.4
Denmark	16.5	11.8
United Kingdom	16.3	11.8
Spain	22.1	3.2

Half of all smoking-related deaths in the developed countries occur in the U.S.

THE HAVOC
Deaths resulting from smoking per year

Country	Deaths
United States	400,000
Japan	110,186
United Kingdom	94,680
Germany	76,005
Italy	54,813
France	35,853
Canada	30,000
Australia	23,000
Spain	20,230
East Germany	18,571
Netherlands	16,032
Belgium	11,569
Sweden	11,443
Austria	8,881
Denmark	8,842
Greece	7,023
Finland	5,994
Switzerland	5,909

Who's drinking?

"There's no question but that few Japanese perceive alcoholism as a pathology of any significant magnitude. An international Gallup poll asked the question, 'In your country, today, how serious do you think alcoholism is?' Of the thirteen nations surveyed, the Japanese reported the lowest level of concern: 17 percent very serious, 40 percent quite serious, 32 percent not very/not serious at all. By contrast, Americans reported 74 percent very serious, 26 percent quite serious, 2 percent not very/not at all serious."
—*Stephen R. Smith,* Drinking and Sobriety in Japan

Myth:
Americans have stopped drinking.

Reality:
Their consumption has increased by more than half over the past 30 years.

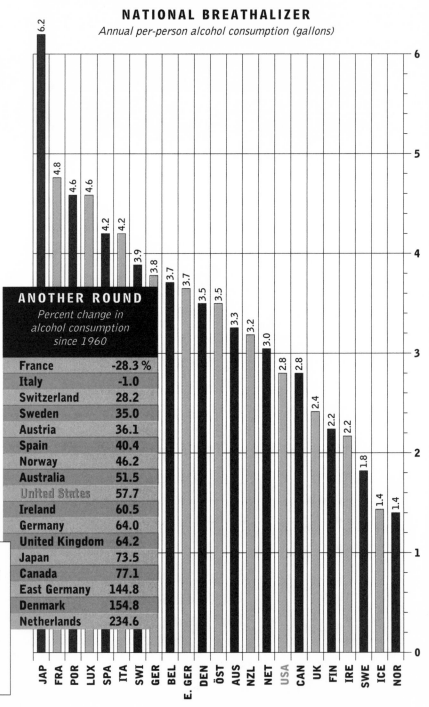

NATIONAL BREATHALIZER

Annual per-person alcohol consumption (gallons)

JAP	6.2
FRA	4.8
POR	4.6
LUX	4.6
SPA	4.2
ITA	4.2
SWI	3.9
GER	3.8
BEL	3.7
E. GER	3.7
DEN	3.5
ÖST	3.5
AUS	3.3
NZL	3.2
NET	3.0
USA	2.8
CAN	2.8
UK	2.4
FIN	2.2
IRE	2.2
SWE	1.8
ICE	1.4
NOR	1.4

ANOTHER ROUND
Percent change in alcohol consumption since 1960

France	-28.3 %
Italy	-1.0
Switzerland	28.2
Sweden	35.0
Austria	36.1
Spain	40.4
Norway	46.2
Australia	51.5
United States	57.7
Ireland	60.5
Germany	64.0
United Kingdom	64.2
Japan	73.5
Canada	77.1
East Germany	144.8
Denmark	154.8
Netherlands	234.6

ALCOHOLICS
Number of alcoholics per 1,000 people

DWI
Annual alcohol-related traffic accidents

United States	1,844,000
Germany	33,543
United Kingdom	9,222
East Germany	3,313
Austria	3,025
Netherlands	2,721
Denmark	1,929
Belgium	1,052
Iceland	57

MOST DRUNKS: THE JAPANESE

175.0

71.0

37.5

36.5

26.2

18.3

15.0

Japan	Soviet Union	United States	Sweden	Poland	Switzerland	United Kingdom

DEAD DRUNK
Number of people killed in alcohol-related accidents, per year

United States	20,208	Austria	184
Germany	1,498	Finland	126
Denmark	228	Netherlands	118
East Germany	216	Belgium	45

What's cooking?

There are more extremely fat people—people who weigh more than 40 percent above their recommended body weight—in the United States than in any other country in the world.

In one of the ironies of progress, a generous national girth, which once marked a land of wealth and plenty, now indicates poverty. The lower a person's socioeconomic status, the more likely he is to eat foods whose caloric content is primarily derived from fats.

But Campbell's soup, Häagen-Dazs ice cream, and McDonald's Big Macs (along with Pizza Hut pizzas, KFC wings, and Mrs. Field's cookies) are making it big in Europe and Japan. The microwave, one-person households, and working women are helping to homogenize food (usually bad-for-you food) across the developed world. According to a report in the journal *Consumer Markets Abroad*, processed foods now account for 40 percent of a European family's food budget.

ROLLS OF FAT

Average daily per capita consumption of butter, oil, and fat (ounces)

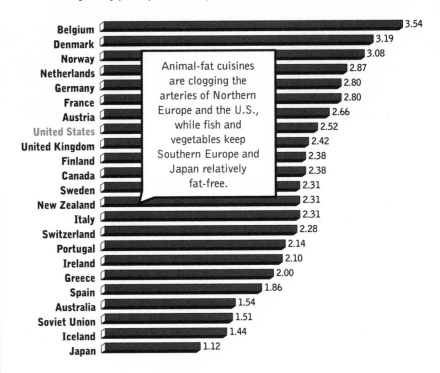

Belgium	3.54
Denmark	3.19
Norway	3.08
Netherlands	2.87
Germany	2.80
France	2.80
Austria	2.66
United States	2.52
United Kingdom	2.42
Finland	2.38
Canada	2.38
Sweden	2.31
New Zealand	2.31
Italy	2.31
Switzerland	2.28
Portugal	2.14
Ireland	2.10
Greece	2.00
Spain	1.86
Australia	1.54
Soviet Union	1.51
Iceland	1.44
Japan	1.12

Animal-fat cuisines are clogging the arteries of Northern Europe and the U.S., while fish and vegetables keep Southern Europe and Japan relatively fat-free.

CALORIE COUNT

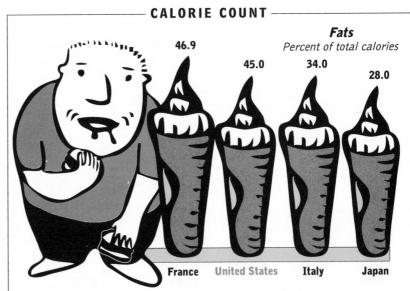

Fats
Percent of total calories

France	United States	Italy	Japan
46.9	45.0	34.0	28.0

RED MEAT

Average daily per capita consumption of meat (ounces)

United States	10.64
New Zealand	10.57
Australia	9.97
Canada	9.52
Belgium	8.47
France	8.44
Ireland	8.37
Germany	7.70
Switzerland	7.42
Austria	7.18
United Kingdom	6.90
Netherlands	6.58
Denmark	5.85
Italy	5.81
Finland	5.29
Sweden	5.29
Spain	5.25
Greece	5.18
Soviet Union	5.08
Norway	4.45
Portugal	4.20
Japan	2.24
Turkey	1.86

In *41 Years of Life*, a Japanese best-seller, Nishimaru Shinya contends that of all Japanese born after 1959, half will be dead from their new Western diets by the age of 41. "Instant foods and fast food with their additives are upsetting Japanese metabolism," he maintains.

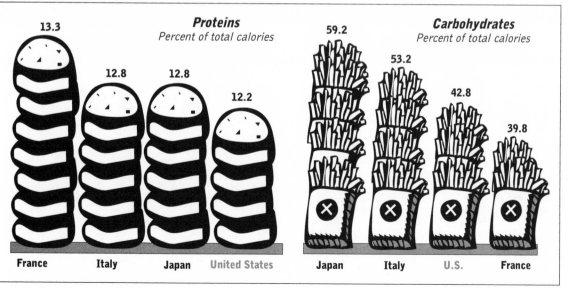

Proteins
Percent of total calories

- 13.3 — France
- 12.8 — Italy
- 12.8 — Japan
- 12.2 — United States

Carbohydrates
Percent of total calories

- 59.2 — Japan
- 53.2 — Italy
- 42.8 — U.S.
- 39.8 — France

What's cooking?

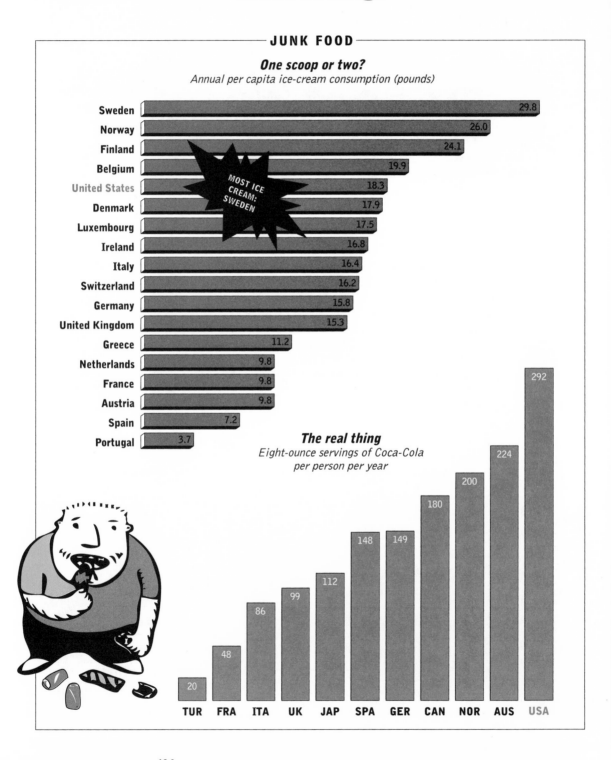

JUNK FOOD

One scoop or two?
Annual per capita ice-cream consumption (pounds)

Country	Pounds
Sweden	29.8
Norway	26.0
Finland	24.1
Belgium	19.9
United States	18.3
Denmark	17.9
Luxembourg	17.5
Ireland	16.8
Italy	16.4
Switzerland	16.2
Germany	15.8
United Kingdom	15.3
Greece	11.2
Netherlands	9.8
France	9.8
Austria	9.8
Spain	7.2
Portugal	3.7

MOST ICE CREAM: SWEDEN

The real thing
Eight-ounce servings of Coca-Cola per person per year

Country	Servings
TUR	20
FRA	48
ITA	86
UK	99
JAP	112
SPA	148
GER	149
CAN	180
NOR	200
AUS	224
USA	292

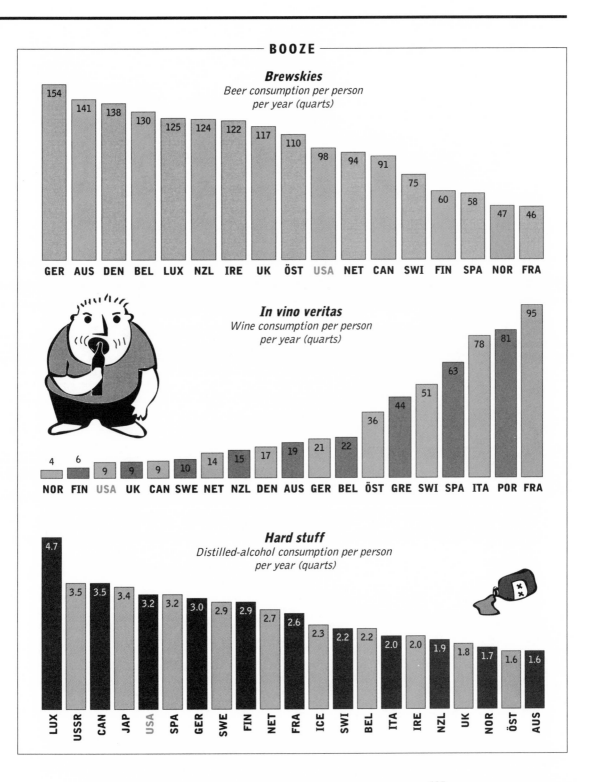

BOOZE

Brewskies
Beer consumption per person
per year (quarts)

GER	AUS	DEN	BEL	LUX	NZL	IRE	UK	ÖST	USA	NET	CAN	SWI	FIN	SPA	NOR	FRA
154	141	138	130	125	124	122	117	110	98	94	91	75	60	58	47	46

In vino veritas
Wine consumption per person
per year (quarts)

NOR	FIN	USA	UK	CAN	SWE	NET	NZL	DEN	AUS	GER	BEL	ÖST	GRE	SWI	SPA	ITA	POR	FRA
4	6	9	9	9	10	14	15	17	19	21	22	36	44	51	63	78	81	95

Hard stuff
Distilled-alcohol consumption per person
per year (quarts)

LUX	USSR	CAN	JAP	USA	SPA	GER	SWE	FIN	NET	FRA	ICE	SWI	BEL	ITA	IRE	NZL	UK	NOR	ÖST	AUS
4.7	3.5	3.5	3.4	3.2	3.2	3.0	2.9	2.9	2.7	2.6	2.3	2.2	2.2	2.0	2.0	1.9	1.8	1.7	1.6	1.6

What's cooking?

YOU ARE WHAT YOU EAT

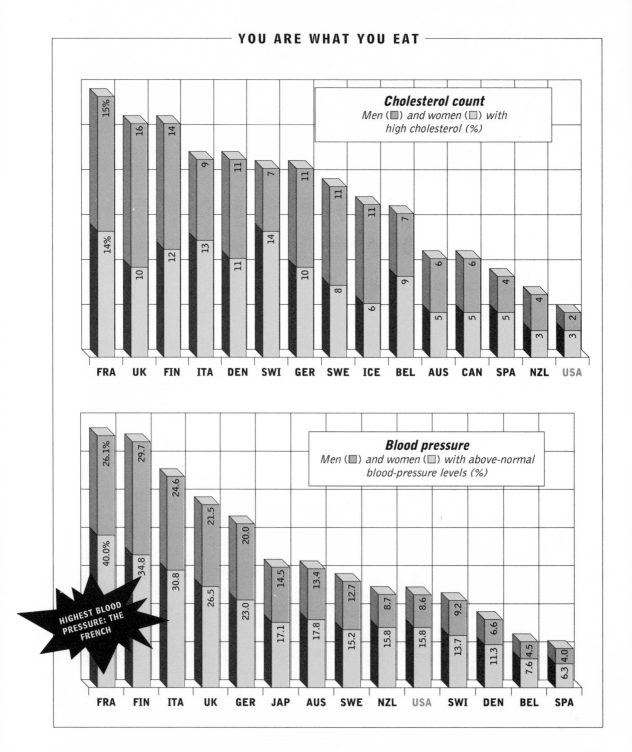

Cholesterol count
Men (■) and women (□) with
high cholesterol (%)

FRA: 15% / 14%
UK: 16 / 10
FIN: 14 / 12
ITA: 9 / 13
DEN: 11 / 11
SWI: 7 / 14
GER: 11 / 10
SWE: 11 / 8
ICE: 11 / 6
BEL: 7 / 9
AUS: 6 / 5
CAN: 6 / 5
SPA: 4 / 5
NZL: 4 / 3
USA: 2 / 3

Blood pressure
Men (■) and women (□) with above-normal
blood-pressure levels (%)

HIGHEST BLOOD PRESSURE: THE FRENCH

FRA: 26.1% / 40.0%
FIN: 29.7 / 34.8
ITA: 24.6 / 30.8
UK: 21.5 / 26.5
GER: 20.0 / 23.0
JAP: 14.5 / 17.1
AUS: 13.4 / 17.8
SWE: 12.7 / 15.2
NZL: 8.7 / 15.8
USA: 8.6 / 15.8
SWI: 9.2 / 13.7
DEN: 6.6 / 11.3
BEL: 7.6 / 4.5
SPA: 6.3 / 4.0

─ IT SHOWS ─

In shape
Men (■) and women (■) with a normal body mass (%)

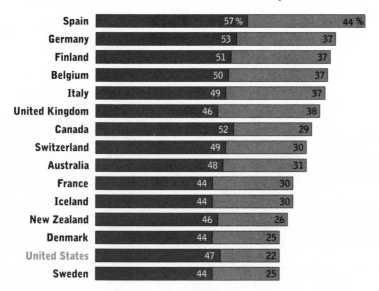

Country	Men	Women
Spain	57 %	44 %
Germany	53	37
Finland	51	37
Belgium	50	37
Italy	49	37
United Kingdom	46	38
Canada	52	29
Switzerland	49	30
Australia	48	31
France	44	30
Iceland	44	30
New Zealand	46	26
Denmark	44	25
United States	47	22
Sweden	44	25

Death from malnutrition (men)
Per million people

United States	7
Canada	5
France	4
Portugal	3
Australia	3
Japan	2
Spain	2
United Kingdom	1
New Zealand	1
East Germany	1
Ireland	1
Norway	0

In the fridge
Men (■) and women (■) who are obese (%)

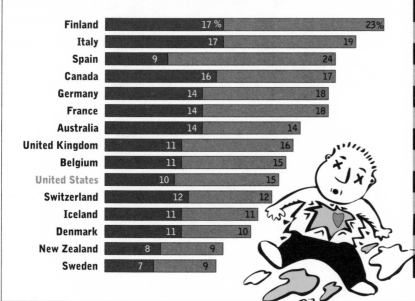

Country	Men	Women
Finland	17 %	23 %
Italy	17	19
Spain	9	24
Canada	16	17
Germany	14	18
France	14	18
Australia	14	14
United Kingdom	11	16
Belgium	11	15
United States	10	15
Switzerland	12	12
Iceland	11	11
Denmark	11	10
New Zealand	8	9
Sweden	7	9

Death from malnutrition (women)
Per million people

United States	13
France	9
Canada	7
New Zealand	4
Portugal	3
Spain	3
Australia	3
United Kingdom	2
Japan	1
East Germany	1
Norway	1
Ireland	0

— Killer skyline —

"Asthma is the most prevalent chronic disease of adults and children in the developed world."
—The Lancet, *July 1989*

Both Alzheimer's and adult-onset diabetes have become more common as the population has aged (and because of improved diagnostic techniques). While 2 percent of all Americans will contract adult-onset diabetes between the ages of 20 and 44, and 6 percent between 40 and 60, almost 20 percent of all Americans will get it in their eighties.

Myth:
Tuberculosis has been eradicated.

Reality:
It is making a dramatic comeback almost everywhere.

Death from:
Stroke (■), asthma (■), diabetes (■), Alzheimer's disease (■),
and tuberculosis (■) in an average community of 200,000 people, per year

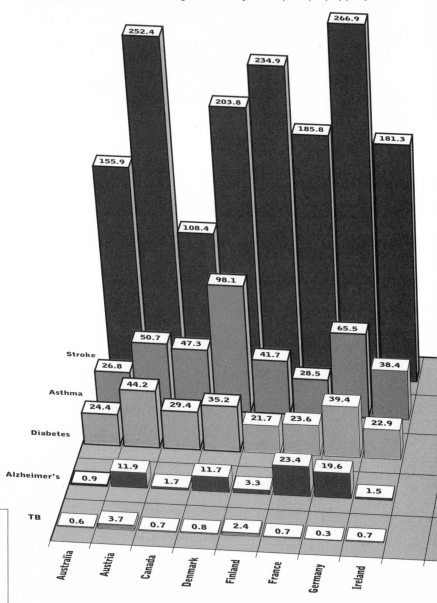

	Australia	Austria	Canada	Denmark	Finland	France	Germany	Ireland
Stroke	155.9	252.4	108.4	203.8	234.9	185.8	266.9	181.3
Asthma	26.8	50.7	47.3	98.1	41.7	28.5	65.5	38.4
Diabetes	24.4	44.2	29.4	35.2	21.7	23.6	39.4	22.9
Alzheimer's	0.9	11.9	1.7	11.7	3.3	23.4	19.6	1.5
TB	0.6	3.7	0.7	0.8	2.4	0.7	0.3	0.7

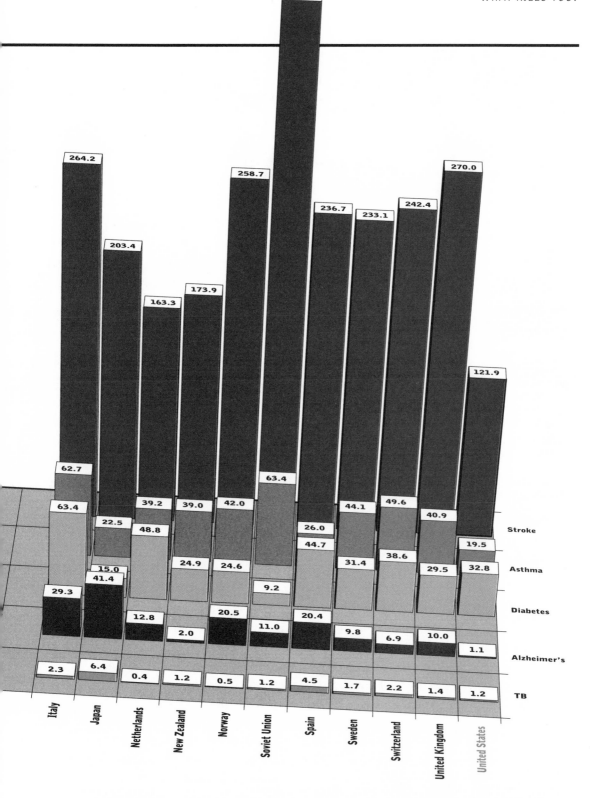

381.0

264.2
203.4
163.3
173.9
258.7
236.7
233.1
242.4
270.0
121.9

62.7
63.4
22.5
39.2
39.0
42.0
63.4
26.0
44.1
49.6
40.9
19.5

Stroke

48.8
24.9
24.6
44.7
38.6
29.5
32.8

Asthma

15.0
41.4
12.8
20.5
9.2
31.4

29.3
2.0
11.0
20.4
9.8
6.9
10.0
1.1

Diabetes

Alzheimer's

2.3
6.4
0.4
1.2
0.5
1.2
4.5
1.7
2.2
1.4
1.2

TB

Italy
Japan
Netherlands
New Zealand
Norway
Soviet Union
Spain
Sweden
Switzerland
United Kingdom
United States

What health-care system works?

Most striking among the national imbalances of the twentieth century is the inability of the U.S. to provide its citizens with an effective health-care system. Indeed, it has failed even to satisfy the general notions of effectiveness: wide access, equal quality, and low cost.

No developed country is as unhappy with its health-care system as the U.S. Public disenchantment with the U.S. health-care system, suggests a Harvard University study, reflects not so much doubts about the quality of care as fears about the availability of any care at all. Health-care-related strikes went from 18 percent of all strikes in the mid-1980s to 78 percent in 1989. Voters in Pennsylvania elected an underdog U.S. Senate candidate, Harris Wofford, in part because of his calls for national health insurance. Even the American Medical Association, traditionally the group most resistant to any change in the system, has issued a series of proposals for radical reform.

America pays the most and gets the least. But what makes America's massive health-care expenditures most painful is the great number of its citizens who are excluded from the health-care system—by most counts, 30 million to 40 million Americans, 12 million of them children.

"The fact is that despite all our advances in health-care technology, the United States lags behind other industrialized countries on such basic measures of health status as life expectancy and maternal and infant mortality," says James O. Mason, assistant secretary of Health and Human Services. "And, surely, inadequate access to care for some Americans—especially minorities, the poor, the homeless—is a primary reason for this lag."

In many respects, the U.S. health-care system shows cowboy capitalism at its best and worst: America will spend hundreds of thousands of dollars helping one-and-a-half-pound babies survive, but it is unwilling to provide poor mothers with adequate prenatal care.

Health care is a fundamental need. The illogic and unfairness of a system will eventually undermine a government's credibility. Indeed, the decline—and in some cases virtual collapse—of the health-care systems in the Soviet Union and Eastern Europe contributed heavily to the economic and social bankruptcy that ended those regimes.

Rating the systems

WHO'S HAD ENOUGH?
Percent of people who believe their health-care system needs fundamental change

60% United States
58 Sweden
52 United Kingdom
47 Japan
46 Italy
46 Netherlands
43 Australia
42 France
38 Canada

WHO'S SAFE?
Percent of people eligible for government-funded hospital care

United States	40
Netherlands	77
Germany	92
Switzerland, Spain, Belgium	98
France, Austria	99
All other countries	100%

Who lives?

The classic advertisements for Dannon Yogurt, featuring spry 106-year-olds on the farms of rural Georgia, tried to make the life expectancy of a Georgian the wonder of the world (or of those in the world who saw the commercial). The truth, however, is that the life expectancy of a citizen of the former Soviet Union is developmentally some 50 years behind his counterpart in the West. America, too, with an infant-mortality rate higher than in Singapore and life expectancy levels on a par with Cuba's, has failed to keep pace with other modern nations. For America to reach a life expectancy of 85 years—the World Health Organization's goal for developed nations—it will have to cut its death rate by 65 percent. On the other hand, the Japanese, who a century ago lived only to 35, now have the highest life expectancy in the history of the world, thanks to improved life-style and diet, and equitable medical care.

THE OUTER LIMITS

Male (■) and female (■) life expectancy (years)

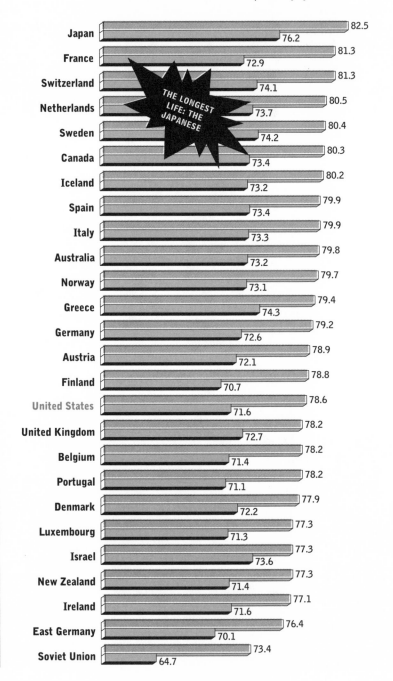

Japan	82.5	76.2
France	81.3	72.9
Switzerland	81.3	74.1
Netherlands	80.5	73.7
Sweden	80.4	74.2
Canada	80.3	73.4
Iceland	80.2	73.2
Spain	79.9	73.4
Italy	79.9	73.3
Australia	79.8	73.2
Norway	79.7	73.1
Greece	79.4	74.3
Germany	79.2	72.6
Austria	78.9	72.1
Finland	78.8	70.7
United States	78.6	71.6
United Kingdom	78.2	72.7
Belgium	78.2	71.4
Portugal	78.2	71.1
Denmark	77.9	72.2
Luxembourg	77.3	71.3
Israel	77.3	73.6
New Zealand	77.3	71.4
Ireland	77.1	71.6
East Germany	76.4	70.1
Soviet Union	73.4	64.7

THE LONGEST LIFE: THE JAPANESE

WHO GETS TO BE OLD?

Years of life lost prematurely (before the age of 64) per 100 people

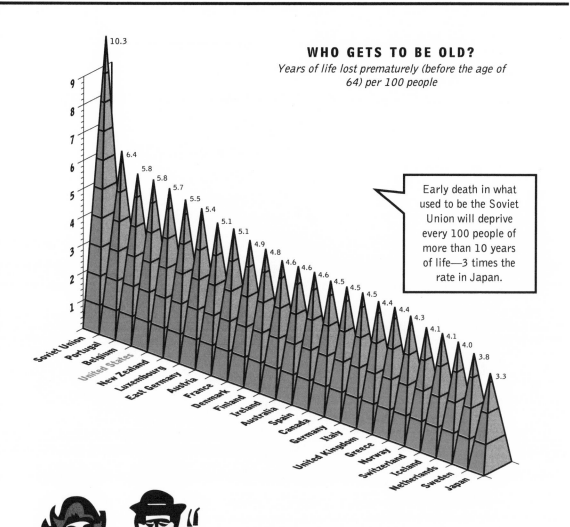

10.3																											

Soviet Union 10.3, Portugal 6.4, Belgium 5.8, United States 5.8, New Zealand 5.7, Luxembourg 5.5, East Germany 5.4, Austria 5.1, France 5.1, Denmark 4.9, Finland 4.8, Ireland 4.6, Australia 4.6, Spain 4.6, Canada 4.5, Germany 4.5, Italy 4.5, United Kingdom 4.4, Greece 4.4, Norway 4.3, Switzerland 4.1, Iceland 4.1, Netherlands 4.0, Sweden 3.8, Japan 3.3

> Early death in what used to be the Soviet Union will deprive every 100 people of more than 10 years of life—3 times the rate in Japan.

LIVING WELL

Average number of sick days per person per year

Country	Days		Country	Days
Norway	32		Canada	16
Sweden	25		Finland	13
United Kingdom	24		New Zealand	13
Netherlands	22		Austria	12
Australia	20		Ireland	11
United States	19			

Who dies?

COUNTED OUT

Annual death rate for men (■) and women (□) per 100,000 people

> "Europe today is commonly described as a continent drawing together. Yet recent data from the World Health Organization still delineate a deadly barrier cutting through the center of Europe. Never before, in fact, have the health and longevity prospects of Europe's peacetime population been so separate, or their levels so politically distinct.... For the whole of [Eastern Europe], death rates for men in their 60s rose by about 10 percent between 1965 and 1985; for those in their 30s, by more than 20 percent; for those in their 50s, by more than 30 percent; for men in their 40s, by more than half."
> —*Nicholas Eberstadt, Harvard's Center for Population Studies*

Because the infant-mortality rate is so strongly a function of access to care, it is one of the most common measures of the overall fairness of a health-care system. At 10.4 per 1,000 live births, the U.S. has one of ➤+

Country	Men	Women
Soviet Union	1,099.2	621.9
East Germany	854.4	518.5
Ireland	780.0	485.8
Luxembourg	771.9	439.8
New Zealand	742.1	469.1
Finland	794.7	412.0
Belgium	759.9	432.9
Portugal	745.9	431.2
Denmark	714.7	452.0
United Kingdom	700.5	439.9
United States	715.2	423.9
Austria	709.6	408.6
Israel	639.7	473.9
Germany	698.2	399.5
Norway	668.4	381.4
Italy	658.8	373.4
Australia	649.4	378.2
Canada	646.3	365.8
Spain	637.8	370.5
Netherlands	647.8	356.0
Greece	599.6	390.4
France	654.0	330.3
Sweden	615.9	359.3
Switzerland	604.7	329.5
Iceland	522.0	365.3
Japan	518.5	295.2

LOST BABIES
Infant mortality per 1,000 live births

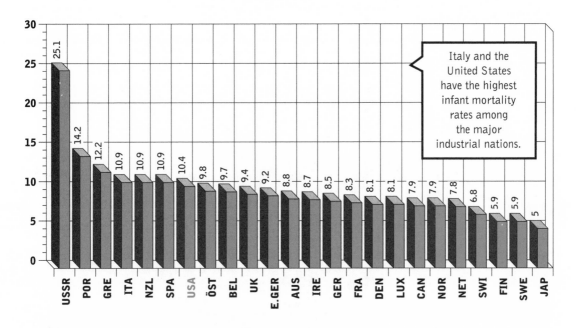

> Italy and the United States have the highest infant mortality rates among the major industrial nations.

''NOW I LAY ME...''
Annual death rate of 1-to-4-year-olds in an average community of 200,000 people

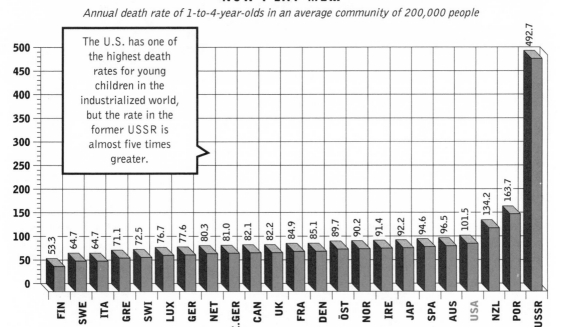

> The U.S. has one of the highest death rates for young children in the industrialized world, but the rate in the former USSR is almost five times greater.

Who dies?

the highest infant-mortality rates among the major industrial nations.

Young adults should be the healthiest age group in any nation. High death rates in this group most often result from factors other than disease, including accidents, drugs, and violence—in other words, man-made death. The U.S. Centers for Disease Control describes the critically high homicide rates among young men as not only a crime concern but a significant public-health crisis. The murder rate among U.S males 15 to 24 years old is 4 times that of any other industrial country, and 40 times that of Japan.

The mortal effects of life-style—fatty diet, stress, lack of exercise, and hereditary bad luck—"bulge" in the 45–54 age range of a modern man. The former USSR, where bad habits were compounded by the additional curse of lax care, far outdistances all Western nations in death rate, but among the major industrial nations only France surpasses the U.S.

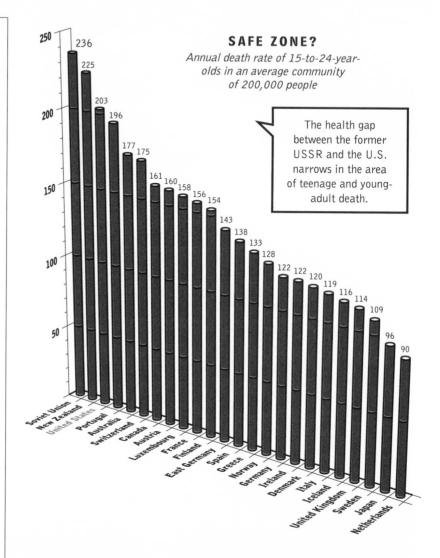

SAFE ZONE?

Annual death rate of 15-to-24-year-olds in an average community of 200,000 people

The health gap between the former USSR and the U.S. narrows in the area of teenage and young-adult death.

CUT DOWN

Murder rate for males age 15 to 24 per 100,000 people

United States	24.4	Norway	2.3	France	1.2
Soviet Union	10.5	Finland	2.3	Netherlands	1.2
New Zealand	4.4	Denmark	2.2	Germany	0.9
Italy	3.2	United Kingdom	2.0	Greece	0.9
Canada	2.6	Spain	1.9	Japan	0.5
Australia	2.4	Ireland	1.6	East Germany	0.4
Sweden	2.3	Austria	1.2	Switzerland	0.3

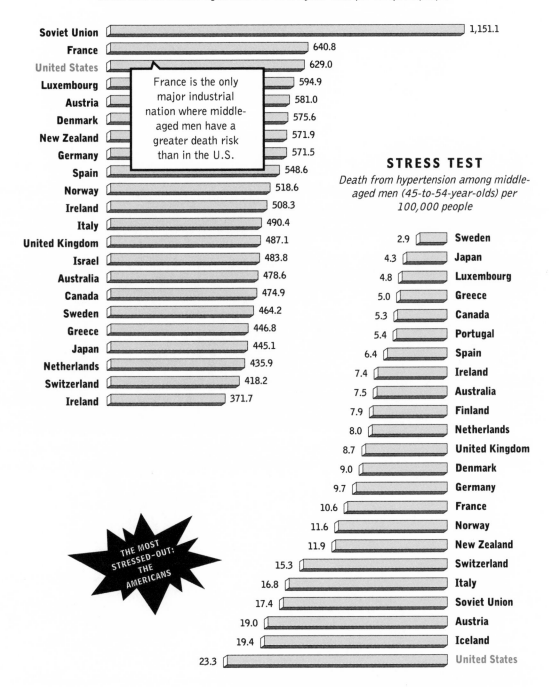

THE DANGER ZONE

Death rate for middle-aged men (45-to-54-year-olds) per 100,000 people

Soviet Union	1,151.1
France	640.8
United States	629.0
Luxembourg	594.9
Austria	581.0
Denmark	575.6
New Zealand	571.9
Germany	571.5
Spain	548.6
Norway	518.6
Ireland	508.3
Italy	490.4
United Kingdom	487.1
Israel	483.8
Australia	478.6
Canada	474.9
Sweden	464.2
Greece	446.8
Japan	445.1
Netherlands	435.9
Switzerland	418.2
Ireland	371.7

France is the only major industrial nation where middle-aged men have a greater death risk than in the U.S.

THE MOST STRESSED-OUT: THE AMERICANS

STRESS TEST

Death from hypertension among middle-aged men (45-to-54-year-olds) per 100,000 people

2.9	Sweden
4.3	Japan
4.8	Luxembourg
5.0	Greece
5.3	Canada
5.4	Portugal
6.4	Spain
7.4	Ireland
7.5	Australia
7.9	Finland
8.0	Netherlands
8.7	United Kingdom
9.0	Denmark
9.7	Germany
10.6	France
11.6	Norway
11.9	New Zealand
15.3	Switzerland
16.8	Italy
17.4	Soviet Union
19.0	Austria
19.4	Iceland
23.3	United States

117

Who will take care of you?

Americans are the most X-rayed, CAT-scanned, hospitalized, and operated-on people on earth, which goes a long way to explaining why U.S. health-care costs are so high. (It is not out of the ordinary for doctors who order up extra CAT scans and other expensive tests to own an interest in the labs that do the tests, or for labs to pay doctors for referrals.) If your insurance is in order—and if your employer hasn't cut back on the plan's coverage—then the U.S. is not a bad place to be sick. But if you don't work for a solid, well-established company with good medical benefits, you're a beggar at the feast.

Bulat Okudzhava, a noted Soviet poet, was struck with critical heart disease while on tour in Los Angeles. Doctors recommended an emergency bypass. The operation was a success, but the uninsured 67-year-old poet suddenly faced bankruptcy. The bill: $56,000.

Admission rates at Japanese hospitals are only 7.5 per 1,000 people, compared ➤➤

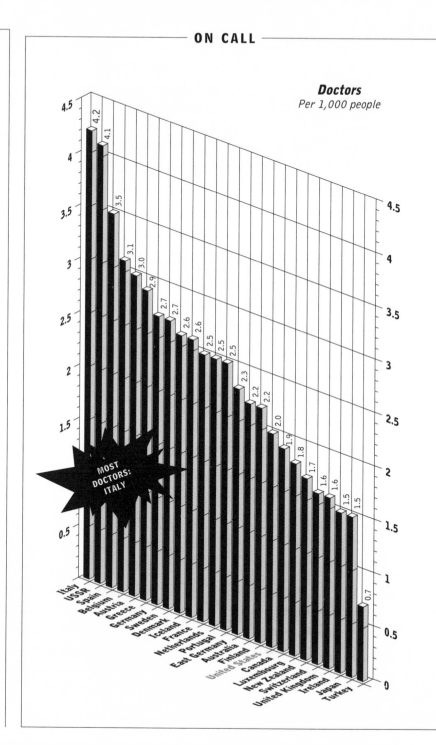

ON CALL

Doctors
Per 1,000 people

MOST DOCTORS: ITALY

Country	Doctors per 1,000
Italy	4.2
USSR	4.1
Spain	3.5
Belgium	3.1
Austria	3.0
Greece	2.9
Germany	2.7
Sweden	2.7
Denmark	2.6
Iceland	2.6
France	2.5
Netherlands	2.5
Portugal	2.5
East Germany	2.3
Australia	2.2
Finland	2.2
United States	2.0
Canada	1.9
Luxembourg	1.8
New Zealand	1.7
Switzerland	1.6
United Kingdom	1.6
Ireland	1.5
Japan	1.5
Turkey	0.7

118

MOST SHRINKS:
THE U.S.

Nurses
Per 1,000 people

New Zealand	12.5
Finland	8.7
Norway	8.5
Australia	8.4
United States	7.9
Switzerland	7.7
Sweden	7.6
Iceland	7.4
Ireland	7.1
Denmark	6.0
Austria	5.7
France	5.3
Japan	5.3
Germany	5.1
Italy	4.0
Spain	3.9
Luxembourg	3.7
Netherlands	3.5
Canada	3.3
United Kingdom	3.2
Greece	2.3
Belgium	1.0
Turkey	0.7

Psychiatrists
Per 100,000 people

United States	12.1
Belgium	10.0
Sweden	9.7
Denmark	8.4
Ireland	6.7
Austria	5.7
Italy	4.4
France	3.7
United Kingdom	3.7
Netherlands	2.3

Dentists
Per 1,000 people

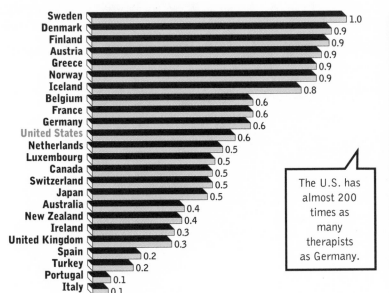

Sweden	1.0
Denmark	0.9
Finland	0.9
Austria	0.9
Greece	0.9
Norway	0.9
Iceland	0.8
Belgium	0.6
France	0.6
Germany	0.6
United States	0.6
Netherlands	0.5
Luxembourg	0.5
Canada	0.5
Switzerland	0.5
Japan	0.5
Australia	0.4
New Zealand	0.4
Ireland	0.3
United Kingdom	0.3
Spain	0.2
Turkey	0.2
Portugal	0.1
Italy	0.1

The U.S. has almost 200 times as many therapists as Germany.

Psychologists
Per 100,000 people

United States	57.6
Norway	7.2
Sweden	6.8
Iceland	6.5
East Germany	5.6
Netherlands	2.1
United Kingdom	1.7
Ireland	1.5
Denmark	1.1
Italy	0.4
Germany	0.3

Who will take care of you?

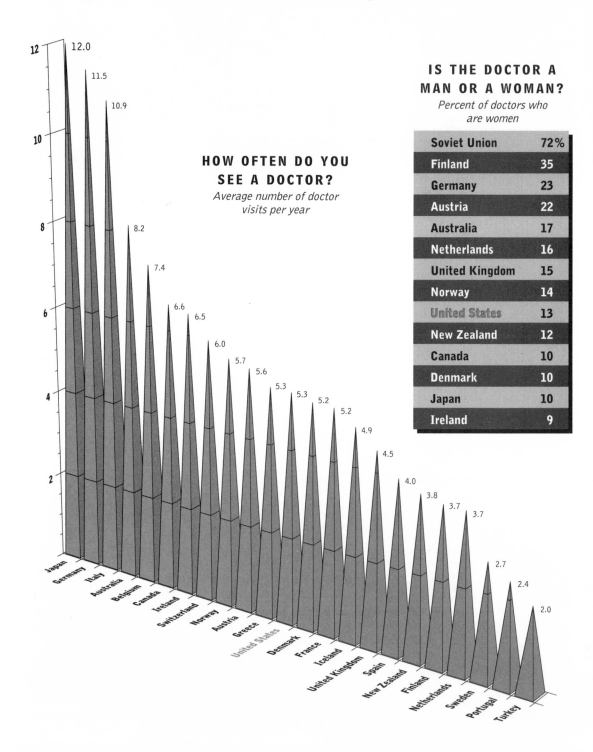

HOW OFTEN DO YOU SEE A DOCTOR?
Average number of doctor visits per year

12.0
11.5
10.9
8.2
7.4
6.6
6.5
6.0
5.7
5.6
5.3
5.3
5.2
5.2
4.9
4.5
4.0
3.8
3.7
3.7
2.7
2.4
2.0

Japan, Germany, Italy, Australia, Belgium, Canada, Ireland, Switzerland, Norway, Austria, Greece, United States, Denmark, France, Iceland, United Kingdom, Spain, New Zealand, Finland, Netherlands, Sweden, Portugal, Turkey

IS THE DOCTOR A MAN OR A WOMAN?
Percent of doctors who are women

Soviet Union	72%
Finland	35
Germany	23
Austria	22
Australia	17
Netherlands	16
United Kingdom	15
Norway	14
United States	13
New Zealand	12
Canada	10
Denmark	10
Japan	10
Ireland	9

HOW LONG IS THE VISIT?
Average duration of a doctor visit (minutes)

Netherlands 5.0

United Kingdom 8.2

Germany 9.0

France 14.0

United States 14.0

Canada 15.0

HOW MANY YEARS OF TRAINING DOES HE/SHE HAVE?
Training necessary to become a general practitioner (years)

Norway	12.5	United States	10.0
Finland	12.0	Austria	9.0
Denmark	11.5	Belgium	9.0
France	11.0	Greece	9.0
Switzerland	11.0	Spain	9.0
Sweden	10.3	Netherlands	8.0
Germany	10.0	United Kingdom	8.0
Ireland	10.0	Italy	6.5

with an average of 16 per 1,000 in the West. The Japanese may well have good reason for not rushing off to the hospital—the average stay lasts 40 days. The average stay in America is five days.

In Japan, according to *The Economist*, doctors are so revered and so secretive that many hardly communicate with their patients. It is quite common not to be told what kind of drugs you're taking—or even whether you have a terminal illness.

In most Western nations, including the U.S., mental-hospital admissions have decreased. In Japan, however, according to a report in *Nature*, the inpatient population has grown more than twenty-fold over the last generation—and 80 percent of the admissions are involuntary. In Japan, commitment can be arranged by a family member solely on the basis of the opinion of the hospital superintendent.

While a visit to the doctor in the U.S. is apt to last fifteen to twenty minutes, the average visit in the U.K. takes little more than eight minutes. ➡

Who will take care of you?

WHAT'S YOUR PROBLEM?
Number of medical complaints per 1,000 people over a three-year period for...

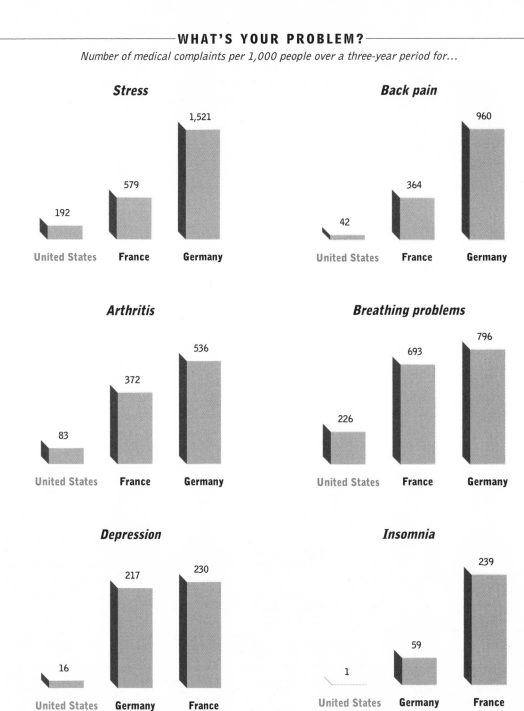

Stress

United States	France	Germany
192	579	1,521

Back pain

United States	France	Germany
42	364	960

Arthritis

United States	France	Germany
83	372	536

Breathing problems

United States	France	Germany
226	693	796

Depression

United States	Germany	France
16	217	230

Insomnia

United States	Germany	France
1	59	239

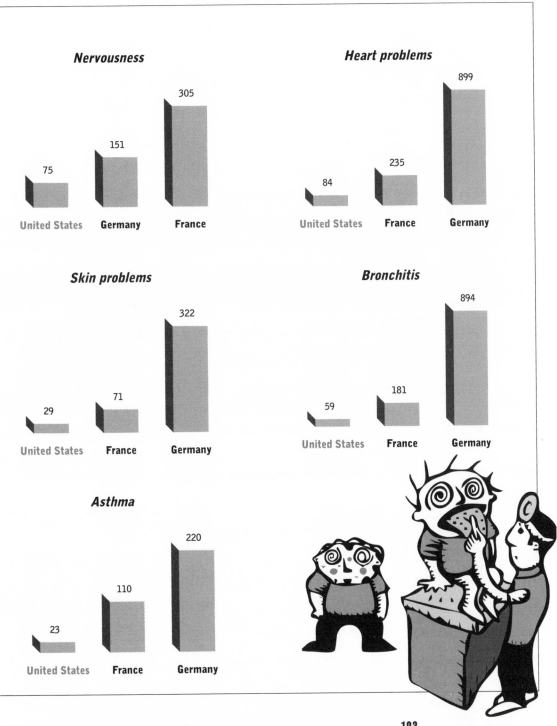

Nervousness

75	151	305
United States	Germany	France

Heart problems

84	235	899
United States	France	Germany

Skin problems

29	71	322
United States	France	Germany

Bronchitis

59	181	894
United States	France	Germany

Asthma

23	110	220
United States	France	Germany

Who will take care of you?

WHAT IF YOU NEED A HOSPITAL BED?

Crowded ward
Hospital beds per 1,000 people

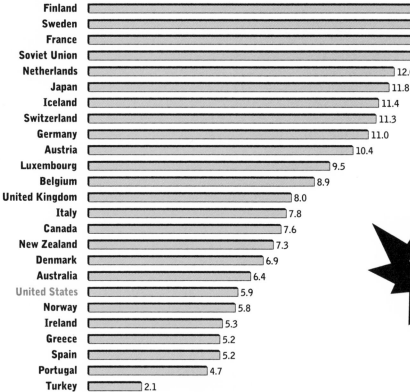

Finland	14.9
Sweden	13.2
France	12.9
Soviet Union	12.8
Netherlands	12.0
Japan	11.8
Iceland	11.4
Switzerland	11.3
Germany	11.0
Austria	10.4
Luxembourg	9.5
Belgium	8.9
United Kingdom	8.0
Italy	7.8
Canada	7.6
New Zealand	7.3
Denmark	6.9
Australia	6.4
United States	5.9
Norway	5.8
Ireland	5.3
Greece	5.2
Spain	5.2
Portugal	4.7
Turkey	2.1

MOST BEDS: FINLAND

Checking in
Hospital admissions per 1,000 people

Austria	22.6	Ireland	16.9	New Zealand	13.0
Finland	22.6	Norway	16.3	Greece	12.1
Australia	21.6	United Kingdom	15.8	Netherlands	11.0
France	21.2	Italy	15.0	Iceland	10.9
Germany	21.1	United States	14.7	Portugal	9.3
Denmark	20.5	Belgium	14.6	Spain	9.0
Sweden	20.0	Canada	14.5	Japan	7.5
Luxembourg	19.0	Switzerland	13.2	Turkey	5.5

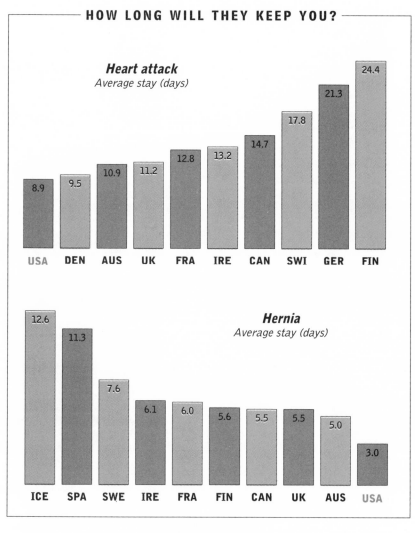

HOW LONG WILL THEY KEEP YOU?

Heart attack
Average stay (days)

USA	DEN	AUS	UK	FRA	IRE	CAN	SWI	GER	FIN
8.9	9.5	10.9	11.2	12.8	13.2	14.7	17.8	21.3	24.4

Hernia
Average stay (days)

ICE	SPA	SWE	IRE	FRA	FIN	CAN	UK	AUS	USA
12.6	11.3	7.6	6.1	6.0	5.6	5.5	5.5	5.0	3.0

The certifiable
Mental-hospital admissions per 10,000 people

Country	Value	Country	Value
Sweden	90.3	Italy	26.3
Switzerland	66.5	Greece	25.0
Germany	35.4	Canada	15.7
Israel	32.5	Japan	13.2
United States	29.7	Portugal	13.2
Norway	27.8	Turkey	4.8

Likewise, the British are only half as likely to be X-rayed or operated on.

In January 1989, claims Dr. James S. Todd of the American Medical Association, more than 1,000 people were on waiting lists for bypass surgery in Toronto, Canada. They could expect to wait eight to nine months for their operations.

"The dedicated doctors who have created much of what is good about [the U.S.] health-care system are increasingly dispirited....More than 30 percent of current [U.S.] physicians say they would not have gone to medical school if they had known what they now know about medicine as a career."
—*Regina E. Herzlinger, "Healthy Competition,"* The Atlantic Monthly

Myth:
U.S. hospitals keep you longer to boost your bill.

Reality:
The average stay is relatively short.

— How much does your care cost? —

THE MEDICAL BILL
What each nation spends annually on health care (% of GDP)

United States	11.2%
Sweden	9.0
Canada	8.6
France	8.6
Netherlands	8.5
Austria	8.4
Germany	8.2
Iceland	7.8
Switzerland	7.7
Luxembourg	7.5
Norway	7.5
Finland	7.4
Ireland	7.4
Belgium	7.2
Australia	7.1
Italy	6.9
New Zealand	6.9
Japan	6.8
Portugal	6.4
United Kingdom	6.1
Denmark	6.0
Spain	6.0
Greece	5.3

TOP HEALTH-CARE SPENDER: THE U.S.

YOUR SHARE
Annual medical spending per person ($)

United States	$2,354
Canada	1,683
Switzerland	1,376
Sweden	1,361
Iceland	1,353
France	1,274
Norway	1,234
Germany	1,232
Luxembourg	1,193
Netherlands	1,135
Austria	1,093
Finland	1,067
Italy	1,050
Japan	1,035
Australia	1,032
Belgium	980
Denmark	912
United Kingdom	836
New Zealand	820
Ireland	658

YOUR PAIN, HIS GAIN
Cost of an average office visit ($)

MOST EXPENSIVE DOCTORS: THE U.S.

United States	Switzerland	Luxembourg	Germany	France	Belgium	Denmark	Japan
$31	24	18	14	13	12	11	10

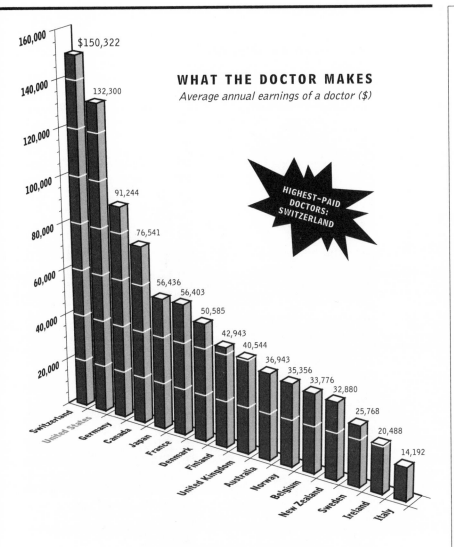

WHAT THE DOCTOR MAKES
Average annual earnings of a doctor ($)

HIGHEST-PAID DOCTORS: SWITZERLAND

- Switzerland $150,322
- United States 132,300
- Germany 91,244
- Canada 76,541
- Japan 56,436
- France 56,403
- Denmark 50,585
- Finland 42,943
- United Kingdom 40,544
- Australia 36,943
- Norway 35,356
- Belgium 33,776
- New Zealand 32,880
- Sweden 25,768
- Ireland 20,488
- Italy 14,192

A DAY IN THE HOSPITAL
Average cost of a hospital bed per day ($)

United States	$360		Netherlands	140
Denmark	220		United Kingdom	140
Norway	220		Iceland	130
Canada	210		Switzerland	125
Australia	200		Germany	110
France	170		Finland	70
Ireland	170		Japan	60

The biggest industry in every advanced nation is health care. The U.K.'s National Health Service can see the day when it will become Europe's biggest employer. The U.S., however, spends by far the most for each of its citizens—double the amount it spends on education, for instance. Even so, it manages to cover less. No doubt all models of health care are imperfect and expensive, but some are more imperfect than others—and more expensive.

"In 1987, if the U.S. had spent the same share of GNP on health care as our international competitors, we could have saved $158 billion," says Dr. Otis R. Bowen, former secretary of Health and Human Services.

If U.S. health-care costs maintain their present rate of growth, they will exceed $1 trillion by the year 2000. Canada, the Netherlands, Germany, and Japan are actually reducing their health-care-cost growth rates.

General practitioners make the most money in Switzerland and the U.S.—approximately twice as much as those in Canada, almost ➤

How much does your care cost?

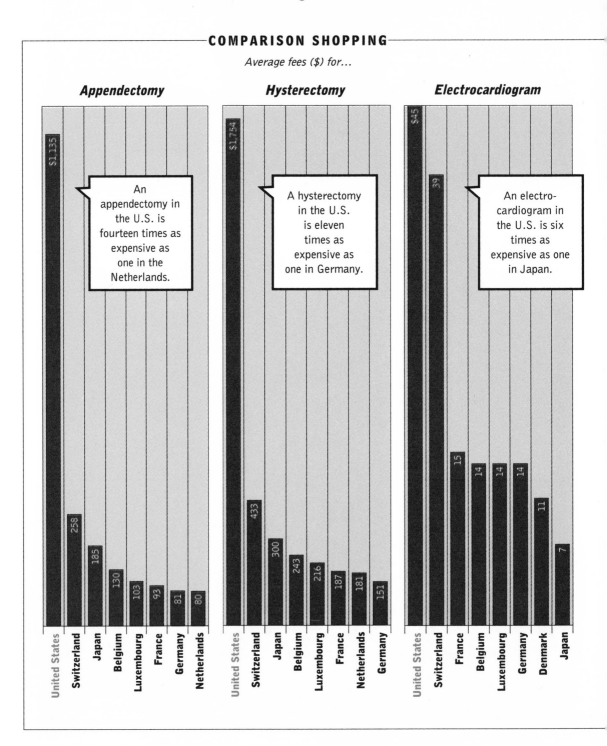

COMPARISON SHOPPING

Average fees ($) for...

Appendectomy

$1,135

An appendectomy in the U.S. is fourteen times as expensive as one in the Netherlands.

United States	Switzerland	Japan	Belgium	Luxembourg	France	Germany	Netherlands
	258	185	130	103	93	81	80

Hysterectomy

$1,754

A hysterectomy in the U.S. is eleven times as expensive as one in Germany.

United States	Switzerland	Japan	Belgium	Luxembourg	France	Netherlands	Germany
	433	300	243	216	187	181	151

Electrocardiogram

$45

39

An electro-cardiogram in the U.S. is six times as expensive as one in Japan.

United States	Switzerland	France	Belgium	Luxembourg	Germany	Denmark	Japan
		15	14	14	14	11	7

Molar extraction

United States	$70
France	15
Denmark	13
Japan	12
Switzerland	8
Belgium	8
Luxembourg	8
Germany	7
Netherlands	5

A molar extraction in the U.S. is fourteen times as expensive as one in the Netherlands.

Tooth filling

United States	$36
Belgium	14
Luxembourg	13
France	12
Germany	12
Netherlands	8

A filling in the U.S. is four times as expensive as one in the Netherlands.

three times as much as those in the U.K., and ten times as much as those in Italy.

Canada spends 25 percent to 50 percent less than the U.S. per capita for hospital costs, without any significant difference in death rates on a large sampling of surgical procedures.

"The U.S. is spending a lot more on hospitals than we are, but they don't seem to be getting as much out of it."
—*University of Manitoba professor of health sciences Lester L. Roos*

Myth:
The high cost of U.S. health care is a complex problem.

Reality:
A big part of the problem is simple—doctors' fees are ridiculously high!

The druggiest

Germany leads the world in the amount it spends, per person, on medication.

"Doctors in France are not well trained to handle psychological problems. And French people are very private; they do not like to consult psychologists or psychiatrists. A Frenchman is like the opposite of Woody Allen, you see."
—*Valérie Lennes, spokeswoman for the pharmaceutical company Produits Roche, trying to explain why the French lead the world in the habitual consumption of sedatives*

HALCION DAZE
Daily doses of tranquilizers per 1,000 people per day

Denmark	110.76
Spain	110.44
United Kingdom	88.04
Italy	73.57
Finland	54.44
Norway	52.21
Sweden	50.62
France	46.74
Australia	45.64
East Germany	43.34
Germany	38.12
Japan	33.59
United States	32.96
Iceland	27.90
Greece	21.91
Belgium	7.80
Canada	3.88
Soviet Union	1.26
Switzerland	0.86
Portugal	0.33

HALF–LIFE
Percent of population who use tranquilizers longer than 12 months

Country	Percent
France	5.0%
Spain	3.8
United Kingdom	3.1
Netherlands	1.7
Italy	1.6
Germany	1.6
United States	1.6
Switzerland	1.2

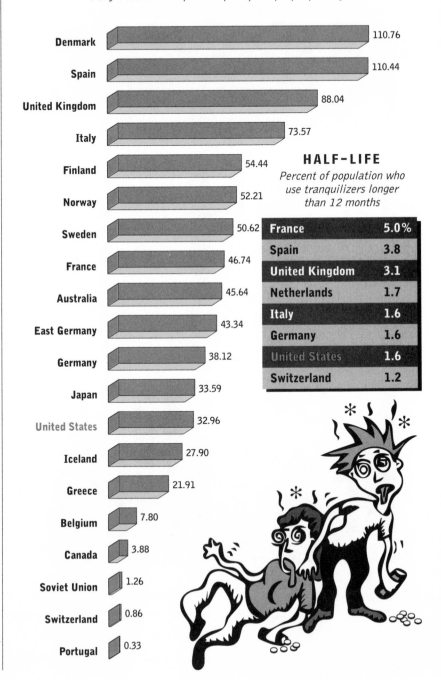

BEHIND THE COUNTER
Number of prescriptions per person per year

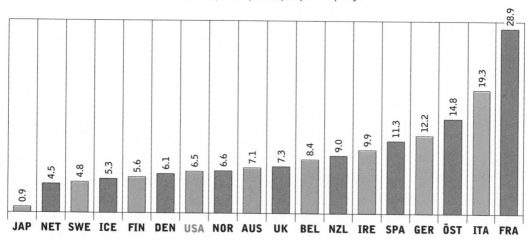

JAP	NET	SWE	ICE	FIN	DEN	USA	NOR	AUS	UK	BEL	NZL	IRE	SPA	GER	ÖST	ITA	FRA
0.9	4.5	4.8	5.3	5.6	6.1	6.5	6.6	7.1	7.3	8.4	9.0	9.9	11.3	12.2	14.8	19.3	28.9

OVER THE COUNTER
Annual per capita spending on medicines ($)

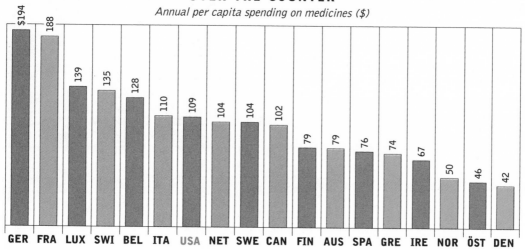

GER	FRA	LUX	SWI	BEL	ITA	USA	NET	SWE	CAN	FIN	AUS	SPA	GRE	IRE	NOR	ÖST	DEN
$194	188	139	135	128	110	109	104	104	102	79	79	76	74	67	50	46	42

VALIUM
Daily doses per 1,000 adults per day

United States	21.8
United Kingdom	18.7
Greece	6.7
Japan	4.5

BILLS FOR PILLS
Index of average drug prices (100=lowest average price)

Greece	100
Spain	105
France	127
Italy	131

United Kingdom	217
Germany	269
United States	279
Netherlands	299

The Cutting Edge

According to *The Economist*, surgical rates are low in Japan because the Japanese have an aversion to being cut up.

Eighty percent fewer bypasses are performed in the U.K. than in the U.S.

"American patients want to be in perfect health. This explains a little of our predilection for surgery. We think that if something bad is taken out, then we're going to be perfect....People should recognize that because America thinks of itself as a can-do society, doctors emphasize the risk of doing nothing and tend to minimize the risk of doing something."
—*Lynn Payer,* Medicine & Culture

Traditionally knife-happy American surgeons perform three times as many hysterectomies as their counterparts in France, and twice as many as doctors in the U.K.

"The brain surgeons are jousting with the bone surgeons, the dermatologists are rubbing plastic surgeons the »

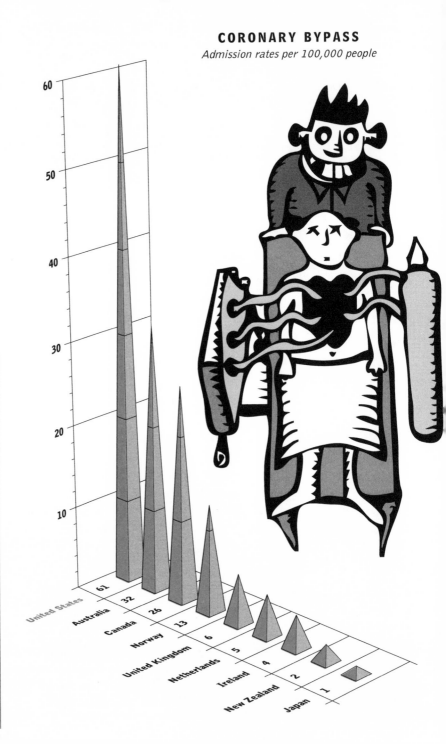

CORONARY BYPASS
Admission rates per 100,000 people

United States 61
Australia 32
Canada 26
Norway 13
United Kingdom 6
Netherlands 5
Ireland 4
New Zealand 2
Japan 1

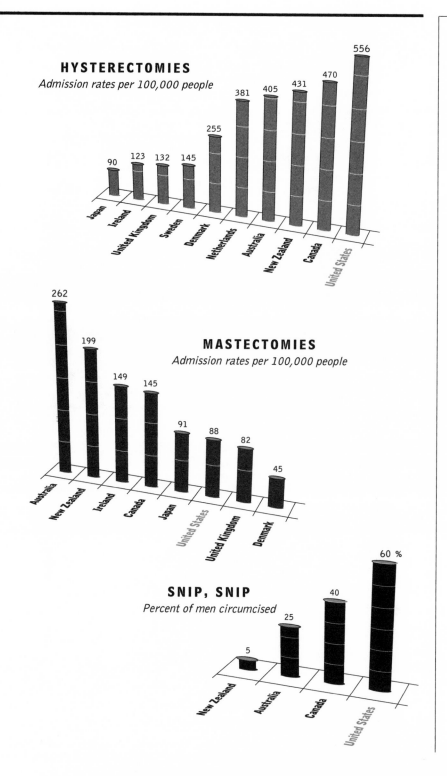

HYSTERECTOMIES
Admission rates per 100,000 people

Japan	90
Ireland	123
United Kingdom	132
Sweden	145
Denmark	255
Netherlands	381
Australia	405
New Zealand	431
Canada	470
United States	556

MASTECTOMIES
Admission rates per 100,000 people

Australia	262
New Zealand	199
Ireland	149
Canada	145
Japan	91
United States	88
United Kingdom	82
Denmark	45

SNIP, SNIP
Percent of men circumcised

New Zealand	5
Australia	25
Canada	40
United States	60 %

wrong way and the radiologists are fighting with nearly all their medical colleagues.... Underused cardiologists and cardiac surgeons fight for the right to insert pacemakers. Gastroenterologists, who refined the art of peering into the upper and lower digestive tracts with scopes, now watch in dismay as surgeons begin to do the peering themselves... Plastic surgeons complain that other specialists are horning in on the performance of rhinoplasties, better known as nose jobs.''
—The New York Times

Screw-ups

In the U.S., malpractice premiums have risen over the last ten years by 345 percent, with the highest at $96,878. Million-dollar awards to plaintiffs have more than quadrupled during that time.

"The perception that individuals cannot bring about certain kinds of change translates into a greater reluctance to challenge the status quo, whether by suing for medical malpractice or for anything else. [In Britain], somehow, a taint of avarice or unethical conduct seems to be attached to litigation, particularly where personal injuries are concerned. Moreover, the British judiciary often fosters this idea by scornful references to the greed of American plaintiffs and their lawyers."
—*Frances H. Miller,* American Journal of Law & Medicine

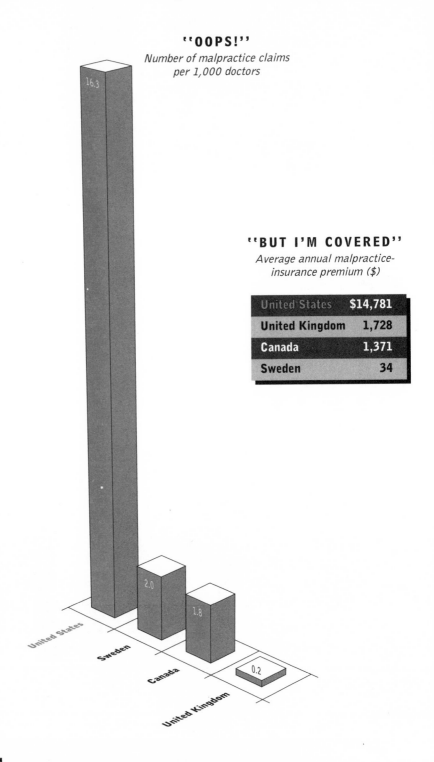

"OOPS!"
Number of malpractice claims per 1,000 doctors

16.3

2.0

1.8

0.2

United States

Sweden

Canada

United Kingdom

"BUT I'M COVERED"
Average annual malpractice-insurance premium ($)

United States	$14,781
United Kingdom	1,728
Canada	1,371
Sweden	34

THE AWARD
Average award ($)

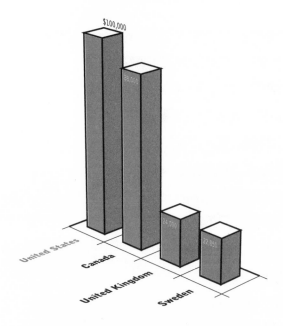

MORE AND MORE
Annual growth in number of claims (%)

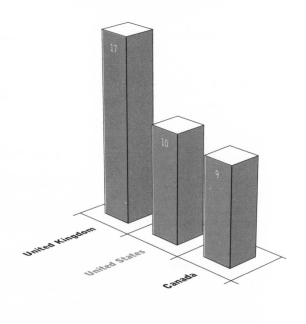

FOR EVER-LARGER AMOUNTS
Annual growth in average awarded compensation (%)

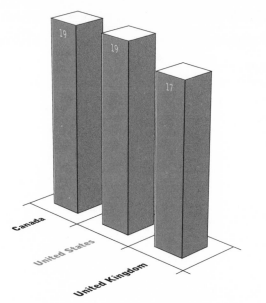

...AND EVER-LARGER PREMIUMS
Annual growth in average malpractice premium (%)

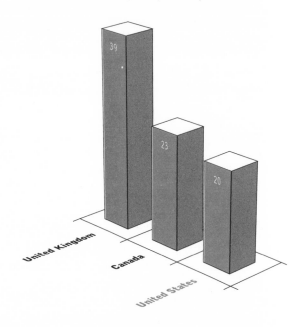

And who pays?

WHAT COMES OUT OF YOUR POCKET
Percent of income spent on health insurance

"How would you like to compete without this albatross around your necks called runaway health care costs? For me, it's $700 a car, and still going up at twice the rate of inflation. Other countries put those costs in their taxes, but we put them into the price of our products. That's not very healthy for competing with the other guys."
—*Lee A. Iacocca, chairman, Chrysler Corp.*

In the U.S., between 1980 and 1987, 90 percent of real income gains were wiped out by rising health-care costs, with household income growing by 6.4 percent, or $1,500, and average real household health-care costs growing by 35 percent, or $1,412.

In the U.S., between 30 million and 40 million people have no health insurance whatsoever—and 12 million of the uninsured are children. Even for the relatively well insured, a catastrophic illness presents the possibility of economic disaster. ➡

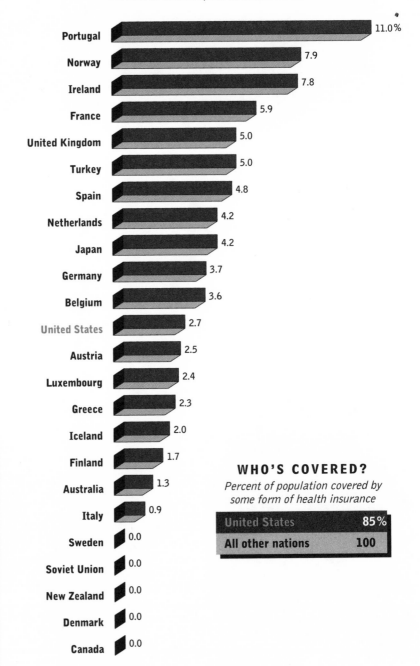

Country	Percent
Portugal	11.0%
Norway	7.9
Ireland	7.8
France	5.9
United Kingdom	5.0
Turkey	5.0
Spain	4.8
Netherlands	4.2
Japan	4.2
Germany	3.7
Belgium	3.6
United States	2.7
Austria	2.5
Luxembourg	2.4
Greece	2.3
Iceland	2.0
Finland	1.7
Australia	1.3
Italy	0.9
Sweden	0.0
Soviet Union	0.0
New Zealand	0.0
Denmark	0.0
Canada	0.0

WHO'S COVERED?
Percent of population covered by some form of health insurance

United States	85%
All other nations	100

WHAT COMES FROM YOUR EMPLOYER'S POCKET?

Percent of wages spent on an employee's health insurance

Portugal	24.5 %
Spain	24.0
Norway	17.2
Netherlands	14.5
France	12.6
Sweden	10.1
Italy	9.6
United States	8.3
Belgium	6.0
Turkey	5.0
United Kingdom	5.0
Greece	4.5
Soviet Union	4.4
Japan	4.2
Germany	3.7
Canada	3.2
Austria	2.5
Luxembourg	2.4
Finland	1.5
Ireland	1.3
Denmark	0.0
Switzerland	0.0
New Zealand	0.0
Iceland	0.0
Australia	0.0

More than 40 percent of corporate operating profits in the U.S. go to health-care costs—compared with 9 percent in 1965.

"Competent, affordable health care—this aspiration is linked to the biggest worry clouding the American dream, particularly for those approaching or in retirement. When we asked respondents what might stand in the way of achieving their dream, catastrophic illness came out at the top of the list, outranking such fears as recession and natural disaster....Even the affluent know that one major illness could wipe them out."

—Money Magazine

WHAT THE GOVERNMENT PAYS

Percent of hospital costs borne by government

Denmark	100 %		Luxembourg	95
Norway	100		France	92
Portugal	100		Austria	90
Sweden	100		Finland	90
Switzerland	100		Greece	90
Italy	99		Spain	84
United Kingdom	99		Netherlands	80
Germany	97		Belgium	68
Ireland	95		United States	55

137

And the winner is...

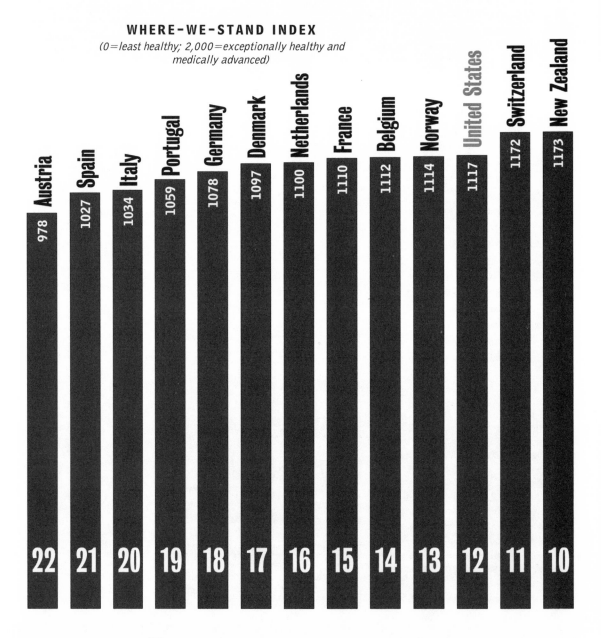

WHERE–WE–STAND INDEX
(0=least healthy; 2,000=exceptionally healthy and medically advanced)

Rank	Country	Index
22	Austria	978
21	Spain	1027
20	Italy	1034
19	Portugal	1059
18	Germany	1078
17	Denmark	1097
16	Netherlands	1100
15	France	1110
14	Belgium	1112
13	Norway	1114
12	United States	1117
11	Switzerland	1172
10	New Zealand	1173

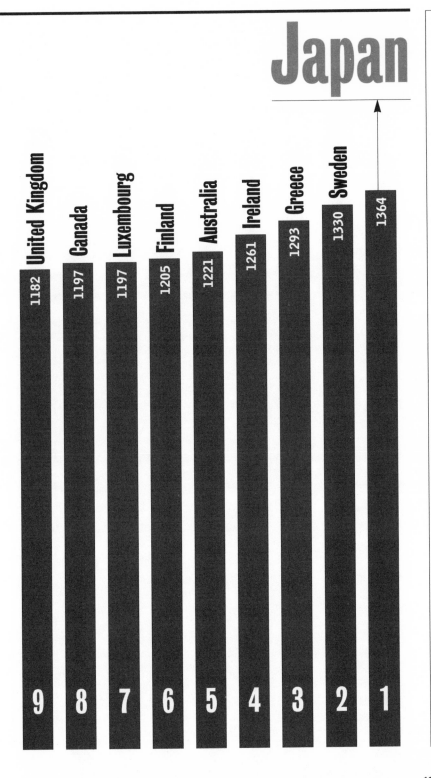

Japan

United Kingdom — 1182

Canada — 1197

Luxembourg — 1197

Finland — 1205

Australia — 1221

Ireland — 1261

Greece — 1293

Sweden — 1330

1364

9 8 7 6 5 4 3 2 1

Japanese men and women live longer than people anywhere else; Japan's death rate is the lowest among industrial nations; its infant-mortality rate the lowest in the world. It has the fewest heart attacks for both men and women (even though Japanese men smoke and drink to excess), the lowest cancer rates (particularly for the big killers: lung cancer, breast cancer, and ovarian cancer), and the second-lowest incidence of death due to hypertension. Its citizens take fewer medicines than almost anyone else—30 times fewer medicines per capita than the French. What's more, its health-care system works better and cheaper— for doctors' fees, for hospital costs, and for most procedures. Overall, Japan spends less than half of what the U.S. spends on health care, and yet it is a fairer system—offering access to everyone.

THE BUSIEST

Is labor working?

The secret of national happiness—or at least of a rising paycheck—is having each worker produce more than he did the year before.

And the world's best workers are...(still; surprise!) the Americans. But that just shows what a true colossus America was—and how far it has had to fall (and how far other nations have had to go to catch up to it). American productivity growth has slipped severely over the past generation, from an average annual gain of 2.8 percent in the 1960s to half that rate through the 1970s and '80s. By 1990, French workers were 85 percent as efficient as American workers, German workers 81 percent, and Japanese workers 70 percent (up from 15 percent in 1950). One restraint on Japan's productivity growth is its continued commitment to full employment, which has created inefficiencies in many areas, especially farming and the distribution of goods. Nevertheless, at present rates, Japan, along with Europe, will surpass the U.S. by early next century.

Increased productivity—less and less input for greater and greater output—is among America's contributions to the twentieth century. The nineteenth-century point of view, held by Marx as well as free-market economists, was that production could increase only with more effort and longer hours. But an American, Frederick W. Taylor, began to analyze manual work. His studies showed how to improve productivity through labor-saving techniques, workplace reorganization, and new technologies.

"In a very real sense, it is Taylor who defeated Marx and Marxism," says economist Peter F. Drucker. "For his *Scientific Management* not only tremendously increased output; it also made possible increasing the worker's wages while at the same time cutting the product's prices and thereby increasing demand."

Productivity is the key to competition among nations; the one who produces the most goods in the shortest period of time wins. It is a game that depends on the skill, experience, and dedication of a nation's work force, the efficiency of its factories, the competence of its managers, and the thoroughness of its planning and research—all areas where the U.S. was once unchallenged.

When the challenge came, it was fraught with ironies: The U.S. found itself with older factories and machinery than Germany and Japan, whose rebuilding the U.S. had financed after the war; the management practices adopted so successfully by Japan and Europe and now other Asian nations are almost all American in origin; and in the U.S., home of the work ethic, "Take this job and shove it" became the motto of the work force.

Making it!

THEY'RE GAINING

*Growth of worker output in the industrial nations, compared
with U.S. productivity growth (U.S.=100)*

STILL THE MOST PRODUCTIVE: THE AMERICANS

FIFTIES
100 77.1 30.8 36.8 32.4 53.9 15.2

SIXTIES
100 80.1 43.9 46.0 49.1 54.3 23.2

SEVENTIES
100 84.2 66.4 61.7 61.8 58.0 45.7

EIGHTIES
100 92.8 80.9 80.1 77.4 65.9 62.6

1990
100 95.5 85.5 85.3 81.1 71.9 70.7

United States   Canada   Italy   France   Germany   United Kingdom   Japan

Making it!

Some analysts have laid America's productivity problems at the feet of the baby-boomers. They say that starting in the 1970s, American industry was forced to absorb a disproportionate number of unskilled, inexperienced, and badly schooled workers. Some even blame drug use for slowing down America's work machine. Others say that America's industrial problems are more than just a demographic glitch, pointing out that among the Group of Seven countries, the U.S. had both the slowest rate of productivity growth and the lowest ratio of public investment from 1973 to 1985. Japan, tops in productivity growth, also led the field in public investment.

"Productivity isn't everything, but in the long run, it is almost everything. A country's ability to improve its standard of living depends almost entirely on its ability to raise its output per worker."
—*MIT economist Paul Krugman*

FASTER AND FASTER
Average percent increase in productivity

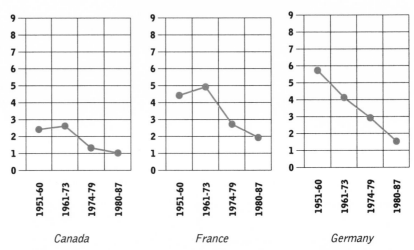

Canada   France   Germany

HOW MANY AMERICANS DOES IT TAKE TO MAKE A CAR?
Average number of job categories per auto plant

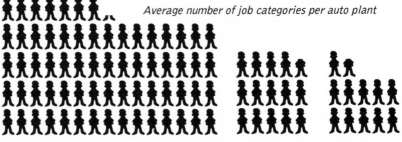

United States: **67.1**   Europe: **14.8**   Japan: **11.8**

HOW LONG DOES IT TAKE?
Average number of hours to make a car

Europe   United States   Japan

By the turn of the century, according to some estimates, America will lose its productivity lead to Europe and Japan.

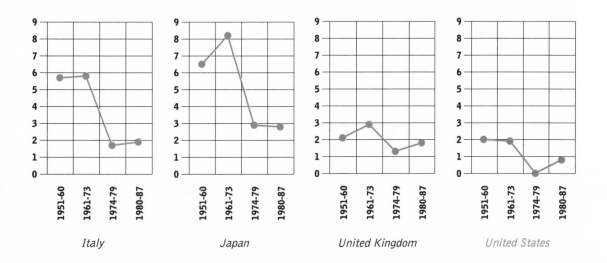

Italy   *Japan*   *United Kingdom*   *United States*

THE KEY TEST: WHAT GETS ACCOMPLISHED IN 60 MINUTES

Value of what an average worker produces in one hour ($)

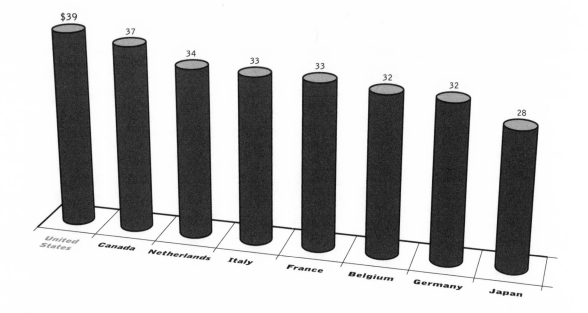

The faithful and diligent

The Japanese work week, at 46.8 hours, is 20.3 percent longer than the American week, at 38.9 hours. In South Korea, the work week is 54.8 hours— 40.9 percent longer than America's. Only one out of three Japanese workers gets a two-day weekend. Japan's economic expansion has relied not only on increased productivity but also on relentlessly long work hours. Even though Japan has one of the highest average per-person incomes, its workers are among the lowest-paid per hour in the industrial world.

While the U.S. work week has stayed at near 40 hours, holidays, vacations, and sick leave shrank by 15 percent during the 1980s. In 1950, the U.S. worker put in fewer hours per year than workers in any other major industrial country. Today, only ➤➤

Myth:
The Japanese work better.

Reality:
The Japanese work longer.

THANK GOD IT'S MONDAY
Average work week (hours)

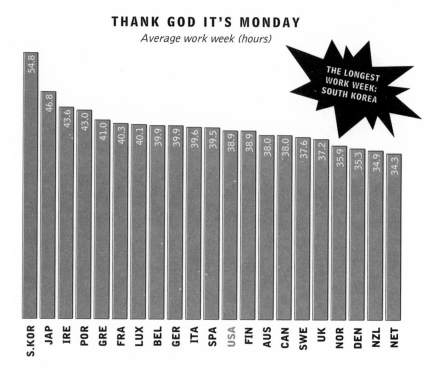

THE LONGEST WORK WEEK: SOUTH KOREA

S.KOR 54.8 · JAP 46.8 · IRE 43.6 · POR 43.0 · GRE 41.0 · FRA 40.3 · LUX 40.1 · BEL 39.9 · GER 39.9 · ITA 39.6 · SPA 39.5 · USA 38.9 · FIN 38.9 · AUS 38.0 · CAN 38.0 · SWE 37.6 · UK 37.2 · NOR 35.9 · DEN 35.3 · NZL 34.9 · NET 34.3

YEAR IN AND YEAR OUT
Average work year (hours)

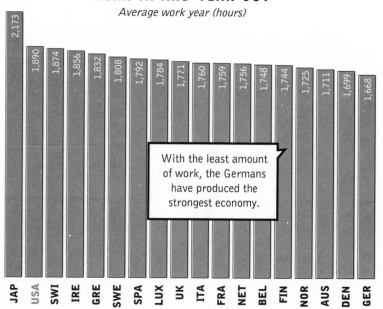

With the least amount of work, the Germans have produced the strongest economy.

JAP 2,173 · USA 1,890 · SWI 1,874 · IRE 1,856 · GRE 1,832 · SWE 1,808 · SPA 1,792 · LUX 1,784 · UK 1,771 · ITA 1,760 · FRA 1,759 · NET 1,756 · BEL 1,748 · FIN 1,744 · NOR 1,725 · AUS 1,711 · DEN 1,699 · GER 1,668

The Italians are the least likely to switch jobs, the Americans the most likely.

TRUE TO THEIR COMPANY

Annual employee turnover in manufacturing (%)

40%

United States

35%

Finland

25%

Germany

20%

United Kingdom

18%

Sweden

18%

Japan

14%

France

11%

Italy

HAPPY CAMPERS

How employers rate their employees (100 = strong identification with company objectives)

Japan	84.69
Switzerland	70.83
Austria	68.59
Denmark	68.38
Germany	64.25
Belgium	61.11
Norway	60.71
Finland	60.42
Netherlands	58.54
France	57.88
United States	56.44
Sweden	56.02
Turkey	55.56
Portugal	55.09
Ireland	54.94
Canada	52.24
New Zealand	50.48
United Kingdom	48.12
Greece	47.31
Australia	46.94
Italy	46.74
Spain	45.00

Japanese workers log more yearly hours.

Japanese managers give their employees an astounding rating of 84.69 on a 100 scale for "strong identification with company objectives." This is the highest rating in the 33 industrial countries surveyed. It is 66 percent higher than the 56 rating American employers give their employees.

While Japanese company loyalty evokes comparisons to the halcyon days of American corporate culture, there are signs of the beginnings of a backlash similar to the rebellion against conformity that began in America in the 1950s.

Myth:
Americans have gotten lazy.

Reality:
Only the Japanese, among major industrial nations, work more hours per year.

147

The suits

THE NEW BREED

"Information workers"— non-manufacturing-sector office workers — as a percent of total work force

| 70.5% | 70.1 | 68.8 | 68.7 | 68.4 | 68.1 | 68.0 | 67.0 | 66.9 |
| USA | CAN | NET | BEL | UK | NOR | AUS | SWE | DEN |

WHO'S THE BOSS?
Percent of managers in the work force

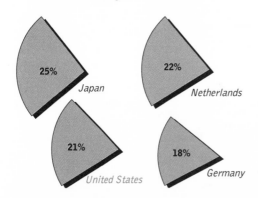

25% Japan

22% Netherlands

21% United States

18% Germany

A SHOESHINE AND A SMILE
Percent of salesmen in the work force

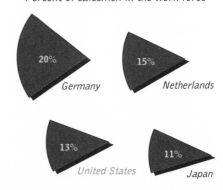

20% Germany

15% Netherlands

13% United States

11% Japan

BAD SUITS
Accountants per 100,000 people

United Kingdom	210
United States	122
Germany	62
France	39
Japan	5

LAW SUITS
Lawyers per 100,000 people

United States	281
Germany	111
United Kingdom	82
Japan	11

Service-sector employment in the U.S. is significantly greater than in Germany and Japan—the smallest white-collar employers among the major industrial nations.

63.5 60.2 59.3 58.2 58.2 56.5 56.5 54.0 29.5

FRA FIN SWI ITA JAP GER IRE SPA TUR

THE COLLEGE KIDS
Percent of population with a university degree

MOST DIPLOMAS: THE U.S.

Country	Percent
United States	19.2%
Norway	17.7
United Kingdom	15.8
Belgium	13.2
Switzerland	12.7
Canada	12.2
Japan	11.3
Sweden	10.9
Finland	10.3
Australia	7.5
Austria	4.8
Italy	4.6
Germany	4.5
Netherlands	4.0
Spain	3.1

The U.S. has increasingly created a two- or even three-tier work force. The bottom is divided between old manufacturing-sector jobs suffering rapid attrition and new low-paid service-sector employment. On top is the information worker, the knowledge provider, the problem solver—the paper pusher. *Yuppie* defines not only a sensibility but a new professional class.

The U.S. has more lawyers than the rest of the world put together, and the number is growing: from 260,000 in 1960 to 756,000 in 1990, from 145 to 281 per 100,000 citizens.

At the University of Pennsylvania's Wharton School and New York University's Stern School of Business, 25 percent of the MBA candidates are foreign—a third of them from Japan. But the MBA is still the most American of degrees, with 70,000 awarded by U.S. universities in 1988.

"Japan graduates ten engineers for every lawyer, and we graduate ten lawyers for every engineer.... They train people to build a better mousetrap, and we ▸▸

149

The suits

train people to sue
the guy with the
mousetrap."
*—Lee A. Iacocca,
chairman, Chrysler
Corporation*

*In Search of Excess,
the Overcompensation
of American
Executives*, by Graef S.
Crystal, charts the rise
of CEO salaries at
major U.S. companies.
During the past twenty
years, as the wages of
U.S. workers fell by 13
percent, CEO
compensation jumped
by more than 400
percent. Even during
the 1991–92 recession,
CEO pay rose faster
than that of any other
group of American
workers. Many CEOs
now earn 70 to 80
times more than the
lowest-paid production
worker—double the
gap of fifteen years
ago. A recent survey
showed that U.S. chief
executives make twice
as much as their
counterparts in second-
and third-ranked
Canada and Germany.

**"Corporate America
operates by the John
Wayne school of
management. There
are one or two
powerful guys at the
top who have the
power to bet the
company on a new** ➦

MBA'S
Number of degrees awarded annually

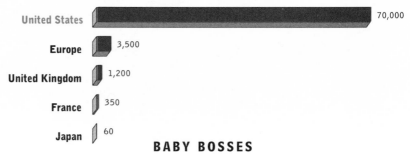

United States — 70,000
Europe — 3,500
United Kingdom — 1,200
France — 350
Japan — 60

BABY BOSSES
Entry-level manager's salary ($)

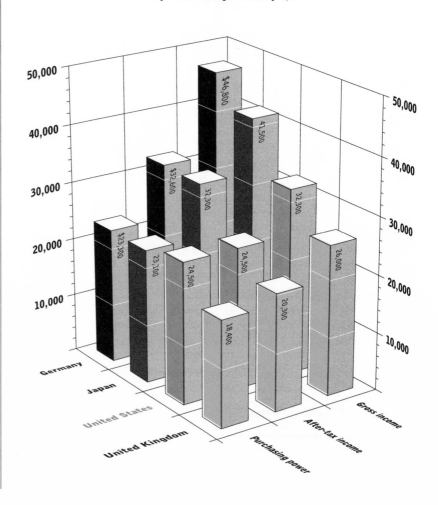

WHAT DOES A CEO MAKE?
Average salary of a CEO ($)

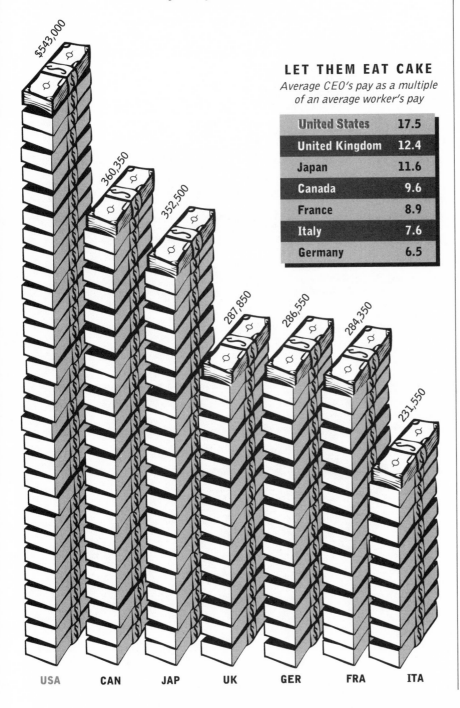

LET THEM EAT CAKE
Average CEO's pay as a multiple of an average worker's pay

United States	17.5
United Kingdom	12.4
Japan	11.6
Canada	9.6
France	8.9
Italy	7.6
Germany	6.5

$543,000

360,350

352,500

287,850

286,550

284,350

231,550

USA   CAN   JAP   UK   GER   FRA   ITA

project or a huge investment, and that requires John Wayne–type pay. The Germans and Japanese, by contrast, run companies collegially, spreading the responsibility around among top managers."
—*Alan M. Johnson, executive-compensation consultant*

"Lee Iacocca is a folk hero, but not to the Chrysler worker. He was a hero until he rightly refused to give wage increases but then he got an enormous bonus himself."
—*Peter Drucker, interviewed in* U.S. News & World Report

When asked by *Industry Week* magazine to rate pay scales, 43 percent of U.S. CEOs said they felt that senior executives were overcompensated. When asked to evaluate their own take, however, a mere 5 percent said they might be paid too much.

The old blue collar

Not only jobs disappear, whole areas of employment, whole aspects of society vanish. One hundred years ago, one of the most common jobs was servant. Fifty years ago, more than half of the population still worked as farmers. Servants now exist only as curiosities, and farmers make up a barely significant part of the work force. Next on the endangered list are factory workers.

According to some estimates, within twenty years, the number of industrial workers in the developed world will dwindle to between 5 percent and 10 percent of the work force. There will be only slightly more factory workers than farmers.

During the glory years—the postwar years—American labor and management fought bitterly. In the end, though, workers kept getting better deals because management was able to pass the added costs on to the consumer— who was getting richer, too. But American labor and American management, locked ➡→

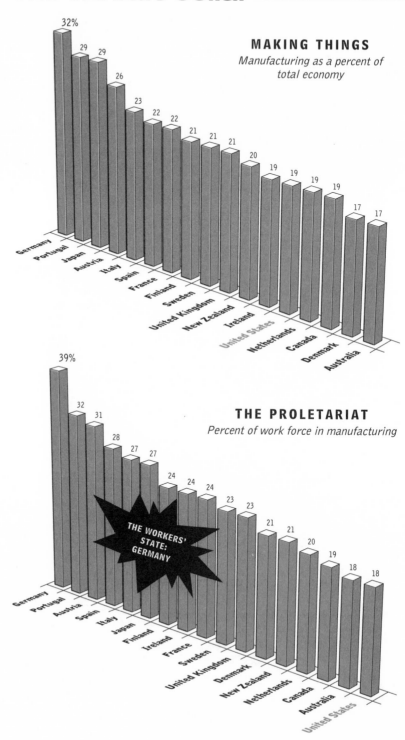

MAKING THINGS
Manufacturing as a percent of total economy

Germany 32% · Portugal 29 · Japan 29 · Austria 26 · Italy 23 · Spain 22 · France 22 · Finland 21 · Sweden 21 · United Kingdom 21 · New Zealand 20 · Ireland 19 · United States 19 · Netherlands 19 · Canada 19 · Denmark 17 · Australia 17

THE PROLETARIAT
Percent of work force in manufacturing

THE WORKERS' STATE: GERMANY

Germany 39% · Portugal 32 · Austria 31 · Spain 28 · Italy 27 · Japan 27 · Finland 24 · Ireland 24 · France 24 · Sweden 23 · United Kingdom 23 · Denmark 21 · New Zealand 21 · Netherlands 20 · Canada 19 · Australia 18 · United States 18

LOST WORKERS

*Change in manufacturing employment
(1960–1989)*

Japan	13.6%
Italy	-6.1
Germany	-7.8
France	-22
United States	-30
Canada	-31
United Kingdom	-40

BUSTED

*Changes in union membership
(1980–1988)*

Sweden	6.6%
Canada	-1.4
Germany	-8.6
Japan	-13.8
Australia	-14.2
United Kingdom	-18.1
Italy	-19.6
United States	-28.6
Netherlands	-29.1
France	-36.8

in perpetual battle, were hardly equipped to deal with a third antagonist: foreign competition. To recover from the effects of the 1973 oil crisis—and the sudden demand for cheap, fuel-efficient cars from Europe and Japan—big business put the squeeze on workers, demanding givebacks and cutting jobs, further eroding union power. One of the seminal events of the Reagan administration, setting the tone for the worker-be-damned decade, was the firing of the striking air-traffic controllers.

THE UNION SHOP

Union members as a percent of the work force

Sweden	85.3%
Australia	42.0
United Kingdom	41.5
Italy	39.6
Canada	34.6
Germany	33.8
Japan	26.8
Netherlands	25.0
United States	16.4
France	12.0

The new blue collar

As manufacturing has shed jobs, especially in the U.S., the relatively constant employment levels indicate that new jobs have replaced them. Some politicians and economists point hopefully to a new frontier of service-industry employment. Over half of U.S. workers will be employed in the "hospitality industries" in the coming years, they say. Others say that nonunionized, low-productivity service jobs are turning vast portions of what was once the middle class into something closer to a nineteenth-century underclass.

As farm economies evolved into industrial ones, farmers became higher-paid manufacturing workers—increasing the wealth of the entire society. But today's factory worker who loses his job and ends up as a hamburger flipper or security guard takes a pay cut, making him—and society—poorer. The danger is that in the postindustrial world, the once prosperous middle class becomes divided, with affluent information workers ➤→

THE OLDEST PROFESSION
Service as a percent of total economy

Country	%	Country	%
Denmark	71.9%	Italy	63.0
United States	68.8	Greece	61.3
United Kingdom	68.3	Norway	61.2
Canada	67.6	Switzerland	60.9
France	67.4	Luxembourg	60.8
Belgium	67.2	Austria	60.2
Sweden	67.0	Germany	59.0
Iceland	65.2	Ireland	57.4
Netherlands	64.7	Japan	56.2
New Zealand	64.6	Spain	55.0
Australia	64.3	Portugal	54.7
Finland	63.2	Turkey	47.7

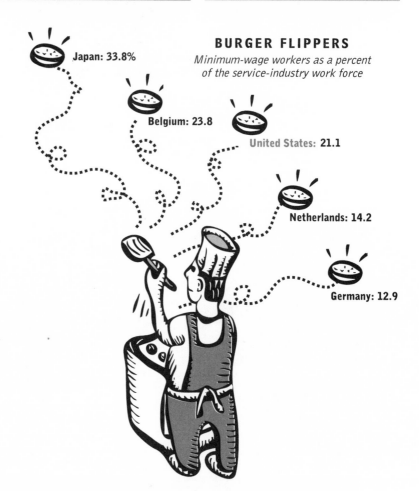

BURGER FLIPPERS
Minimum-wage workers as a percent of the service-industry work force

Japan: 33.8%

Belgium: 23.8

United States: 21.1

Netherlands: 14.2

Germany: 12.9

NINE-TO-FIVERS
Secretaries and clerical workers as a percent of the work force

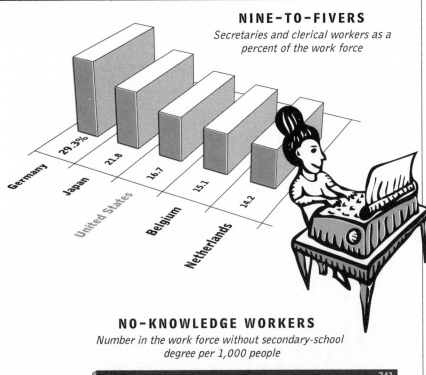

- Germany 29.3%
- Japan 21.8
- United States 16.7
- Belgium 15.1
- Netherlands 14.2

NO-KNOWLEDGE WORKERS
Number in the work force without secondary-school degree per 1,000 people

Austria	741
Germany	716
Turkey	694
New Zealand	665
France	660
Spain	647
Italy	643
United Kingdom	634
Finland	564
Greece	515
Belgium	490
Australia	481
Netherlands	473
Denmark	287
United States	254
Sweden	243
Japan	122

In the German-speaking countries, fewer people complete high school than in any other place in the developed world. But almost all students can attend a wide range of vocational-training programs.

sitting on top of poorly paid, unskilled service workers.

"The concept of 'the service sector' is misleading. A hairdresser, shop assistant, or hot dog vendor has nothing in common, from an economic standpoint, with an airline pilot, software engineer, or investment banker. It is the latter category of 'high value-added' service occupations that is evoked when bullish sociologists and politicians describe their visions of the post-industrial 'information economy.' But in reality, the overwhelming majority of new service jobs have been created in the no-tech first category."
—The Financial Times

"The no-knowledge workers will, in any society, be a very large group—as much as one-half of the working population. That leaves a large percentage of any nation with work that, no matter how well it pays, does not give social status, social recognition, or self-respect."
—*Peter F. Drucker,* The New Realities

──And who's still down on the farm?──

Thanks to modern agriculture, most of the world is awash in food. Not only does no one in the world need to starve, but even in affluent nations, food prices could be steeply cut. But farmers, despite their small numbers, command extraordinary political power—allowing them to choke trade the world over.

Besides costing consumers billions of yen a year, rice subsidies in Japan help maintain constricting real-estate prices. Europeans paid $85 billion more for their food than they would have without subsidies; Americans, $28 billion more. As a whole, the industrialized nations spent $300 billion in 1990 on subsidies to farmers, according to the OECD.

Supporters of subsidies counter that CAP, the EC's Common Agricultural Policy (also known as the Crazy Agricultural Policy), has preserved the European farm culture and the mythic place of farm life in Europe's consciousness.

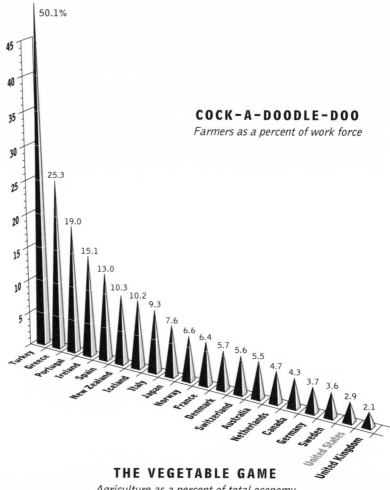

COCK-A-DOODLE-DOO
Farmers as a percent of work force

(Turkey 50.1%, Greece 25.3, Portugal 19.0, Ireland 15.1, Spain 13.0, New Zealand 10.3, Iceland 10.2, Italy 9.3, Japan 7.6, Norway 6.6, France 6.4, Denmark 5.7, Switzerland 5.6, Australia 5.5, Netherlands 4.7, Canada 4.3, Germany 3.7, Sweden 3.6, United States 2.9, United Kingdom 2.1)

THE VEGETABLE GAME
Agriculture as a percent of total economy

Country	%		Country	%
Greece	14%		Netherlands	4
Iceland	10		Austria	3
New Zealand	8		France	3
Portugal	8		Japan	3
Finland	6		Norway	3
Spain	6		Sweden	3
Australia	4		Belgium	2
Canada	4		United States	2
Denmark	4		Germany	1
Italy	4		United Kingdom	1

GOODBYE TO ALL THAT

Decline in number of farmers from 50 years ago (%)

Greece
48%

Sweden
36%

Australia
59%

United
Kingdom
59%

Ireland
61%

Switzerland
66%

Portugal
61%

Spain
73%

Netherlands
76%

France
76%

Canada
77%

Norway
74%

United States
76%

Denmark
77%

Belgium
77%

Italy
77%

Finland
81%

Germany
81%

Austria
79%

Japan
85%

On the job or on the dole

A flash point in a modern society is the clash between productivity and employment. This is a dilemma as old as the Industrial Age. Workers continue to fear that technology, the keystone of greater productivity, will destroy jobs. And it surely does. But technology has the power to create even more jobs and even greater wealth—albeit with much dislocation and pain. Robots, for instance, might put autoworkers on the street but give jobs to robot-builders. And by making auto production cheaper, these same robots would help sell more cars, which means more work for tiremakers and glassmakers, and certainly for accountants and lawyers.

Myth:
*Foreign competition
has put Americans
out of work.*

Reality:
*Overall, the
unemployment rate has
not grown.*

WORKERS OF THE WORLD
Total work force

Perhaps one of the most significant resources of the unified Europe is the size of its work force.

Europe: 162,273,000

Japan: 62,700,000

United States: 125,557,000

WHO'S OUT OF A JOB?
Unemployment rate (%)

Spain	16.0%
Ireland	13.9
Italy	11.4
Turkey	10.9
Denmark	10.2
Canada	9.5
France	9.1
Greece	8.9
Belgium	8.8
Australia	7.7
New Zealand	7.6
United States	6.5
United Kingdom	6.3
Netherlands	6.2
Portugal	5.4
Norway	5.1
Germany	5.0
Finland	4.7
Austria	3.3
Sweden	2.8
Japan	2.3
Iceland	1.5
Luxembourg	1.4
Switzerland	0.7

THE YOUNG AND THE RESTLESS
Percent of unemployed under the age of 24

Country	Percent
Turkey	55%
Italy	50
Portugal	48
Netherlands	45
Greece	43
Australia	43
Spain	42
Norway	39
New Zealand	39
Ireland	38
United States	37
Sweden	36
Austria	31
France	30
Belgium	30
Canada	30
United Kingdom	29
Finland	26
Japan	25
Germany	23
Denmark	21
Switzerland	11

Europe's chronic unemployment began in the 1981 recession and has continued into boom times because of overall increases in productivity and slow growth in low-skill jobs. Spain has brought its rate down to 16 percent from 21.5 percent in 1985.

On the job or on the dole

WHERE THE BOYS WERE

*Women of working age who are employed
outside the home (%)*

Country	%
Sweden	80.5%
Denmark	77.3
Finland	73.3
Norway	71.2
United States	68.1
Canada	67.4
United Kingdom	65.4
Australia	60.8
New Zealand	60.7
Portugal	59.7
Japan	59.3
Switzerland	58.5
France	56.2
Germany	54.8
Austria	54.3
Belgium	51.6
Netherlands	51
Luxembourg	47.6
Italy	44.3
Greece	43.5
Spain	39.9
Ireland	37.6

HELP WANTED

Job growth rate since 1980 (%)

MOST NEW
JOBS: THE
NETHERLANDS

Country	%
Belgium	1.8
Ireland	3.6
France	4.1
Finland	4.4
Sweden	4.8
United Kingdom	6.2
Germany	6.6
Portugal	7.2
Italy	7.6
Denmark	8.2
Austria	10.3
Japan	11.0
Norway	11.1
Switzerland	11.4
Spain	12.3
Greece	15.0
Luxembourg	15.7
United States	15.7
Canada	16.6
Turkey	19.0
New Zealand	20.7
Australia	23.6
Netherlands	24.2%

160

Malcontents

ON STRIKE!

Worker days lost due to strikes in 1989 (thousands)

One measure of labor harmony is that while Italian workers are the least likely to switch jobs, they're the most likely to go on strike.

ITA	29,060
USA	17,014
UK	4,060
CAN	3,663
AUS	1,202
FRA	800
FIN	204
NZL	193

BAD ATTITUDES

Percent of unemployed fired for cause

Denmark	83%	European Community	43
Netherlands	58	France	41
United Kingdom	56	Greece	37
United States	52	Italy	8

PLAYING HOOKY

Days lost each year due to absenteeism, per worker

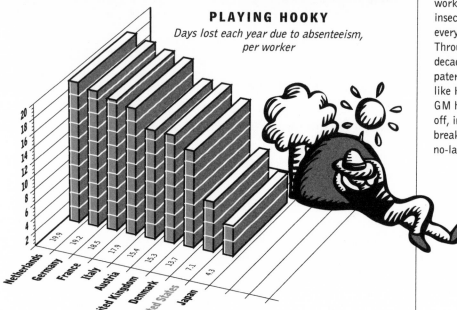

Netherlands	Germany	France	Italy	Austria	United Kingdom	Denmark	United States	Japan
19.9	19.2	18.5	17.9	15.4	15.3	13.7	7.1	4.3

Critics of American industry say that Japanese workers and management are willing to cooperate in pursuit of larger national goals, while American workers maintain adversarial relationships with their bosses. One reason they cite for the loyalty of Japanese workers is the "job for life" system of so many major Japanese companies. In Europe, too, job security is a vital component of the social contract. In contrast, a primary reason for the alienation of American workers is the insecurity of virtually every job today. Throughout the last decade, even big, paternalistic employers like Kodak, IBM, and GM had to lay people off, in some cases breaking longstanding no-layoff pledges.

The universal office

Our progress has been from the farm to the factory to the office. More than half of the working population in the developed world spends more than half of its waking hours in offices—all places with similar cultures, equipment, procedures, and purpose.

In any language, it's still work. Although the promise has been that in the information society, workers will be more independent, more self-actualized, so far the hierarchies, constraints, and demands seem to have increased rather than diminished. While blue-collar alienation was the scourge of the last working generation, the white-collar worker has been the victim in the 1980s and '90s. New York provides perhaps the best example: Former growth industries such as publishing, advertising, broadcasting, financial services, and law are shedding jobs by the thousands. Many predict that whole classes of corporate paperwork jobs that once seemed to carry lifetime tenure— clerical staffs, for example—will disappear. The office of the future will have fewer bodies—from managers to secretaries—and more specialists.

The differences that remain among the world's offices merely await a consensus on what produces better results and bigger gain. America has contributed the automated office, the age of information processing; Europe has tried the more tolerant and equitable office, more rights, and greater benefits; Japan has offered the longer work day.

Perhaps the office is the final melting pot. While families, nationality, ethnicity, religion, customs, and culture preserve and foster differences, the goal of the modern office is to break down all barriers—language problems, style differences, management quirks, technological incompatibilities—to other offices and to other office workers. This is the global village, bound together by fiber optics and the utter sameness of what we all do all day.

As cross-ownership, multicountry production, mobile labor markets, and European unity increase, the international business environment will continue to homogenize. Senior managers will form a class not unlike military officers of the nineteenth century, having more in common with one another than with people who have not been inculcated in their culture.

Then too, of course, there will always be the non-officer class, and the less gung ho, and the inevitably world-weary. They will share the age-old experience of wanting to be anywhere but on the job.

Why they call it "travail"

WHO'S AFRAID OF THE BOSS?
The Power Distance Index
(100=abject terror,
0=blissful coexistence)

France	68
Japan	54
Italy	50
United States	40
Canada	39
Germany	35
UK	35

Why they call it "travail"

"IF THEY ASKED ME…"
Employees who feel free to criticize (%)

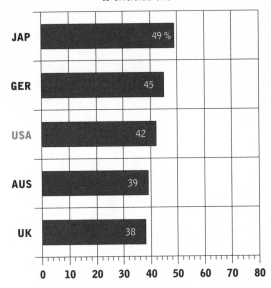

JAP	49 %
GER	45
USA	42
AUS	39
UK	38

0 10 20 30 40 50 60 70 80

A FAIR SHAKE
Employees who think management is fair (%)

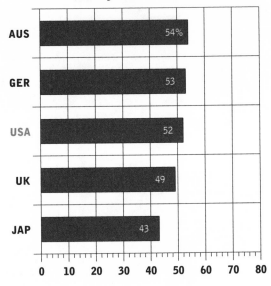

AUS	54%
GER	53
USA	52
UK	49
JAP	43

0 10 20 30 40 50 60 70 80

WHISTLIN' WHILE THEY WORK
Employees who are satisfied with their job (%)

GER	73%
JAP	69
AUS	68
USA	67
UK	64

0 10 20 30 40 50 60 70 80

WHO'S SAFE?
Employees who believe they have job security (%)

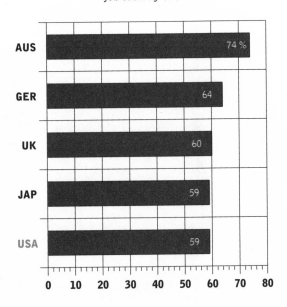

AUS	74 %
GER	64
UK	60
JAP	59
USA	59

0 10 20 30 40 50 60 70 80

THE FRINGE

*Employees who are satisfied
with their benefits (%)*

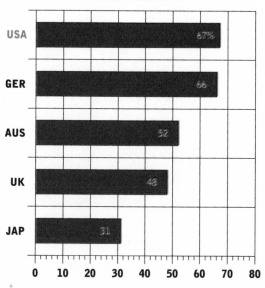

- USA 67%
- GER 66
- AUS 52
- UK 48
- JAP 31

NEVER ENOUGH

*Employees who are satisfied
with their pay (%)*

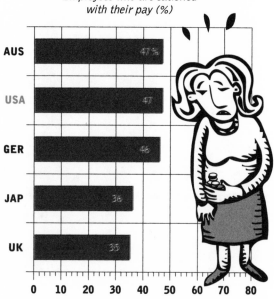

- AUS 47%
- USA 47
- GER 46
- JAP 36
- UK 35

GETTING AHEAD

*Employees who are satisfied with their
opportunities for career advancement (%)*

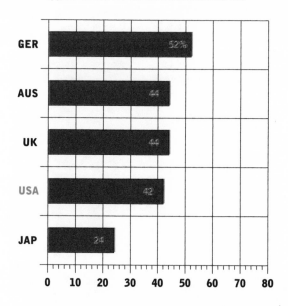

- GER 52%
- AUS 44
- UK 44
- USA 42
- JAP 24

A HELPING HAND

*Employees who are satisfied
with their job training (%)*

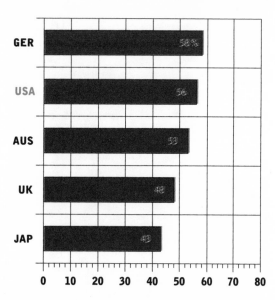

- GER 58%
- USA 56
- AUS 53
- UK 48
- JAP 43

Office tech

From the introduction of the first two-line phone, to the photostat machine with the smelly paper, to the air-conditioned mainframe, to the dedicated word processor, to the PC, the belief has been that (a) there would be much less paper, and (b) the most teched-up company would dominate its field. The first supposition did not come true; computers, faxes, and copying machines produced an explosion of paper (by some estimates, the automated office uses ten times as much paper as the pre-electronic one did). As for the second, the rate of technological obsolescence has not let any company enjoy its lead for long. Indeed, technology changes so fast that by the time your state-of-the-art system is up and running, it is no longer state-of-the-art.

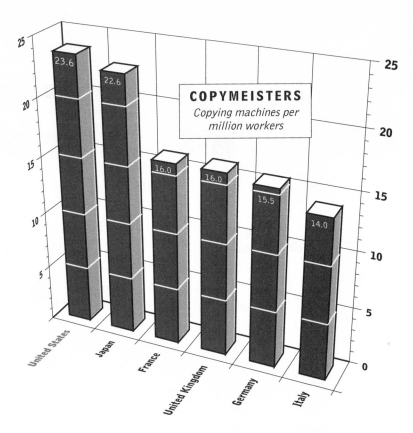

COPYMEISTERS
Copying machines per million workers

INTERNATIONAL BUSINESS MACHINES
Annual purchases of office equipment ($ millions)

United States	$7,279	Sweden	157
Japan	1,899	Belgium	121
Germany	1,311	Austria	113
United Kingdom	856	Finland	95
France	704	Denmark	62
Italy	564	Norway	54
Canada	465	Portugal	54
Netherlands	368	Ireland	51
Spain	318	New Zealand	49
Switzerland	312	Greece	44
Australia	228	Turkey	36

THE BIGGEST BYTE

Share of the world's computers in use (%)

THE MOST SOUPED-UP OFFICE: U.S.

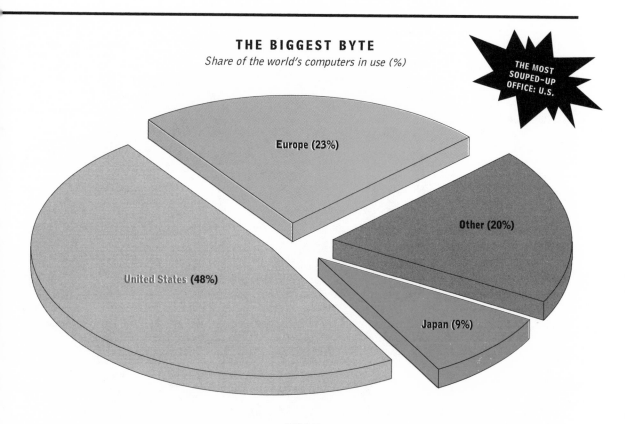

Europe (23%)

Other (20%)

United States (48%)

Japan (9%)

HOLD

Telephone lines per person

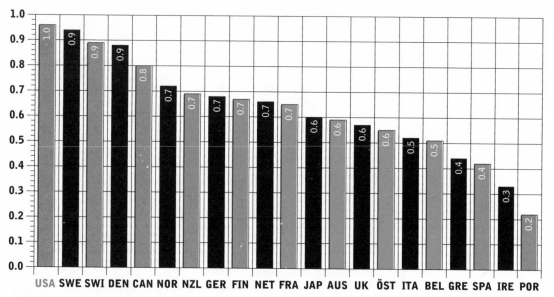

USA	SWE	SWI	DEN	CAN	NOR	NZL	GER	FIN	NET	FRA	JAP	AUS	UK	ÖST	ITA	BEL	GRE	SPA	IRE	POR
1.0	0.9	0.9	0.9	0.8	0.7	0.7	0.7	0.7	0.7	0.7	0.6	0.6	0.6	0.6	0.5	0.5	0.4	0.4	0.3	0.2

Office politics

Europeans have led the way in creating a more sympathetic workplace. Parental leave of many months is standard practically everywhere. Almost every worker gets at least a month's vacation time. And throughout Europe, job training—and retraining—virtually on demand is the rule. In France, any company with more than ten employees must spend a specified portion of its wage costs—from 1.2 percent to 3 percent—on training programs.

Japanese corporations offer lifelong employment—one life, one company—but almost all women are excluded from this social contract.

The Americans take a much less paternalistic approach to the destructive side effects of capitalism: The philosophy in all but the most caring of companies is sink or swim.

QUALITY TIME
Parental leave granted (months)

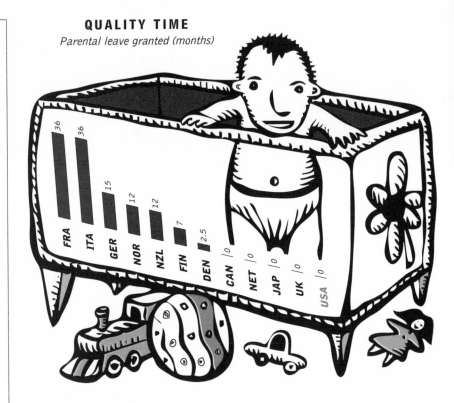

FRA	36	
ITA	36	
GER	15	
NOR	12	
NZL	12	
FIN	7	
DEN	2.5	
CAN	0	
NET	0	
JAP	0	
UK	0	
USA	0	

MOTHER CARE
Average paid maternity leave (weeks)

Country	Weeks
Sweden	32
France	28
Luxembourg	20
Italy	20
United Kingdom	18
Soviet Union	18
Norway	18
Denmark	18
Canada	18
Austria	16
Japan	14
Germany	14
Portugal	13
Netherlands	12
United States	0

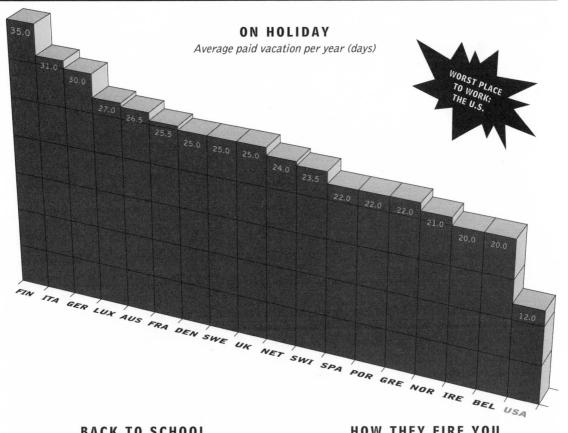

ON HOLIDAY
Average paid vacation per year (days)

WORST PLACE TO WORK: THE U.S.

35.0 FIN
31.0 ITA
30.0 GER
27.0 LUX
26.5 AUS
25.5 FRA
25.0 DEN
25.0 SWE
25.0 UK
24.0 NET
23.5 SWI
22.0 SPA
22.0 POR
22.0 GRE
21.0 NOR
20.0 IRE
20.0 BEL
12.0 USA

BACK TO SCHOOL
Spending on labor training programs as a percent of GDP

Sweden	1.79
Germany	1.05
Italy	0.90
France	0.81
United Kingdom	0.77
Canada	0.52
United States	0.25

HOW THEY FIRE YOU
Average length of termination notice (months)

Denmark	6
Norway	3
Austria	3
Netherlands	2
France	2
Germany	2
Belgium	1
United Kingdom	1
Sweden	1
Australia	0
Ireland	0
United States	0

INTERNATIONAL PIGS
Number of sexual-harassment suits through 1989

United States	38,000
Japan	1

And the winner is...

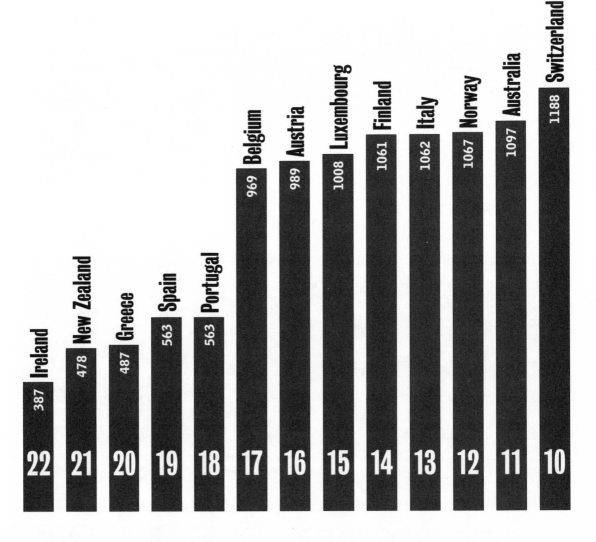

WHERE-WE-STAND INDEX
(0=least productive; 2,000=extremely productive)

Ireland 387 — 22
New Zealand 478 — 21
Greece 487 — 20
Spain 563 — 19
Portugal 563 — 18
Belgium 969 — 17
Austria 989 — 16
Luxembourg 1008 — 15
Finland 1061 — 14
Italy 1062 — 13
Norway 1067 — 12
Australia 1097 — 11
Switzerland 1188 — 10

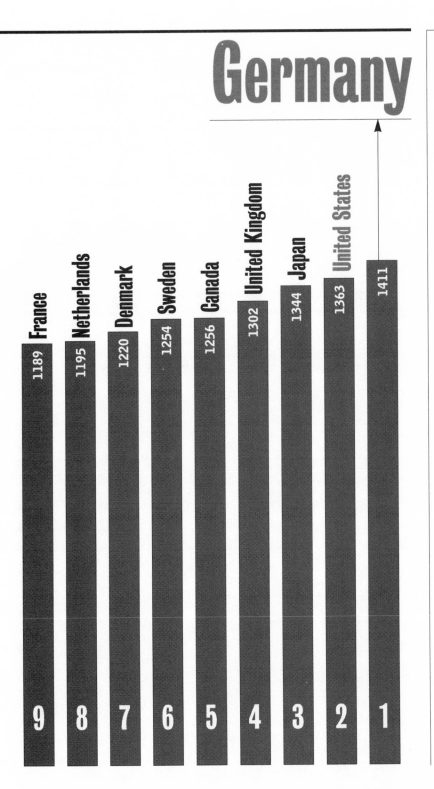

Germany

France 1189
Netherlands 1195
Denmark 1220
Sweden 1254
Canada 1256
United Kingdom 1302
Japan 1344
United States 1363
1411

9 8 7 6 5 4 3 2 1

The world's largest manufacturing society—Germany—is the most productive nation overall. Indeed, the German "*Wirtschaftswunder*"—economic miracle—has triumphed over the Japanese one. More of its work force is engaged in producing high-profit products, and less of it is involved in low-profit, low-end service activities, than in any other nation. While Japan too has built itself into a productivity powerhouse, to a great degree it has advanced its growth on the basis of longer hours. The U.S. maintains an even higher degree of productivity but also at the expense of its work force. In Germany, workers realize the fruits of their labors in short weeks and long vacations. It may be no coincidence that while overall productivity and general worker satisfaction are high in Germany, CEO compensation is the most modest among the industrial nations.

171

THE FREEST

The political life

Americans are mighty proud to claim for themselves the oldest continuous democracy, while brushing off the rest of the world's frequent reminders of America's antidemocratic sins (both of omission and of commission).

Citizens of other democracies are often amazed by how sporadically Americans vote. In the last presidential election, 49 percent of America's eligible voters cast ballots. The average turnout for a national election in virtually all other countries save Switzerland is near 80 percent (while the Swiss don't have much interest in their part-time parliament, they turn out in droves to vote on referenda). Cynicism, apathy, boredom, and lack of choice are among the reasons that Americans go to the polls in ever-diminishing numbers. Another: America is one of the few democracies where registration is the ➤+

Myth:
The U.S. is the world's premier democracy.

Reality:
Fewer than half of its eligible voters bother to vote.

With its focus on personalities over ideology, the U.S. has created a political system of obvious strengths—stability first and foremost—and great idiocies: a circus atmosphere, deadly pieties, massive cash requirements, and television personalities. Many say the Reagan presidency represents the most glaring instance of personality triumphing over all other considerations.

Europe, on the other hand, has always reveled in the nuances of ideology. European nations have often moved from one form of government to its diametric opposite (causing several of history's great catastrophes along the way). But since the Second World War, Europe has organized itself into an oddly tolerant mix of left, center, and right political forces.

The postimperial Japanese system, offering a third alternative, is a democracy based on the American model that eschews both personality and ideology in a famously dull combination of consensus and status quo.

In the U.S., Western Europe, and Japan, the past decade has been a time of political quietude—or inertia. Leaders have stayed in office longer, center parties have gotten larger, and, perhaps most notably, voters have gotten richer, at least in Europe and Japan. According to a recent poll, 44 percent of people in the European Community are "not much" or "not at all" interested in politics. Indeed, both left and right in Europe seem to have arrived at the same new political faith—European economic and political unity.

But some regard the quiet as worrisome. In the U.S., there is sweeping anti-incumbent sentiment; in Europe, an alarming increase in far-right parties and an anti-immigrant backlash; and in Japan, a growing generational split.

By the people

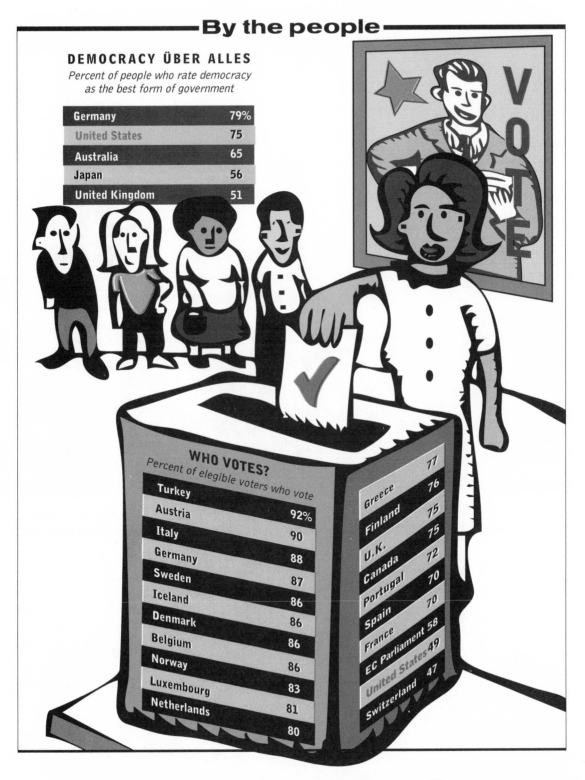

DEMOCRACY ÜBER ALLES
*Percent of people who rate democracy
as the best form of government*

Germany	79%
United States	75
Australia	65
Japan	56
United Kingdom	51

WHO VOTES?
Percent of elegible voters who vote

Turkey	
Austria	92%
Italy	90
Germany	88
Sweden	87
Iceland	86
Denmark	86
Belgium	86
Norway	86
Luxembourg	83
Netherlands	81
	80

	77
Greece	76
Finland	75
U.K.	75
Canada	72
Portugal	70
Spain	70
France	
EC Parliament	58
United States	49
Switzerland	47

By the people

voter's responsibility. Most other countries make voting a clearer obligation—something like paying taxes. In Italy, for instance, it's illegal not to vote. And there are no absentee ballots—if you're out of town, even abroad, the government will pay your fare home. Some observers, looking to put a more positive spin on an appalling statistic, contend that Americans' lack of enthusiasm for voting demonstrates their contentment with the system. They say that faced with potential disaster, or clear choice—for instance, the specter of David Duke and his neo-Nazism in Louisiana— Americans turn out in record numbers.

Myth:
Democracy is deeply rooted in the industrial world.

Reality:
Democracy as we know it is hardly half a lifetime old.

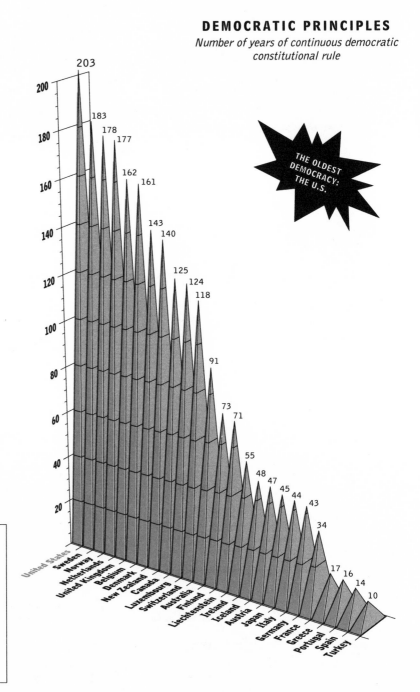

DEMOCRATIC PRINCIPLES
Number of years of continuous democratic constitutional rule

THE OLDEST DEMOCRACY: THE U.S.

203 — United States
183 — Sweden
178 — Norway
177 — Netherlands
162 — United Kingdom
161 — Belgium
143 — Denmark
140 — New Zealand
125 — Canada
124 — Luxembourg
118 — Switzerland
91 — Australia
73 — Finland
71 — Liechtenstein
55 — Ireland
48 — Iceland
47 — Austria
45 — Japan
44 — Italy
43 — Germany
34 — France
17 — Greece
16 — Portugal
14 — Spain
10 — Turkey

AND NOT JUST WHITE MALES

The year women got the right to vote

	New Zealand
	Australia
	Finland
	Norway
	Denmark
	Iceland
	Soviet Union
	United Kingdom
	Austria
	Canada
	Ireland
	Netherlands
	Luxembourg
	Germany
	United States
	Sweden
	Spain
	Portugal
	Turkey
	France
	Japan
	Italy
	Belgium
	Greece
	Switzerland

1890 · 1900 · 1910 · 1920 · 1930 · 1940 · 1950 · 1960 · 1970 · 1980

LET US VOTE

VOX POPULI

Average number of national referenda per year

Switzerland	169
Australia	18
New Zealand	17
Denmark	11
France	10
Ireland	8
Italy	4
Sweden	3
Austria	1
Belgium	1
Norway	1
United Kingdom	1
Canada	0
Finland	0
Germany	0
Iceland	0
Japan	0
Luxembourg	0
Netherlands	0
United States	0

By the people

WHAT ARE THE ISSUES?

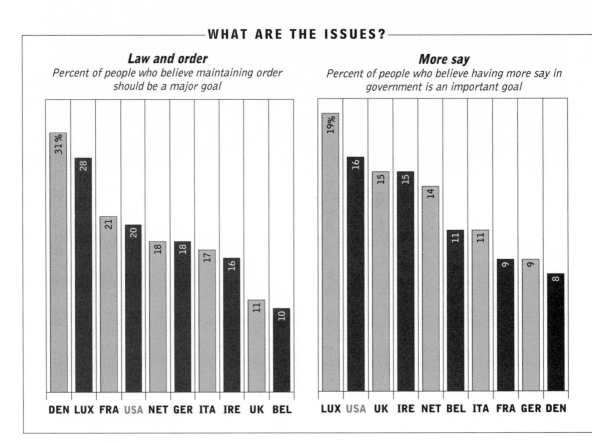

Law and order
Percent of people who believe maintaining order should be a major goal

31% DEN · 28 LUX · 21 FRA · 20 USA · 18 NET · 18 GER · 17 ITA · 16 IRE · 11 UK · 10 BEL

More say
Percent of people who believe having more say in government is an important goal

19% LUX · 16 USA · 15 UK · 15 IRE · 14 NET · 11 BEL · 11 ITA · 9 FRA · 9 GER · 8 DEN

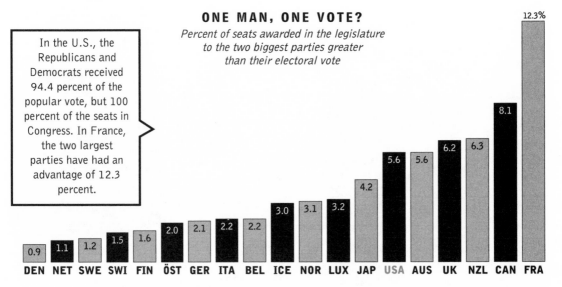

ONE MAN, ONE VOTE?
Percent of seats awarded in the legislature to the two biggest parties greater than their electoral vote

In the U.S., the Republicans and Democrats received 94.4 percent of the popular vote, but 100 percent of the seats in Congress. In France, the two largest parties have had an advantage of 12.3 percent.

0.9 DEN · 1.1 NET · 1.2 SWE · 1.5 SWI · 1.6 FIN · 2.0 ÖST · 2.1 GER · 2.2 ITA · 2.2 BEL · 3.0 ICE · 3.1 NOR · 3.2 LUX · 4.2 JAP · 5.6 USA · 5.6 AUS · 6.2 UK · 6.3 NZL · 8.1 CAN · 12.3% FRA

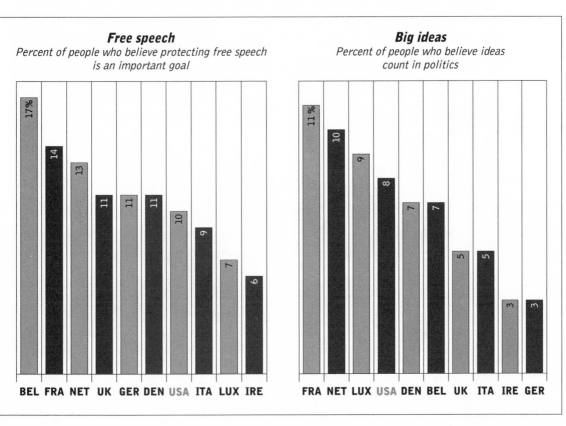

Free speech
Percent of people who believe protecting free speech is an important goal

BEL	FRA	NET	UK	GER	DEN	USA	ITA	LUX	IRE
17%	14	13	11	11	11	10	9	7	6

Big ideas
Percent of people who believe ideas count in politics

FRA	NET	LUX	USA	DEN	BEL	UK	ITA	IRE	GER
11%	10	9	8	7	7	5	5	3	3

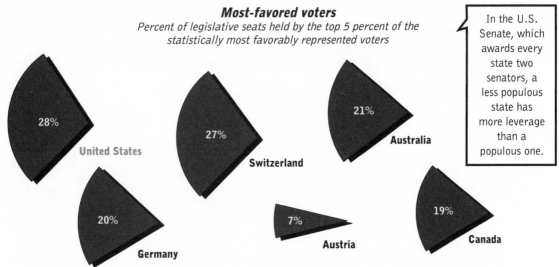

Most-favored voters
Percent of legislative seats held by the top 5 percent of the statistically most favorably represented voters

28% United States

20% Germany

27% Switzerland

7% Austria

21% Australia

19% Canada

In the U.S. Senate, which awards every state two senators, a less populous state has more leverage than a populous one.

179

Who's in charge?

POWER PLAYS

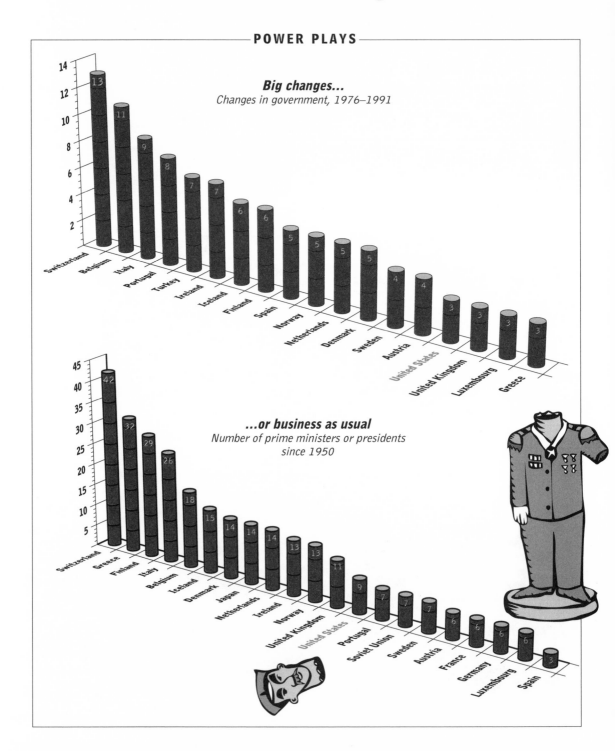

Big changes...
Changes in government, 1976–1991

Switzerland 13
Belgium 11
Italy 9
Portugal 8
Turkey 7
Ireland 7
Iceland 6
Finland 6
Spain 5
Norway 5
Netherlands 5
Denmark 5
Sweden 4
Austria 4
United States 3
United Kingdom 3
Luxembourg 3
Greece 3

...or business as usual
*Number of prime ministers or presidents
since 1950*

Switzerland 42
Greece 32
Finland 29
Italy 26
Belgium 18
Iceland 15
Denmark 14
Japan 14
Netherlands 14
Ireland 13
Norway 13
United Kingdom 11
United States 9
Portugal 7
Soviet Union 7
Sweden 7
Austria 6
France 6
Germany 6
Luxembourg 6
Spain 3

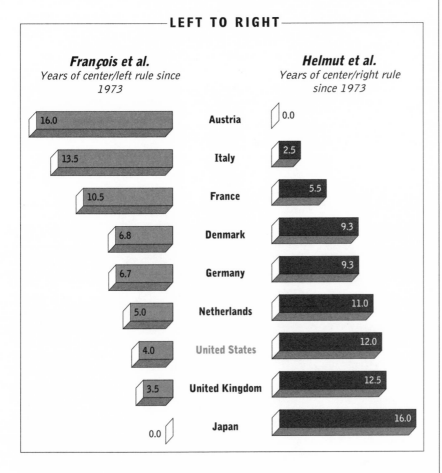

━ LEFT TO RIGHT ━

François et al.
Years of center/left rule since 1973

Helmut et al.
Years of center/right rule since 1973

16.0	Austria	0.0	
13.5	Italy	2.5	
10.5	France	5.5	
6.8	Denmark	9.3	
6.7	Germany	9.3	
5.0	Netherlands	11.0	
4.0	United States	12.0	
3.5	United Kingdom	12.5	
0.0	Japan	16.0	

UNCERTAIN TERMS
Average length of a chief executive's term in office (years)

Portugal	7.8	Ireland	4.0
France	7.5	Norway	3.8
Soviet Union	6.4	Netherlands	3.4
Canada	6.2	Denmark	3.1
Germany	6.0	Greece	2.5
Sweden	6.0	Spain	2.5
Austria	5.4	Japan	2.2
United States	5.1	Italy	1.7
United Kingdom	4.5	Switzerland	1.0

An unanticipated development in the American system is the frequency with which the presidency is controlled by one party and Congress by the other. Adding to the confusion, U.S. presidents are often elected with overwhelming majorities, while they are denied, also by convincing majorities, congressional support. According to some political analysts, this split is at the heart of America's inability to respond to its long-standing domestic problems. Where presidents traditionally function unimpeded in areas of foreign policy, they must forge a consensus at home. The paralysis arising from this balance of power is precisely what the parliamentary system, favored by most other democracies, is designed to avoid. Americans, on the other hand, almost always rate their personal vote for president as one of the main symbols of political freedom. Likewise, the Russians embraced the popularly elected Boris Yeltsin over Mikhail Gorbachev, whose mandate came from the Supreme Soviet.

Who's in charge?

"Margaret Thatcher's successor, John Major, was selected in a manner that...most Americans would find about as palatable as steak-and-kidney pie and a pint of bitter."
—*Ross K. Baker, professor of political science, Rutgers University*

Where are the smoke-filled rooms today? In Japan, many say. Dutch journalist Karel van Wolferen, in his book *The Enigma of Japanese Power,* argues that in Japan, elected representatives are merely tools for the business special-interest groups. "The system," he says, "is run on the basis of informal, personal relationships rather than by procedures and laws." The result, he concludes, is that the political system itself is nearly powerless.

"No one in power in Japanese politics can see to it that promises made to other countries can be carried out, that Japanese national priorities can be reestablished.... There is no center of accountability, no place where the »+

CHANGING HORSES
Average time the Cabinet remains in office (years)

Canada	8.6
Australia	8.5
Austria	8.3
United Kingdom	6.8
United States	6.4
Sweden	6.2
Ireland	5.8
New Zealand	5.3
Luxembourg	4.8
Japan	4.8
Norway	4.6
Germany	3.9
Iceland	3.1
Netherlands	2.8
Denmark	2.8
France	2.4
Belgium	2.2
Italy	1.4
Finland	1.1

TOP BUREAUCRAT SALARIES: THE U.S.

WHAT DO THEY PAY YOU FOR DOING THIS?
Average salary of a Cabinet member ($)

United States	$138,900
Japan	133,466
Germany	132,029
Italy	80,000
United Kingdom	62,269

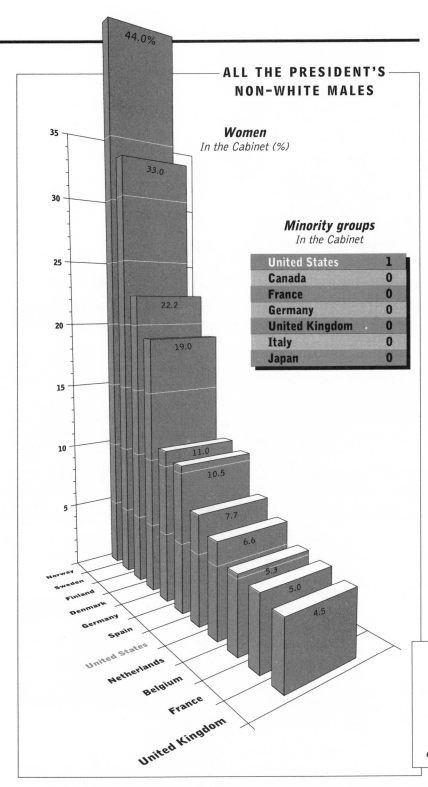

ALL THE PRESIDENT'S NON-WHITE MALES

Women
In the Cabinet (%)

44.0%

33.0

22.2

19.0

11.0

10.5

7.7

6.6

5.3

5.0

4.5

35
30
25
20
15
10
5

Norway
Sweden
Finland
Denmark
Germany
Spain
United States
Netherlands
Belgium
France
United Kingdom

Minority groups
In the Cabinet

United States	1
Canada	0
France	0
Germany	0
United Kingdom	0
Italy	0
Japan	0

buck stops, no person or institution that has ultimate responsibility."
—*Karel van Wolferen,* The Enigma of Japanese Power

"There appears to be a strong relationship today between regular elections and economic success. Elections convey information from the political marketplace, often to the surprise of pollsters and others, just as the financial markets now transmit information (and surprises) to the global economy. If your economy or your politics are locked into a false model, the odds are great now that you will suffer losses. The tempering discipline of elections can alert countries to mistakes before the damage becomes unmanageable."
—The Wall Street Journal

Myth:
The U.S. is an equal-opportunity employer.

Reality:
Not in the highest echelons of government.

Monarchs, dictators, and scandals

The century that made monarchs all but obsolete (Egypt's King Farouk said only five monarchs would survive the twentieth century—the kings of spades, hearts, diamonds, clubs, and England) may do the same with dictators. The headlong rush to freedom has as much to do with paychecks and grocery shelves as it does with essential human longings. Democracy turns out to be the basic requirement of modern economic life, offering nothing less than the difference between wealth and poverty.

The European and Japanese monarchs continue to flourish as cultural if not political institutions—at no small cost. The monarch of all monarchs, Queen Elizabeth II, costs the British taxpayers some $9.2 million annually—causing hardly even a peep of republicanism in recent years (hers is, after all, less than the compensation received by many American CEOs.) Spain, the Netherlands, ➤

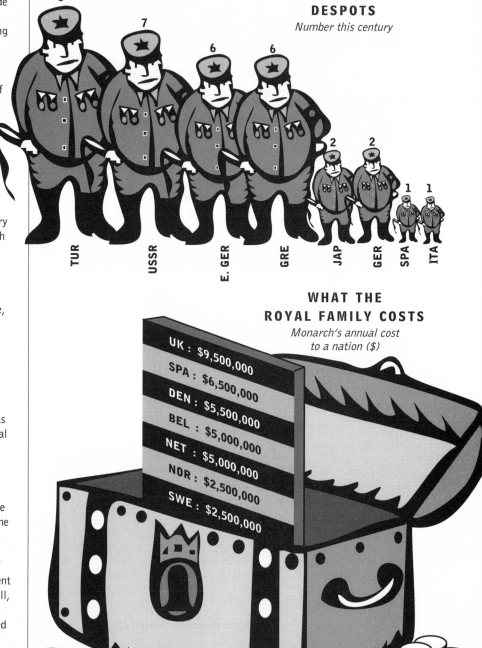

DESPOTS
Number this century

8 TUR
7 USSR
6 E. GER
6 GRE
2 JAP
2 GER
1 SPA
1 ITA

WHAT THE ROYAL FAMILY COSTS
Monarch's annual cost to a nation ($)

UK : $9,500,000
SPA : $6,500,000
DEN : $5,500,000
BEL : $5,000,000
NET : $5,000,000
NOR : $2,500,000
SWE : $2,500,000

WORLDGATE
*Number of political scandals
since 1945*

IN THIS DAY AND AGE
Number since 1945

Monarchs

Greece	3
Denmark	3
Netherlands	3
Sweden	3
Belgium	2
United Kingdom	2
Luxembourg	2
Norway	2
Japan	2
Italy	1
Spain	1

Despots

Turkey	7
Portugal	6
Soviet Union	5
East Germany	4
Spain	1

The high number of scandals and causes célèbres in the U.S. is primarily the result of an aggressive press corps, but it is also due to a greedy, self-serving, and immoral political culture—of course.

MOST SCANDALS: THE U.S.

NOR	NET	IRE	SWE	SPA	JAP	BEL	ITA	GER	GRE	CAN	AUS	ÖST	FRA	UK	USA
1	1	1	2	2	2	2	3	3	4	5	5	8	16	42	53

Norway, Belgium, and Sweden manage to hold the cost down to $3 million to $5 million a year.

With the fall of communism in the Soviet Union and Eastern Europe, numerous pretenders to the countless titles and thrones from Albania to Moldavia have indicated they would accept the long-awaited call home—including a Romanoff heir who has offered to return to Moscow.

Question: What do all democracies have in common? Answer: Scandal. Watergate in America; Profumo in England; P-2 in Italy; the Rainbow Warrior Affair in France; Lockheed in Japan and the Netherlands; Recruit in Japan; the Flick Affair in Germany...to name only the cream.

How the center holds

In Europe, while Socialist and Communist parties have been influential players in virtually every post-World War II democracy, the real power has been held by the Christian Democratic parties. In theory neither liberal nor conservative but "Christian" in values and inspiration, the Christian Democrats—in Belgium, Holland, Luxembourg, Germany, Austria, Switzerland, and Italy—pulled together a political and economic middle ground, the "social market economy," that is capitalism with a strong foundation of social programs.

In virtually every postwar democracy, the bonds holding voters to their parties have weakened—resulting in declining party membership, increasing crossover voting, and a surge in voters who classify themselves as independents. The causes of this "partisan dealignment" lie in the weakening of class and religious ties and the emergence of voters without traditional social identifications and political loyalties.

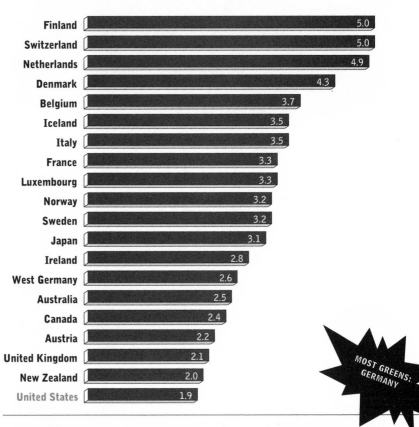

PARTY TIME

Average number of parties in the legislature since 1945

Finland	5.0
Switzerland	5.0
Netherlands	4.9
Denmark	4.3
Belgium	3.7
Iceland	3.5
Italy	3.5
France	3.3
Luxembourg	3.3
Norway	3.2
Sweden	3.2
Japan	3.1
Ireland	2.8
West Germany	2.6
Australia	2.5
Canada	2.4
Austria	2.2
United Kingdom	2.1
New Zealand	2.0
United States	1.9

MOST GREENS: GERMANY

EXTREME RIGHT

Organization or party membership

France	75,000
Germany	34,000
Austria	20,000
United Kingdom	20,000
United States	19,500
Switzerland	5,000
Japan	3,000
Finland	100

GREENS

Party membership

Germany	42,000
Sweden	5,000
Spain	2,500
Switzerland	2,000
New Zealand	2,000
Denmark	1,000
Belgium	1,000
France	700
Austria	500
Finland	500

PARTY LINE
Membership in the largest party as a percent of the population

Austria	15.4%
Sweden	13.0
Japan	12.2
United Kingdom	10.9
United States	8.3
Finland	6.3
New Zealand	5.7
Italy	3.5
Denmark	2.1
Ireland	2.0
Belgium	1.9
Switzerland	1.8
France	1.5
Germany	1.5
Netherlands	1.0
Greece	0.3
Spain	0.3
Norway	0.0
Portugal	0.0

> Unlike in the U.S., political-party membership in Europe and Japan implies a strong personal and financial commitment.

MOST REDS: ITALY

EXTREME LEFT
Organization or party membership

Portugal	115,000
Japan	55,000
Spain	39,000
France	21,300
Sweden	19,000
Italy	11,000
United States	10,000
Norway	10,000
United Kingdom	4,500
Australia	1,000
Germany	1,000
Netherlands	900

COMMUNISTS
Party membership

Italy	800,000	United Kingdom	7,500
Japan	470,000	Denmark	7,400
France	200,000	United States	6,000
Portugal	199,275	Belgium	5,000
Spain	53,300	Switzerland	4,500
Greece	50,000	Netherlands	4,000
Finland	34,700	Canada	3,000
Germany	27,500	Iceland	3,000
Sweden	22,800	Australia	1,000
Austria	15,000	Luxembourg	600
Norway	7,750	New Zealand	100

─────Parliaments of whores?─────

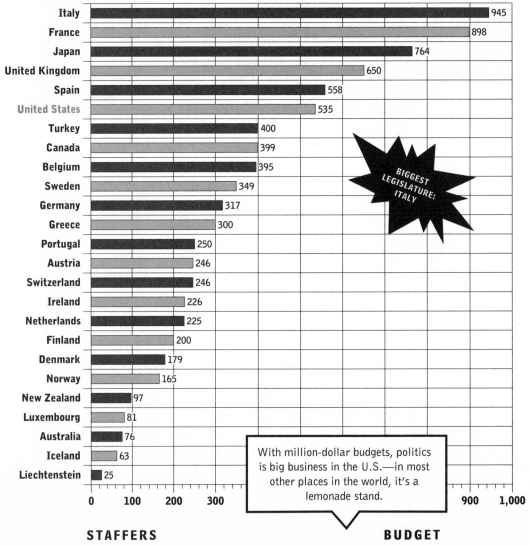

POLS

Total number of legislators

Italy	945
France	898
Japan	764
United Kingdom	650
Spain	558
United States	535
Turkey	400
Canada	399
Belgium	395
Sweden	349
Germany	317
Greece	300
Portugal	250
Austria	246
Switzerland	246
Ireland	226
Netherlands	225
Finland	200
Denmark	179
Norway	165
New Zealand	97
Luxembourg	81
Australia	76
Iceland	63
Liechtenstein	25

BIGGEST LEGISLATURE: ITALY

With million-dollar budgets, politics is big business in the U.S.—in most other places in the world, it's a lemonade stand.

STAFFERS

Average number of full-time employees per legislator

United States	18.0
Japan	2.0
United Kingdom	1.7
Germany	1.5
Italy	1.0

BUDGET

Estimated allocation for a legislative office ($)

United States	$1,000,000
United Kingdom	75,000
Germany	70,000
France	45,000
Japan	29,000

POWER OF THE PURSE
Women in the legislature (%)

Soviet Union	34.5 %
Norway	34.4
East Germany	32.2
Finland	31.5
Denmark	29.0
Sweden	28.5
Iceland	20.6
Netherlands	20.0
Germany	15.4
New Zealand	14.4
Luxembourg	14.1
Switzerland	14.0
Italy	12.8
Austria	11.5
Canada	9.6
Ireland	8.4
Portugal	7.6
Belgium	7.5
France	6.4
Spain	6.4
United Kingdom	6.3
Australia	6.1
United States	5.3
Greece	4.3
Turkey	3.0
Japan	1.4

Japan is run almost exclusively by men.

Alan Ehrenhalt, in his book *The United States of Ambition*, asks perhaps the central question about American politicians: "Who sent these people?" He points out that politicians in the U.S. are self-selected, ambitious, local, professional talent (usually lawyers) with the entrepreneurial drive and marketing skills to promote themselves into office.

This is in high contrast to practically all other democratic systems, where the greatest number of representatives come up through a party structure and, on the basis of consistency and loyalty, are selected to stand up for the party's policies, programs, and ideals. Success and failure belong mainly to the party rather than the politician.

Myth:
In the political process, American women have come into their own.

Reality:
The prevalence of women lawmakers in the U.S. is no greater than in the world's most unliberated societies—e.g., Greece, Turkey, and Japan.

Parliaments of whores?

Almost 18,000 people work for the U.S. Congress: chiefs of staff, special assistants, press secretaries, committee counsels, researchers, aides, secretaries, receptionists, interns—and congressmen and senators too. Another 6,500 or so registered lobbyists join them.

In no other democracy do legislators enjoy the prestige, the cachet, and the financial resources of American members of Congress. Each member runs a multimillion-dollar organization, with staff to advise him or her on every aspect of the job—policy questions, constituent matters, and media relations. In addition, each member has access to vast communications resources—sophisticated production studios, printing offices, subsidized telecommunications systems, and free postage. Many U.S. senators have more than 200 people working for them full-time. In most other democracies, legislators tend to be solo practitioners who work a second job.

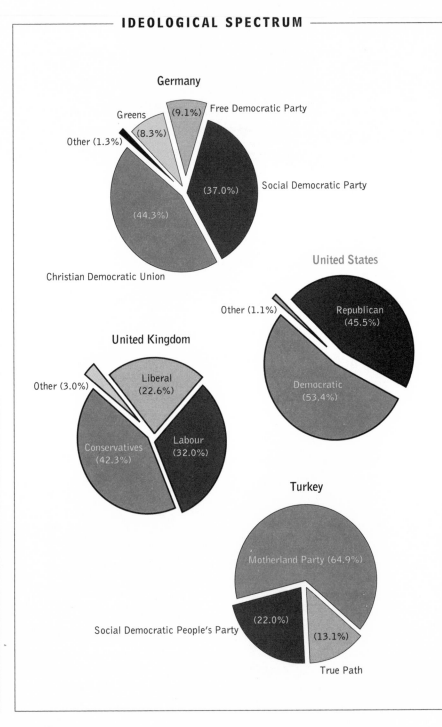

IDEOLOGICAL SPECTRUM

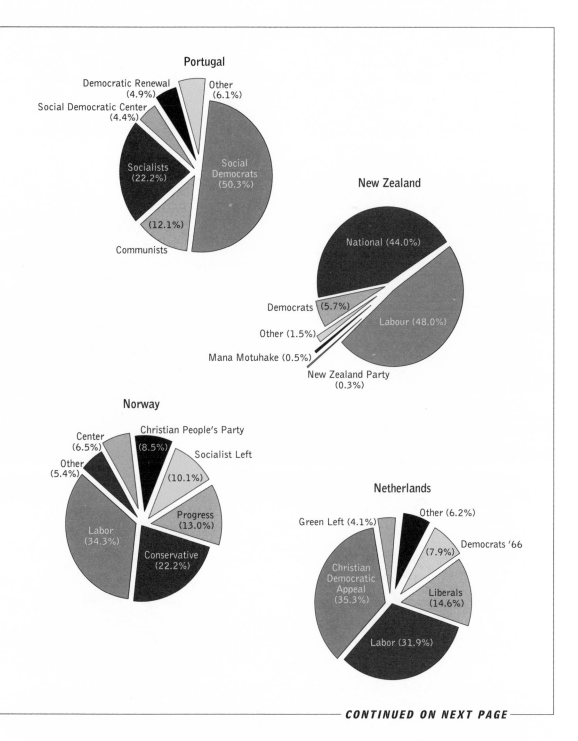

Portugal

Democratic Renewal (4.9%)

Social Democratic Center (4.4%)

Other (6.1%)

Socialists (22.2%)

Social Democrats (50.3%)

(12.1%)

Communists

New Zealand

National (44.0%)

Democrats (5.7%)

Labour (48.0%)

Other (1.5%)

Mana Motuhake (0.5%)

New Zealand Party (0.3%)

Norway

Center (6.5%)

Christian People's Party (8.5%)

Socialist Left

Other (5.4%)

(10.1%)

Progress (13.0%)

Labor (34.3%)

Conservative (22.2%)

Netherlands

Green Left (4.1%)

Other (6.2%)

Democrats '66 (7.9%)

Christian Democratic Appeal (35.3%)

Liberals (14.6%)

Labor (31.9%)

CONTINUED ON NEXT PAGE

Parliaments of whores?

IDEOLOGICAL SPECTRUM

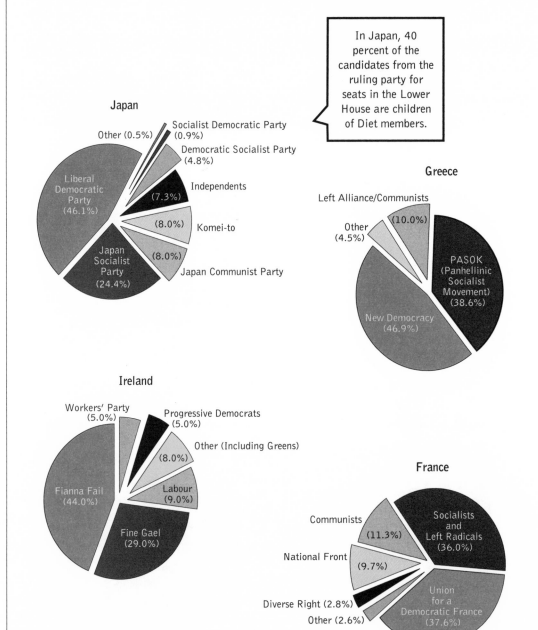

Japan

Other (0.5%)

Socialist Democratic Party (0.9%)

Democratic Socialist Party (4.8%)

Independents (7.3%)

Komei-to (8.0%)

Japan Communist Party (8.0%)

Liberal Democratic Party (46.1%)

Japan Socialist Party (24.4%)

In Japan, 40 percent of the candidates from the ruling party for seats in the Lower House are children of Diet members.

Greece

Left Alliance/Communists (10.0%)

Other (4.5%)

PASOK (Panhellinic Socialist Movement) (38.6%)

New Democracy (46.9%)

Ireland

Workers' Party (5.0%)

Progressive Democrats (5.0%)

Other (Including Greens) (8.0%)

Labour (9.0%)

Fianna Fail (44.0%)

Fine Gael (29.0%)

France

Communists (11.3%)

National Front (9.7%)

Diverse Right (2.8%)

Other (2.6%)

Socialists and Left Radicals (36.0%)

Union for a Democratic France (37.6%)

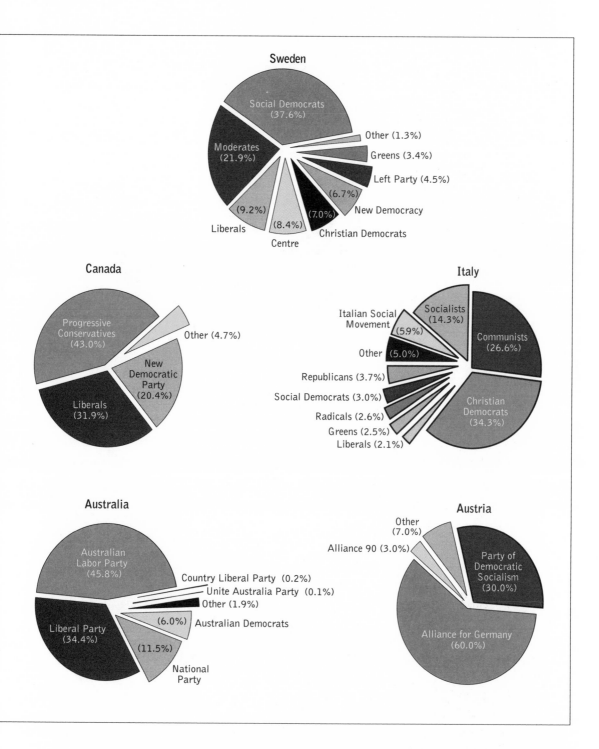

——What makes Johnny run?—

Political races are longer, harder, and more expensive in the U.S. than any other place in the world. They are longer because of the American political tradition of meeting the voters—"see me, touch me, feel me" campaigns, in the words of President Bush's former chief of staff John Sununu. They are harder because there is more ground to cover— literally: Presidential candidates in the U.S. fly millions of miles crisscrossing the country. And they are more expensive because of television— with a 30-second prime-time spot costing upwards of $200,000. In the U.S. in 1988, political candidates spent $500 million on their coast-to-coast campaigns. ➽

Myth:
U.S. politicians spend enormous sums to buy their votes.

Reality:
Compared with their Japanese counterparts, U.S. politicians get off cheap.

WHAT DOES IT COST TO BE PRESIDENT?
Money spent on last presidential race by winning candidate ($)

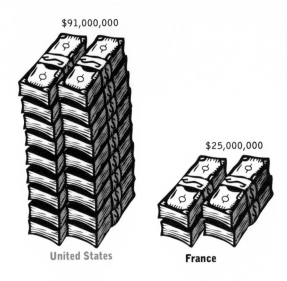

$91,000,000

$25,000,000

United States   **France**

WHAT DOES IT COST TO BE A LEGISLATOR?
Money spent on an average legislative race per elected legislator ($)

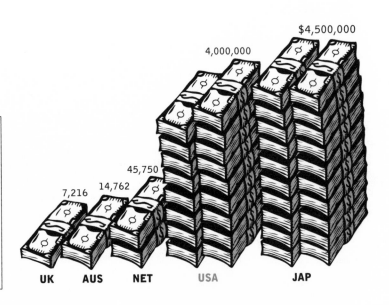

$4,500,000

4,000,000

45,750

7,216   14,762

UK   AUS   NET   USA   JAP

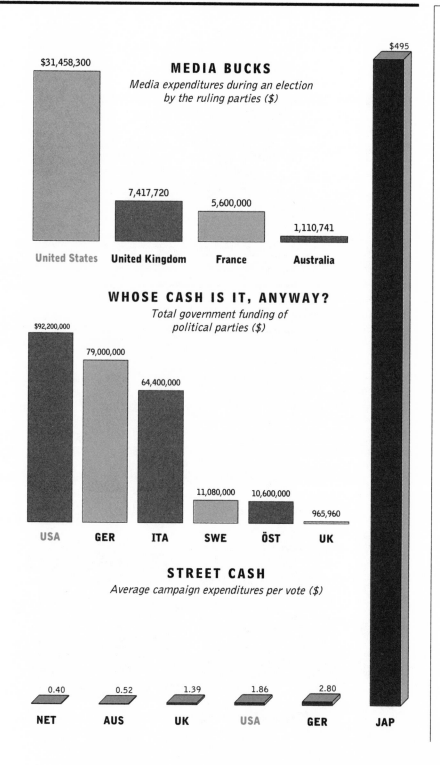

MEDIA BUCKS

*Media expenditures during an election
by the ruling parties ($)*

$31,458,300 — United States
7,417,720 — United Kingdom
5,600,000 — France
1,110,741 — Australia
$495 — JAP

WHOSE CASH IS IT, ANYWAY?

*Total government funding of
political parties ($)*

$92,200,000 — USA
79,000,000 — GER
64,400,000 — ITA
11,080,000 — SWE
10,600,000 — ÖST
965,960 — UK

STREET CASH

Average campaign expenditures per vote ($)

0.40 — NET
0.52 — AUS
1.39 — UK
1.86 — USA
2.80 — GER

Even legislative contests in the U.S. are major financial undertakings. A race for the House of Representatives can cost $3 million to $4 million; an Assembly seat in California goes for more than $1 million.

France is the next most costly political arena, with a presidential candidate looking at a tab of at least $25 million (which an American candidate will spend before he's even nominated).

One soaring U.S. export is its legions of political consultants teaching the world the latest in political marketing techniques—including demographic analysis, voter targeting, direct mail, and telemarketing. These new techniques are of particular interest to the many countries where political advertising on television is prohibited or closely controlled.

Permanent government

In Russia, observes Joseph LaPolombara of Yale University, it's *blat* (literally "pull" or "influence"); in Africa, *dash*; in Italy, public servants might get passed *la bustarella* ("the little envelope"); in Spain, there's *la modida* ("the bite"); in parts of Asia, *baksheesh*. In the U.S., try *grease, graft, bribe, payola, kickback*—the currency of permanent governments everywhere.

Getting government off of people's backs, that American piety ("That government governs best which governs least," said Jefferson), has resulted not only in fewer social programs in the U.S. but also in a smaller bureaucracy than in virtually any other country. It is a companion article of American faith that the "private sector" can do any government job more efficiently.

Myth:
The U.S. government reaches into everybody's life.

Reality:
It's relatively hands-off.

THE BUCK STOPS HERE

Total government spending as a percent of GDP

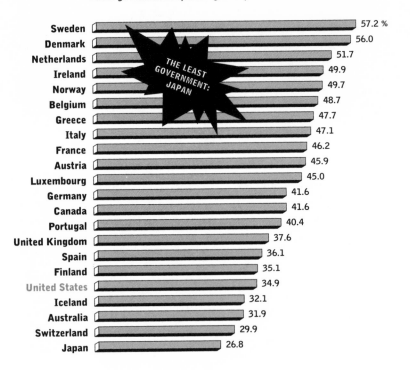

Sweden	57.2 %
Denmark	56.0
Netherlands	51.7
Ireland	49.9
Norway	49.7
Belgium	48.7
Greece	47.7
Italy	47.1
France	46.2
Austria	45.9
Luxembourg	45.0
Germany	41.6
Canada	41.6
Portugal	40.4
United Kingdom	37.6
Spain	36.1
Finland	35.1
United States	34.9
Iceland	32.1
Australia	31.9
Switzerland	29.9
Japan	26.8

THE LEAST GOVERNMENT: JAPAN

THE CENTRALIZED NIGHTMARE

Local rule

Average number of people covered by the most local level of government

United Kingdom	115,300	Germany	7,800
Ireland	39,100	Italy	7,100
Portugal	32,400	United States	6,400
Sweden	29,700	Canada	5,400
Denmark	18,500	Spain	4,100
Netherlands	17,400	Austria	3,300
Belgium	16,400	Switzerland	2,100
Finland	10,400	Greece	1,600
Norway	9,000	France	1,500

SUPER EMPLOYER
*Government employees as a percent
of the total work force*

31.7%
29.8
25.7
22.8
21.9
20.6
20.4
20.3
19.4
18.1
17.4
16.7
15.6
15.5
15.1
15.0
14.4
13.9
12.8
11.3
11.2
6.3

Sweden
Denmark
Norway
France
Finland
Austria
Belgium
United Kingdom
Canada
New Zealand
Iceland
Australia
Italy
Germany
Netherlands
Ireland
United States
Spain
Portugal
Luxembourg
Switzerland
Japan

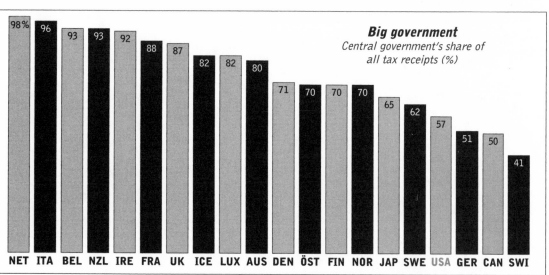

Big government
*Central government's share of
all tax receipts (%)*

NET	ITA	BEL	NZL	IRE	FRA	UK	ICE	LUX	AUS	DEN	ÖST	FIN	NOR	JAP	SWE	USA	GER	CAN	SWI
98%	96	93	93	92	88	87	82	82	80	71	70	70	70	65	62	57	51	50	41

Order or disorder

The Red Brigades in Italy, Bader-Meinhof and Red Army Faction in Germany, CCC in Belgium, Action Directe in France, the IRA in Northern Ireland, and the Basque separatists in Spain are merely the best known of Europe's violent political organizations of the 1970s and '80s. Those homegrown terrorists, together with the traffic from the Middle East—the bombing of Berlin's LaBelle Discotheque, the destruction of Pan Am Flight 103, the hijacking of the *Achille Lauro*, the Paris bombings of the late 1980s, the hunting of Salman Rushdie, and the killing of Iran's former prime minister Bani Sadr—and the recent threat of neo-Nazism in Germany, have made Europe terrorism's capital.

Many hope that with the opening of secret police records throughout the former East-bloc nations—and possibly the KGB's files too—the West will learn how terrorism came to thrive in Europe. Early indications are that former East German ➡

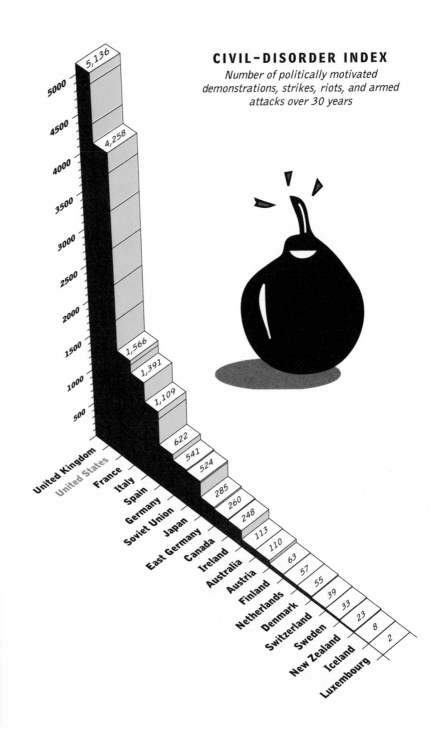

CIVIL–DISORDER INDEX
Number of politically motivated demonstrations, strikes, riots, and armed attacks over 30 years

United Kingdom — 5,136
United States — 4,258
France — 1,566
Italy — 1,391
Spain — 1,109
Germany — 622
Soviet Union — 541
Japan — 524
East Germany — 285
Canada — 260
Ireland — 248
Australia — 113
Austria — 110
Finland — 63
Netherlands — 57
Denmark — 55
Switzerland — 39
Sweden — 33
New Zealand — 23
Iceland — 8
Luxembourg — 2

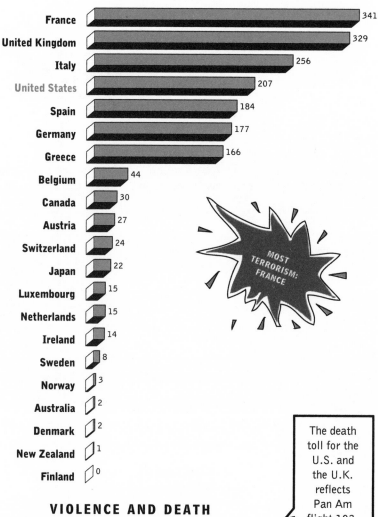

FIRST BLOOD
Terrorist attacks (1980–1991)

Country	Attacks
France	341
United Kingdom	329
Italy	256
United States	207
Spain	184
Germany	177
Greece	166
Belgium	44
Canada	30
Austria	27
Switzerland	24
Japan	22
Luxembourg	15
Netherlands	15
Ireland	14
Sweden	8
Norway	3
Australia	2
Denmark	2
New Zealand	1
Finland	0

MOST TERRORISM: FRANCE

The death toll for the U.S. and the U.K. reflects Pan Am flight 103.

VIOLENCE AND DEATH
Deaths from terrorism (1980–1991)

United States	278	Canada	20	Switzerland	1
U.K.	195	Belgium	8	Australia	0
Italy	179	Austria	7	Denmark	0
Greece	77	Japan	2	Finland	0
Spain	71	Ireland	2	Luxembourg	0
France	65	New Zealand	1	Norway	0
Germany	38	Sweden	1	Netherlands	0

strongman Erich Honecker was the godfather of Euro-terrorism. According to *Newsweek*, German officials have characterized Honecker's shepherding of various extremist groups as his "personal hobby." Likewise, virtually every former East-bloc regime played host to the notorious Ilyich Ramírez Sánchez, aka Carlos. Czechoslovakian president Vaclav Havel revealed that his predecessors sold 1,000 tons of Semtex—the explosive probably used in the bombing of Pan Am Flight 103—to Libyan dictator Muammar Qaddafi.

It remains to be seen whether the fall of the East-bloc nations will mean less support for terrorists in Europe and the Middle East. Or will 1992 and Europe's open borders make it easier for operatives to penetrate, circulate, and increase the threat?

Order or disorder

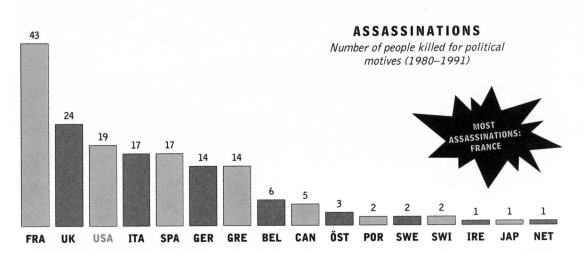

ASSASSINATIONS
*Number of people killed for political
motives (1980–1991)*

| 43 | 24 | 19 | 17 | 17 | 14 | 14 | 6 | 5 | 3 | 2 | 2 | 2 | 1 | 1 | 1 |
| FRA | UK | USA | ITA | SPA | GER | GRE | BEL | CAN | ÖST | POR | SWE | SWI | IRE | JAP | NET |

MOST
ASSASSINATIONS:
FRANCE

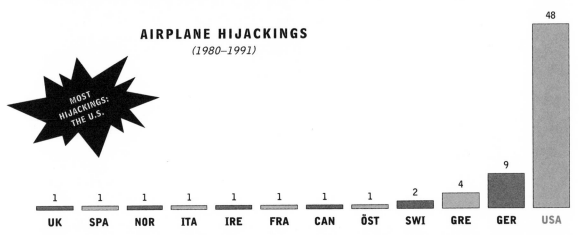

AIRPLANE HIJACKINGS
(1980–1991)

MOST
HIJACKINGS:
THE U.S.

| 1 | 1 | 1 | 1 | 1 | 1 | 1 | 1 | 2 | 4 | 9 | 48 |
| UK | SPA | NOR | ITA | IRE | FRA | CAN | ÖST | SWI | GRE | GER | USA |

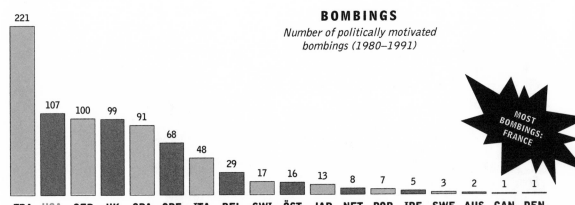

BOMBINGS
*Number of politically motivated
bombings (1980–1991)*

MOST
BOMBINGS:
FRANCE

| 221 | 107 | 100 | 99 | 91 | 68 | 48 | 29 | 17 | 16 | 13 | 8 | 7 | 5 | 3 | 2 | 1 | 1 |
| FRA | USA | GER | UK | SPA | GRE | ITA | BEL | SWI | ÖST | JAP | NET | POR | IRE | SWE | AUS | CAN | DEN |

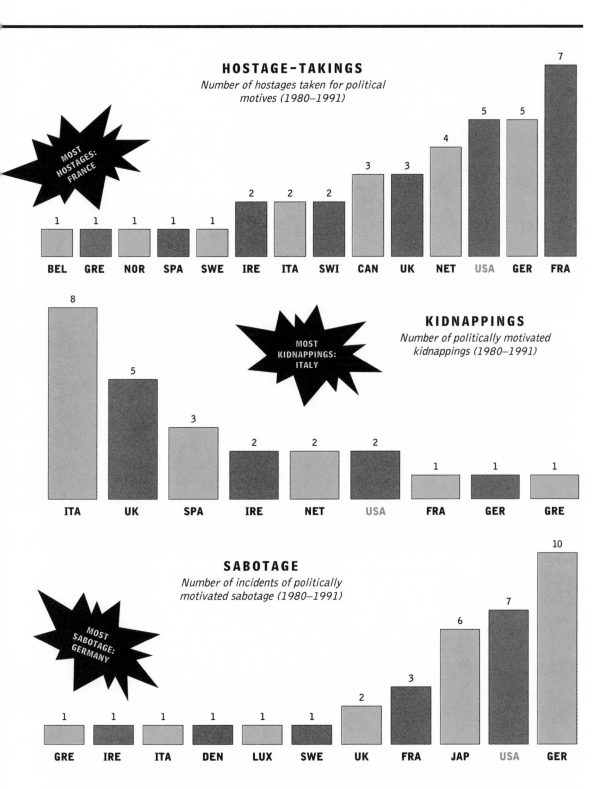

HOSTAGE-TAKINGS

Number of hostages taken for political motives (1980–1991)

MOST HOSTAGES: FRANCE

BEL	GRE	NOR	SPA	SWE	IRE	ITA	SWI	CAN	UK	NET	USA	GER	FRA
1	1	1	1	1	2	2	2	3	3	4	5	5	7

KIDNAPPINGS

Number of politically motivated kidnappings (1980–1991)

MOST KIDNAPPINGS: ITALY

ITA	UK	SPA	IRE	NET	USA	FRA	GER	GRE
8	5	3	2	2	2	1	1	1

SABOTAGE

Number of incidents of politically motivated sabotage (1980–1991)

MOST SABOTAGE: GERMANY

GRE	IRE	ITA	DEN	LUX	SWE	UK	FRA	JAP	USA	GER
1	1	1	1	1	1	2	3	6	7	10

Freedom's just another word

Once the U.S. and it's allies were the only players. But with the overturn of Eastern Europe, the breakup of the Soviet Union, and the passing of the generals in Latin America, democracy has become a part of the competitive game.

The United Nations Development Program issues two evaluations of freedom around the world. The Human Development Index measures the conditions needed for freedom to flourish. It ranks nations on the basis of poverty levels, nutrition, health, education, gender disparities, and income distribution. The Human Freedom Index compares the amount of freedom that citizens of different countries actually enjoy. It considers the right to travel, assemble, and speak; the absence of forced labor, torture, and extreme legal punishment (such as the death penalty); freedom of political opposition, the press, and trade unions; an independent judiciary; gender equality; and the legal right to trial, counsel of choice, privacy, religion, and sexual practice.

The nation that can fully enfranchise more of its citizens is the nation that will achieve the greater economic success and social harmony. Such an incentive may raise the freedom standard higher and higher.

On the other hand, just a short while ago, the rich countries of Europe were bragging that economic unification, together with the collapse of communism, booming economies, and stable governments, would give Europe the competitive advantage over an indebted and racially divided U.S. But Europe is learning one of the twentieth century's ironic truths: that affluence attracts poverty. Having achieved perhaps the world's highest standard of living, and having offered a measure of economic fairness to most of its citizens, it is now faced with large-scale immigration from Asia, the subcontinent, Africa, and the former East-bloc nations.

Will it tolerate the ethnic hordes, or will a backlash challenge Europe's social and democratic values?

"Either we can try to become 'fortress Europe,' turning in on ourselves," says Gianni de Michelis, Italy's foreign minister, "or we can accept the fact that Europe will continue to have immigrants, that we need many of these immigrants, and that we are destined, like the United States, to become multicultural societies."

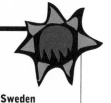

Rights

The Human Freedom Index gives Sweden the highest ranking and Iraq—courtesy of Saddam Hussein—the lowest.

HUMAN FREEDOM INDEX

From 0 to 40, with 40 indicating the most freedom

38	**Sweden**
38	**Denmark**
37	**Netherlands**
36	**Austria**
36	**Finland**
35	**France**
35	**Germany**
34	**Canada**
34	**Switzerland**
33	**Australia**
33	**United States**
32	**Japan**
32	**United Kingdom**
29	**Italy**
27	**Ireland**
26	**Spain**
7	**Turkey**

HUMAN DEVELOPMENT INDEX

Ranking of socioeconomic progress

Japan	1	**Finland**	13	
Canada	2	**Germany**	14	
Iceland	3	**New Zealand**	15	
Sweden	4	**Belgium**	16	
Switzerland	5	**Austria**	17	
Norway	6	**Italy**	18	
United States	7	**Luxembourg**	19	
Netherlands	8	**Spain**	20	
Australia	9	**Ireland**	23	
France	10	**Greece**	24	
U.K.	11	**Soviet Union**	31	
Denmark	12			

The Human Development Index gives Japan the highest ranking and Romania, as a legacy of the Ceausescu regime, the lowest.

Religion

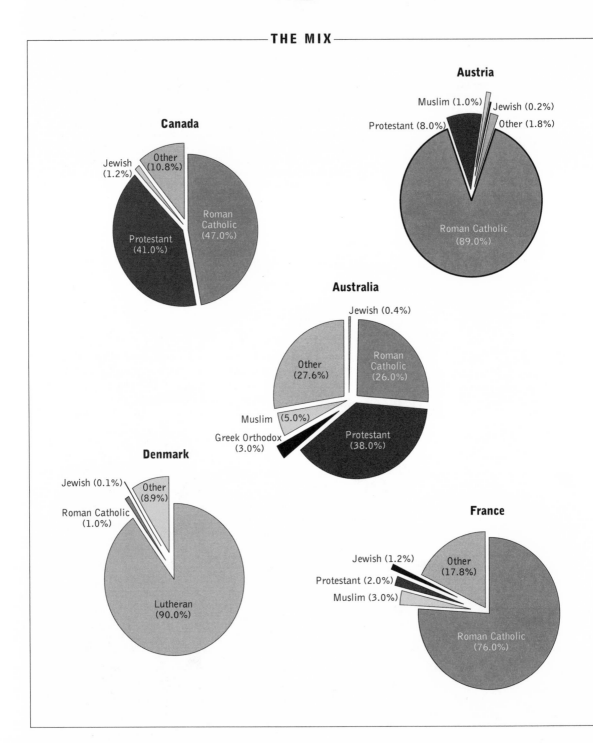

Canada

Jewish (1.2%)
Other (10.8%)
Protestant (41.0%)
Roman Catholic (47.0%)

Austria

Muslim (1.0%)
Jewish (0.2%)
Protestant (8.0%)
Other (1.8%)
Roman Catholic (89.0%)

Australia

Jewish (0.4%)
Other (27.6%)
Roman Catholic (26.0%)
Muslim (5.0%)
Greek Orthodox (3.0%)
Protestant (38.0%)

Denmark

Jewish (0.1%)
Other (8.9%)
Roman Catholic (1.0%)
Lutheran (90.0%)

France

Jewish (1.2%)
Other (17.8%)
Protestant (2.0%)
Muslim (3.0%)
Roman Catholic (76.0%)

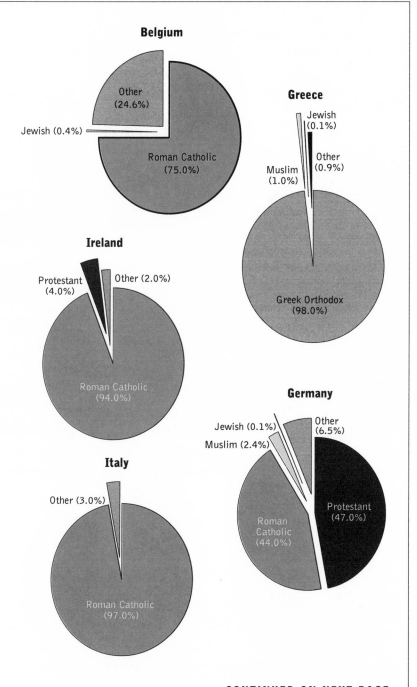

Belgium

Other (24.6%)

Jewish (0.4%)

Roman Catholic (75.0%)

Greece

Jewish (0.1%)

Other (0.9%)

Muslim (1.0%)

Greek Orthodox (98.0%)

Ireland

Protestant (4.0%)

Other (2.0%)

Roman Catholic (94.0%)

Germany

Other (6.5%)

Jewish (0.1%)

Muslim (2.4%)

Protestant (47.0%)

Roman Catholic (44.0%)

Italy

Other (3.0%)

Roman Catholic (97.0%)

"Americans are almost alone in the industrial world in still taking religion seriously."
—*Michael Prowse,* Financial Times

The secularization of Europe has been one of the profound postwar occurrences. Europeans now tend to look on America and its religious preoccupations—its abortion and school-prayer debate, its sexual prudery, and the rise of religious fundamentalism—with both fascination and condescension.

The fall of communism, however, promises at least an initial surge in religious behavior and in religious intolerance in Europe. New outbreaks of anti-Semitic incidents have been reported in virtually every European country.

In Japan, although Shintoism claims almost 100 million adherents and Buddhism nearly 90 million (more than the total Japanese population), polls indicate that fewer than 30 percent of the Japanese people have any real religious beliefs. Most prefer what is called *chuto-hanpa* (a bit of this, ➥

CONTINUED ON NEXT PAGE

Religion

a bit of that). Some religious scholars have said that traditional—prewar—Japanese spiritual intensity has found a new home in the drive to achieve high levels of education.

"I owe respect to my ancestors and show it through Buddhism. I'm a Japanese, so I do all the little Shinto rituals. And I thought a Christian marriage would be real pretty. It's a contradiction, but so what?"
—*Keiko Shirato, age 26*

Seven in ten people in the U.S. belong to a church or synagogue, one of the highest levels of formal religious affiliation in the world. Four in ten Americans have been to a religious service in the past seven days.

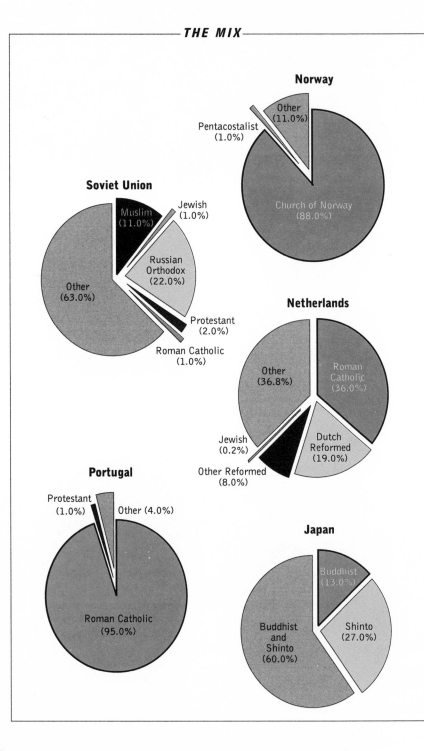

THE MIX

Norway
Other (11.0%)
Pentacostalist (1.0%)
Church of Norway (88.0%)

Soviet Union
Muslim (11.0%)
Jewish (1.0%)
Russian Orthodox (22.0%)
Other (63.0%)
Protestant (2.0%)
Roman Catholic (1.0%)

Netherlands
Other (36.8%)
Roman Catholic (36.0%)
Jewish (0.2%)
Dutch Reformed (19.0%)
Other Reformed (8.0%)

Portugal
Protestant (1.0%)
Other (4.0%)
Roman Catholic (95.0%)

Japan
Buddhist (13.0%)
Shinto (27.0%)
Buddhist and Shinto (60.0%)

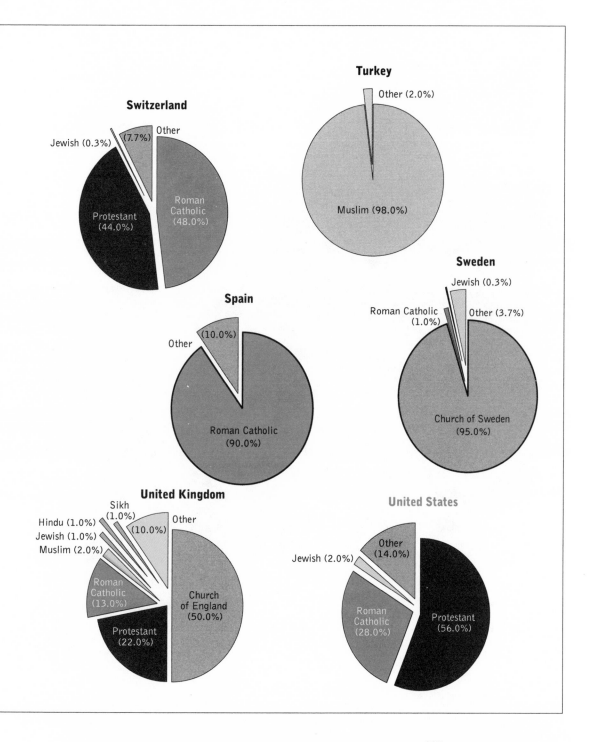

Religion

THE DOMINANT FORCE
*Largest religion's percent of
total population*

98% 98 97 97 95 95 94 90 90 89 88 87 76 75 56 50 48 47 47 36

Greece Turkey Italy Finland Portugal Sweden Ireland Denmark Spain Austria Norway Japan France Belgium United States United Kingdom Switzerland Canada Germany Netherlands

OPIUM

*Percent of people who believe in
God; their religious leaders; and hell*

God   United States: 91%   United Kingdom: 48   Japan: 47

Leaders   United States: 43%   Japan: 6   United Kingdom: 3   Germany: 3

Hell   United States: 76%   Japan: 53   Australia: 38   United Kingdom: 35   Germany: 16

HOLOCAUST LEGACY

Jewish population annihilated during World War II

Poland	3,000,000	Greece	54,000
Soviet Union	1,252,000	Belgium	40,000
Germany/Austria	210,000	Italy	8,000
Netherlands	105,000	Luxembourg	1,000
France	90,000	Norway	900

Ethnicity

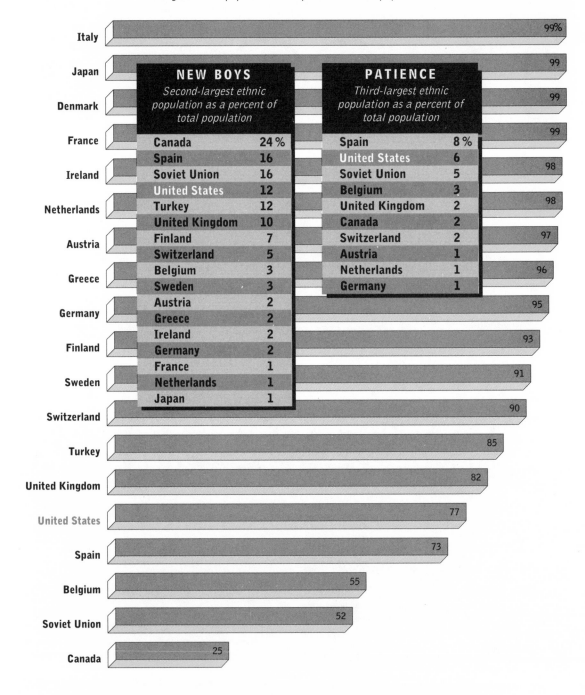

OLD BOYS
Largest ethnic population as a percent of total population

Italy	99%
Japan	99
Denmark	99
France	99
Ireland	98
Netherlands	98
Austria	97
Greece	96
Germany	95
Finland	93
Sweden	91
Switzerland	90
Turkey	85
United Kingdom	82
United States	77
Spain	73
Belgium	55
Soviet Union	52
Canada	25

NEW BOYS
Second-largest ethnic population as a percent of total population

Canada	24 %
Spain	16
Soviet Union	16
United States	12
Turkey	12
United Kingdom	10
Finland	7
Switzerland	5
Belgium	3
Sweden	3
Austria	2
Greece	2
Ireland	2
Germany	2
France	1
Netherlands	1
Japan	1

PATIENCE
Third-largest ethnic population as a percent of total population

Spain	8 %
United States	6
Soviet Union	5
Belgium	3
United Kingdom	2
Canada	2
Switzerland	2
Austria	1
Netherlands	1
Germany	1

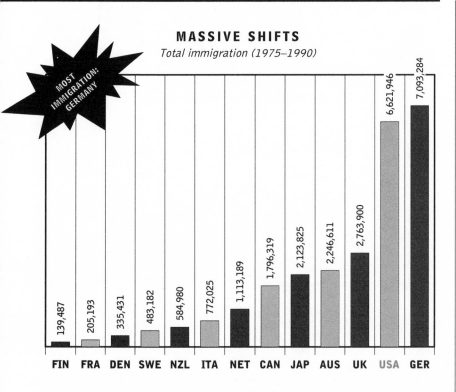

MASSIVE SHIFTS
Total immigration (1975–1990)

MOST IMMIGRATION: GERMANY

FIN	FRA	DEN	SWE	NZL	ITA	NET	CAN	JAP	AUS	UK	USA	GER
139,487	205,193	335,431	483,182	584,980	772,025	1,113,189	1,796,319	2,123,825	2,246,611	2,763,900	6,621,946	7,093,284

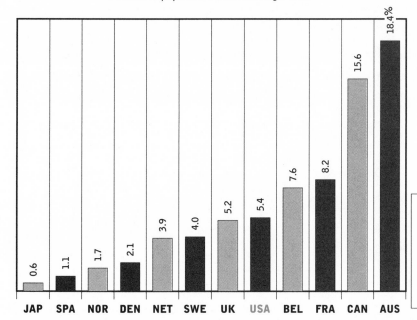

GREENHORNS
Percent of population that is foreign-born

JAP	SPA	NOR	DEN	NET	SWE	UK	USA	BEL	FRA	CAN	AUS
0.6	1.1	1.7	2.1	3.9	4.0	5.2	5.4	7.6	8.2	15.6	18.4%

Walk in London's Hyde Park on Sunday and you might think you were in a Muslim country. A flood of Albanians has strained Italy's usual tolerance. In France—where one in five Frenchmen has a foreign-born grandparent—all political parties are embracing some form of xenophobia (some call for immigrant repatriation). In Germany, immigrants are subject to an outbreak of neo-Nazi hysteria.

America's ethnic mix, now three-quarters of European descent, is expected to be half European by 2050. But Europe is even more in transition.

"Europe has become the real immigration continent."
—*François Heisbourg, director of the International Institute for Strategic Studies*

Myth:
America is the world's melting pot.

Reality:
Now Europe is.

Sexual equality

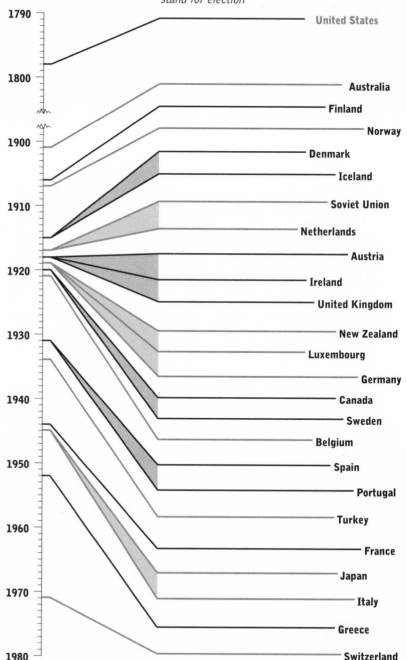

THE RIGHT
Year women gained the right to stand for election

1790	United States
1800	Australia
	Finland
	Norway
1900	Denmark
	Iceland
1910	Soviet Union
	Netherlands
	Austria
1920	Ireland
	United Kingdom
1930	New Zealand
	Luxembourg
	Germany
1940	Canada
	Sweden
	Belgium
1950	Spain
	Portugal
	Turkey
1960	France
	Japan
1970	Italy
	Greece
1980	Switzerland

In only sixteen nations do women hold more than 20 percent of the seats in parliament—Sweden, Norway, Finland, and Denmark, along with twelve communist or formerly communist nations (among them China and North Korea). As democracy grows, observers wonder whether women's participation will decline. Women hold between 10 percent and 20 percent of seats in twenty parliaments, including those of Germany, New Zealand, and Switzerland. The under-10-percenters include Canada, with 9.9 percent; the U.K., with 6.3 percent; and the U.S., with 5.3 percent. Twenty years ago, when the National Women's Political Caucus was founded to promote the election of women, women held only 1 percent of the seats in Congress.

Japan's record on women's rights is among the worst in the world. Although women make up a significant part of the work force, there is almost no opportunity for career advancement. The ➤➤

212

LEAST WOMEN IN POWER: JAPAN

THE MONEY
Average woman's salary as a percent of the average man's

Country	Percent
Sweden	90 %
United Kingdom	79
Australia	75
Germany	72
France	71
Soviet Union	70
United States	66
Canada	64
Japan	54

> In the U.S., only one out of ten economic, political, and legal decision-makers is a woman. In many industrial nations, there are still virtually no women in these jobs.

THE POWER
Women as a percent of elected officials

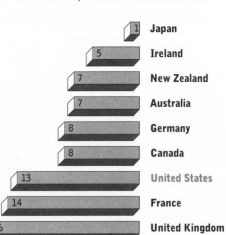

Country	Percent
Japan	1
Ireland	5
New Zealand	7
Australia	7
Germany	8
Canada	8
United States	13
France	14
United Kingdom	16
Netherlands	17
Denmark	20
Norway	29
Sweden	31 %

THE STATUS
Percent of women holding a decision-making economic, political, or legal position

Country	Percent
Norway	18.5
United States	11.5
Finland	11.1
Netherlands	9.5
Sweden	8.8
Canada	6.2
Austria	5.5
Portugal	5.0
Germany	4.9
Iceland	4.9
Belgium	4.6
Denmark	4.1
United Kingdom	4.1
East Germany	4.1
Ireland	3.7
France	3.4
Switzerland	2.9
Australia	1.0
Soviet Union	0.3
Japan	0.0
Italy	0.0

MOST WOMEN IN CHARGE: NORWAY

Sexual equality

ratio of women's to men's pay is among the lowest anywhere—and the gap is widening. No major Japanese company has a woman board member. Nissan has only one female manager. Yet most Japanese women receive the same amount of education— at public expense—as Japanese men. Economists point out the inherent wastefulness of educating women but not letting them make a contribution, and they also cite the disadvantages a lack of women executives imposes when trying to do business with the increasing numbers of managerial women in other parts of the world.

"If women are second-class citizens in most industrial countries, they are third-class ones in Japan. Far from scaling the peaks, they have failed to reach even the foothills in politics, the bureaucracy and business. This waste of the talents of 60 million Japanese will cost the country increasingly dear."
—The Economist

SCIENTISTS
Percent who are women

82.4%
58.3
57.1
52.2
50.0
46.2
37.5
33.3
33.3
33.3
28.6
23.1
22.2
20.0
20.0
16.7
12.5

80
70
60
50
40
30
20
10

Denmark
France
Greece
Netherlands
Norway
Germany
Austria
Finland
Belgium
Italy
Sweden
Canada
United States
Ireland
United Kingdom
Switzerland
Portugal

MANAGERS
Percent who are women

Canada	31 %
United States	30
Sweden	20
Australia	13
New Zealand	9

LAWYERS
Percent who are women

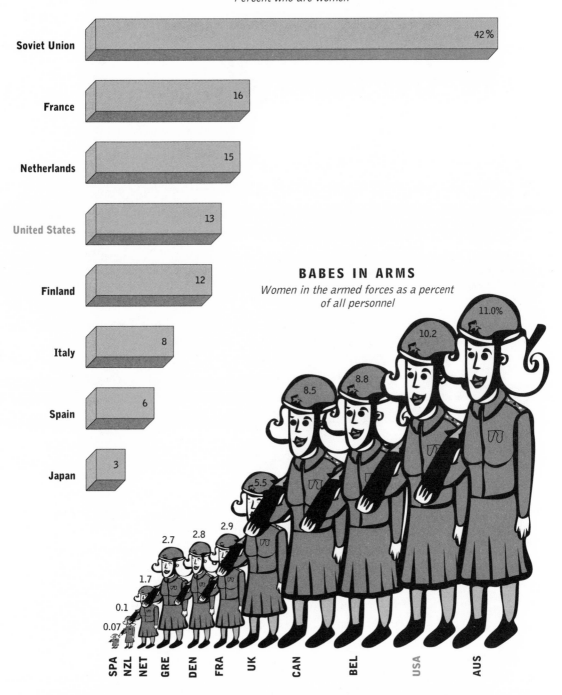

Soviet Union	42%
France	16
Netherlands	15
United States	13
Finland	12
Italy	8
Spain	6
Japan	3

BABES IN ARMS
Women in the armed forces as a percent of all personnel

AUS	11.0%
USA	10.2
BEL	8.8
CAN	8.5
UK	5.5
FRA	2.9
DEN	2.8
GRE	2.7
NET	1.7
NZL	0.1
SPA	0.07

Defense— safe or sorry?

While Western Europe and Japan have invested in the social and industrial infrastructure that ultimately produces wealth, the U.S. has invested the bulk of its available resources in armies and weaponry.

The big contradiction in American politics has been the voter's and politician's belief in a strong defense (and mighty offense) without a corresponding willingness to pay for it. Many believe that Lyndon Johnson's decision to go full steam in Vietnam without raising taxes to cover the cost began America's economic decline. Likewise, Ronald Reagan whipped the nation into a Star Wars military-spending frenzy and plunged it into vast and hopeless debt.

Understanding its limitations, the U.S. persuaded its allies to finance the campaign against Iraq. The allies provided $54 billion—$33 billion more than the war cost—causing cynics to speculate on a new role for the U.S.: that of a mercenary power.

Conservative theoreticians maintain that it was precisely this "overkill" that ultimately persuaded Gorbachev to adopt glasnost and perestroika: He knew the Soviet Union couldn't match U.S. spending and feed its people at the same time. Liberals say the cost of assuming this responsibility has been both painful (causing a winnowing away at the U.S. middle class and its standard of living) and ironic (our allies became our most determined economic foes).

This analysis—"imperial overstretch"—in *The Rise and Fall of the Great Powers,* by Paul Kennedy, that hit Americans and American policymakers squarely in the eye. Kennedy's thesis—all great military powers inevitably try to extend their power too far; in the end, their commitments are too grand and costly—was both convincing and devastating. In the cool light of day, military adventurism is almost always a bad investment decision.

The Gulf War might be one of the more sublime examples of "overstretch." The technology, equipment, readiness, and manpower that the U.S. brought into the region account for a good part of America's $3.5 trillion debt. And who benefits from America's financial outlays and dazzling displays of firepower? Well, most of the flow of oil that the U.S. intervention protected goes to Europe and Japan.

What has it cost?

THE NUT	
Defense spending as percent of GDP	
Soviet Union	11.5%
United States	6.2
Greece	5.9
United Kingdom	4.0
France	3.1
Norway	3.0
Netherlands	2.9
Portugal	2.6
Germany	2.5
Sweden	2.4
Belgium	2.2
Australia	2.1
Denmark	2.1
Italy	2.1
Finland	1.4
Austria	1.2
Japan	0.9
Iceland	0.0

YOUR SHARE	
Per capita defense spending ($)	
United States	$1,061
Soviet Union	1,047
Germany	552
United Kingdom	402
France	395
Sweden	364
Canada	307
Switzerland	282
Netherlands	274
Denmark	257
Belgium	254
Australia	254
Greece	218
Italy	194
Finland	184
New Zealand	148
Luxembourg	134
Japan	125
Spain	107
Austria	107
Portugal	77

PIECE OF THE PIE	
Percent of tax dollars spent on defense	
Soviet Union	47.5%
United States	26.5
Turkey	17.6
Greece	16.8
United Kingdom	12.7
Germany	10.5
Switzerland	10.0
Portugal	9.4
Australia	9.3
France	9.0
Canada	8.2
Spain	7.7
Norway	7.1
Sweden	6.4
Belgium	5.5
Japan	5.4
Netherlands	5.4
Denmark	5.3
Finland	5.0
Italy	4.7
New Zealand	4.5
Austria	3.3

Body count

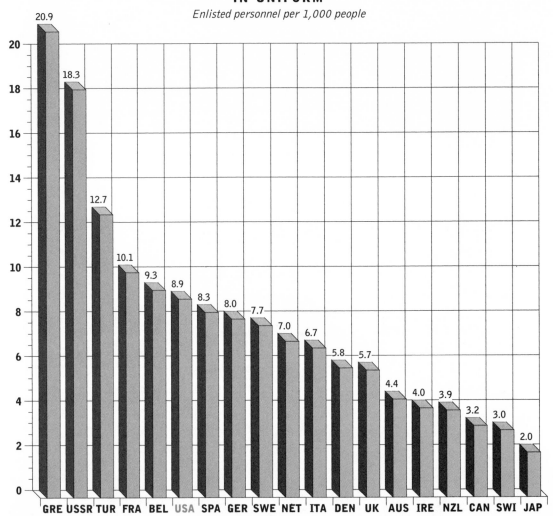

IN UNIFORM
Enlisted personnel per 1,000 people

GRE	20.9
USSR	18.3
TUR	12.7
FRA	10.1
BEL	9.3
USA	8.9
SPA	8.3
GER	8.0
SWE	7.7
NET	7.0
ITA	6.7
DEN	5.8
UK	5.7
AUS	4.4
IRE	4.0
NZL	3.9
CAN	3.2
SWI	3.0
JAP	2.0

GREETINGS!
Military draft requirement (months)

Portugal	20	Norway	15	Finland	10
Germany	18	Netherlands	14	Sweden	9
Greece	18	Belgium	12	Austria	8
Italy	18	Denmark	12	Canada	0
Turkey	18	France	12	United States	0

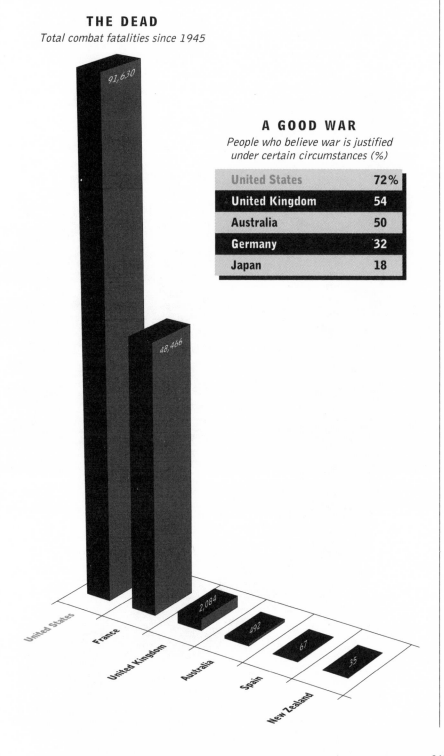

THE DEAD

Total combat fatalities since 1945

91,630

48,466

2,084

492

67

35

United States

France

United Kingdom

Australia

Spain

New Zealand

A GOOD WAR

*People who believe war is justified
under certain circumstances (%)*

United States	72%
United Kingdom	54
Australia	50
Germany	32
Japan	18

"With an army less than two-thirds the size of France's, Britain deployed to the Arabian peninsula a two-brigade-strong armoured division, reinforced with corps-level assets, while France was able to deploy only a single brigade-sized division which had to be strengthened with the addition of an American airborne infantry brigade and field artillery brigade."
—*International Institute for Strategic Studies*

Engagements

In the first days of the Gulf War, Italy sent three jet fighters into battle. Two were unable to complete their midair refueling and had to abort. The third was shot down.

"Ideas of sending a 30,000 strong force (into Yugoslavia) have been greatly watered down....The most that can be expected at the moment is a decision in principle (by the European Community) to give the 400 to 500 EC cease-fire monitors protection involving no more than a few thousand lightly-armed military personnel."
—Financial Times

The 45 years of Cold War between East and West was perhaps the longest period in history without a major hot war between big powers.

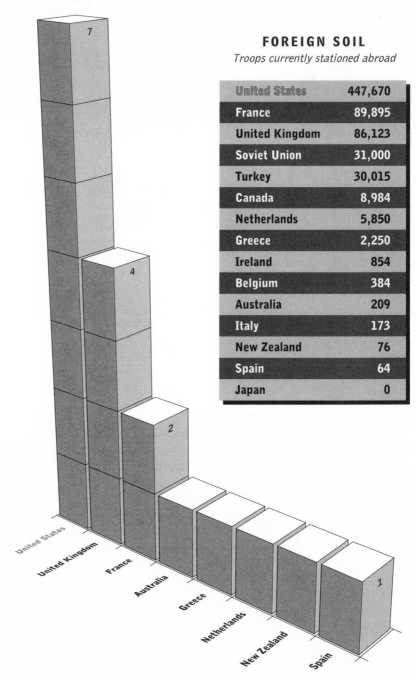

COLD WARS
Combat engagements since 1945

7
4
2
1

United States
United Kingdom
France
Australia
Greece
Netherlands
New Zealand
Spain

FOREIGN SOIL
Troops currently stationed abroad

United States	447,670
France	89,895
United Kingdom	86,123
Soviet Union	31,000
Turkey	30,015
Canada	8,984
Netherlands	5,850
Greece	2,250
Ireland	854
Belgium	384
Australia	209
Italy	173
New Zealand	76
Spain	64
Japan	0

Nukes

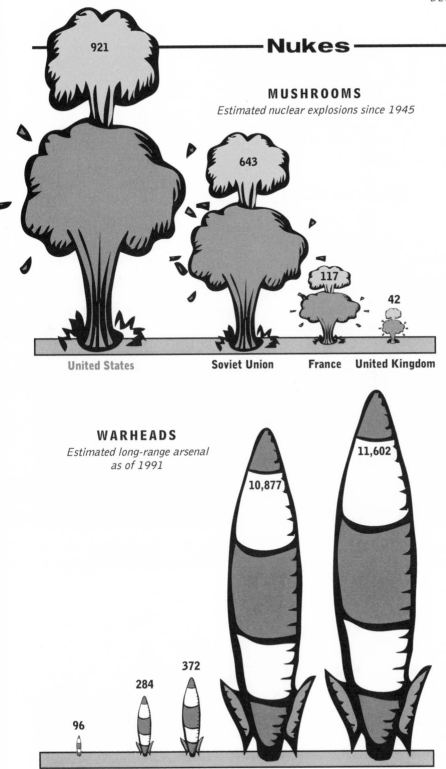

MUSHROOMS
Estimated nuclear explosions since 1945

921 — United States

643 — Soviet Union

117 — France

42 — United Kingdom

WARHEADS
Estimated long-range arsenal as of 1991

96 — United Kingdom

284 — China

372 — France

10,877 — Soviet Union

11,602 — United States

As the prospect of nuclear holocaust recedes into twentieth-century nostalgia (bomb shelters and nuclear-free zones), a new anxiety takes its place. How close was Saddam to having the bomb? What capabilities do the North Koreans possess? What about Pakistan? And now the collapse of the Soviet Union raises the chance that warheads from the old empire's arsenal will come under unknown and less stable control. Such uncertainties, such growing possibilities, have given new life to Ronald Reagan's Star Wars vision—perhaps not unreasonably. The big objection to the original plan was that it would be impossible to build a system that could defend against an all-out Soviet attack. But it is not at all unlikely that an antiballistic system could be built to protect America against a renegade ICBM or two.

Arms sales

The U.S., the Soviet Union, the U.K., France, and China are the big five arms dealers, responsible for 85 percent of the trade in the world's big-ticket military hardware. But the U.S. is the world's greatest exporter of military technology. The $14.3 billion worth of weaponry exported by the U.S. in 1988 was three times the amount exported by all other NATO members combined.

"We are the big Kahuna...the folks that have not only been technologically the most innovative, but we have entrepreneurially ...been the most aggressive (in exporting weapons technology)."
—*Senator Joseph R. Biden Jr.*

Myth:
The U.S. is the most ardent campaigner for controlling the arms trade.

Reality:
It is also the biggest exporter of military technology.

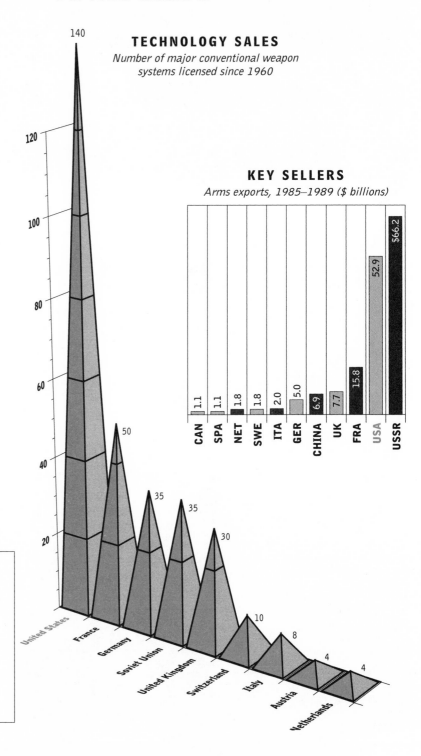

TECHNOLOGY SALES
Number of major conventional weapon systems licensed since 1960

United States — 140
France — 50
Germany — 35
Soviet Union — 35
United Kingdom — 30
Switzerland — 10
Italy — 8
Austria — 4
Netherlands — 4

KEY SELLERS
Arms exports, 1985–1989 ($ billions)

CAN — 1.1
SPA — 1.1
NET — 1.8
SWE — 1.8
ITA — 2.0
GER — 5.0
CHINA — 6.9
UK — 7.7
FRA — 15.8
USA — 52.9
USSR — $66.2

Other methods

THOSE OLD DOLLARS FOR PEACE
Total foreign aid ($ millions)

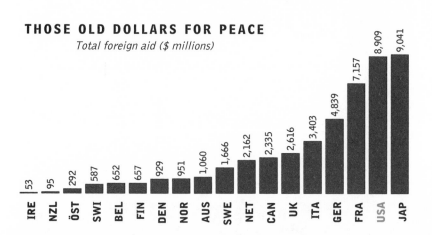

IRE	NZL	ÖST	SWI	BEL	FIN	DEN	NOR	AUS	SWE	NET	CAN	UK	ITA	GER	FRA	USA	JAP
53	95	292	587	652	657	929	951	1,060	1,666	2,162	2,335	2,616	3,403	4,839	7,157	8,909	9,041

YOUR SHARE
Foreign aid per capita ($)

SWE	DEN	NET	FIN	FRA	NOR	CAN	SWI	GER	JAP	BEL	AUS	ITA	UK	ÖST	USA	NZL	IRE
$196	181	146	132	127	92	89	87	78	73	66	63	59	46	38	36	28	15

PEACEKEEPING FORCE
Annual United Nations contribution ($)

USA	$212,875,525	SPA	17,285,493	NOR	4,598,112
JAP	92,302,828	NET	14,816,137	FIN	4,257,511
USSR	86,853,215	AUS	14,134,935	GRE	3,746,610
GER	70,334,074	E.GER	11,324,978	TUR	2,895,108
FRA	54,240,684	SWE	10,643,777	NZL	2,043,606
UK	41,383,003	BEL	10,047,725	IRE	1,532,704
ITA	32,271,930	ÖST	6,301,116	POR	1,432,704
CAN	26,055,965	DEN	6,130,816	LUX	425,752

The U.S. has long held the top spot on the list of donors of foreign aid—that is to say, financial assistance for the purpose of promoting economic development. But in recent years, Japan has taken over. In 1990, the U.S. jealously guarded its claim on aid supremacy by including in its tally forgiveness of $1.3 billion in loans to Egypt—money the Egyptians used to buy American arms.

Throughout the 1980s, the Reagan administration withheld large portions of America's dues to the United Nations because of its anger over what it called the "anti-American" policies of the world body. The Bush administration only recently began payment of the overdue U.S. debt after it perceived a softening in attitude toward the United States by the U.N.'s member states.

And the winner is...

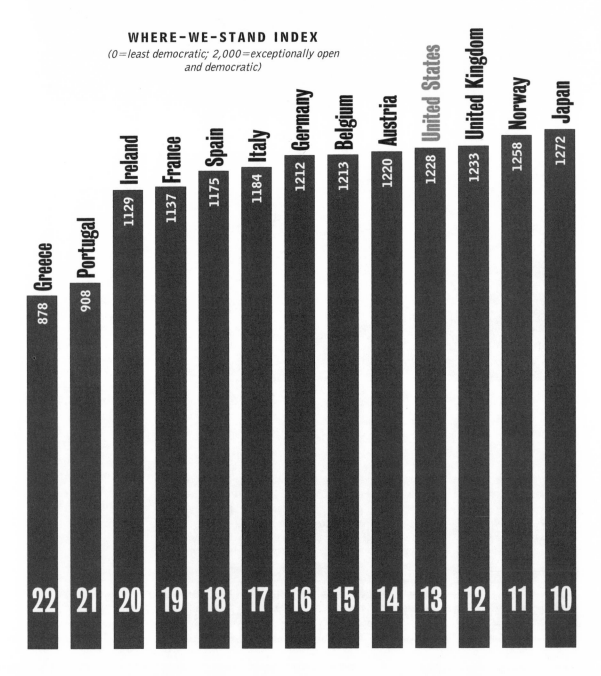

WHERE-WE-STAND INDEX

(0=least democratic; 2,000=exceptionally open and democratic)

Greece 878 — 22
Portugal 908 — 21
Ireland 1129 — 20
France 1137 — 19
Spain 1175 — 18
Italy 1184 — 17
Germany 1212 — 16
Belgium 1213 — 15
Austria 1220 — 14
United States 1228 — 13
United Kingdom 1233 — 12
Norway 1258 — 11
Japan 1272 — 10

Australia

Luxembourg — 1273 — 9

Switzerland — 1286 — 8

New Zealand — 1291 — 7

Sweden — 1292 — 6

Denmark — 1301 — 5

Canada — 1339 — 4

Finland — 1366 — 3

Netherlands — 1367 — 2

1397 — 1

The U.S. may still be the leader of the free world, but the indicators say that Australia is the freest nation. Not only is it one of the few nations (along with the U.S.) to have avoided monarchs and despots this century, but its permanent government, its bureaucracy, is among the smallest, and its overall government spending as a percent of GDP among the lowest in the world. It has been free of terrorism and has limited its involvement in military conflicts and defense spending. Perhaps most important, and most indicative of the freedom it offers, there are more foreign-born citizens in Australia than anywhere else—indeed, it appears to be one of the world's most popular refuges.

THE BEST LOVERS

Who lives with whom?

The twentieth century has been marked by constantly shifting national borders, the result of wars, revolutions, and ethnic and nationalistic divisions. But the most significant dislocation of the century may turn out to be the breakdown of family borders.

The pressures on marriage have been substantially the same in the U.S. and Europe. Education, careers, birth control, and the high cost of owning a home and starting a family have led couples to delay marriage. The need to be married itself—marriage as a social-welfare unit—has vastly diminished, as has the importance of childbearing. As for divorce, laws have been liberalized, and the opprobrium that once accompanied it has all but disappeared. While the U.S. has certainly been the world leader in the dismantling of the marital unit, its divorce rates have leveled off while Europe's continue to rise.

The new relationship freedoms have meant drastic shifts not only in mores, customs, and sensibilities, but in demography too. Family size has been cut in half throughout most of the industrial world. Divorce rates have skyrocketed almost everywhere. Single person households have become one of the key social and economic forces. The family, as a reliable social unit, is as outdated as village life.

Almost everywhere in the industrial world, people live differently from their parents—and more similarly to one another. Quite possibly, changing relationships and demographics have done as much for integrating cultures as any other single development in the history of man. Indeed, the continuing struggle to forge new and workable sexual and family relationships has become one of the defining issues of our time, in many ways taking the place of religious and political struggles.

In large measure, the 2,000-year primacy of the Roman Catholic Church in Western life was swept away by relationship issues—divorce, sex, birth control—in less than two decades.

Now, with the dismantling of the family ideal complete, the drama revolves around what will take its place—because societies seem to need an entity between the individual and the government that can nurture young and care for old, and because the free world turns out to be a very lonely place.

Myth:
Americans don't get married anymore.

Reality:
Americans get married over and over again.

Between marriage and divorce

WHO'S STILL GETTING MARRIED?

That world...
Marriage rate per 1,000 people, 1960

Japan	14.5
United States	14.1
Germany	13.9
Netherlands	12.7
Canada	12.4
Denmark	12.2
Italy	11.7
United Kingdom	11.5
France	11.3
Sweden	10.2

...and this
Marriage rate per 1,000 people, 1990

United States	15.1
United Kingdom	10.6
Canada	10.2
Denmark	9.0
Germany	8.7
Netherlands	8.7
Japan	8.6
Italy	7.5
France	7.3
Sweden	7.2

Multiple marriages keep the U.S. wedding rate high.

Between marriage and divorce

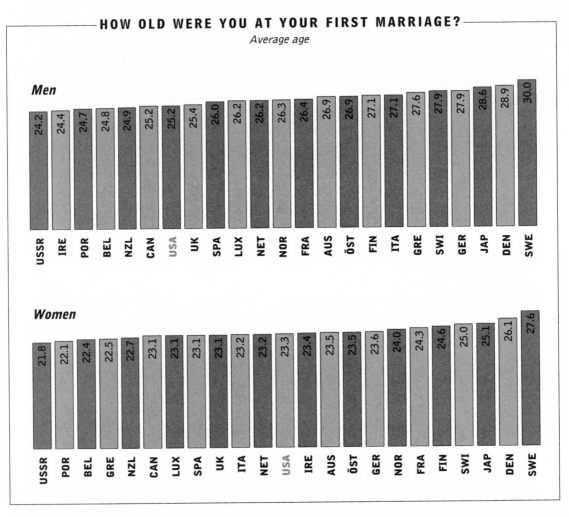

HOW OLD WERE YOU AT YOUR FIRST MARRIAGE?
Average age

Men

USSR	IRE	POR	BEL	NZL	CAN	USA	UK	SPA	LUX	NET	NOR	FRA	AUS	ÖST	FIN	ITA	GRE	SWI	GER	JAP	DEN	SWE
24.2	24.4	24.7	24.8	24.9	25.2	25.2	25.4	26.0	26.2	26.2	26.3	26.4	26.9	26.9	27.1	27.1	27.6	27.9	27.9	28.6	28.9	30.0

Women

USSR	POR	BEL	GRE	NZL	CAN	LUX	SPA	UK	ITA	NET	USA	IRE	AUS	ÖST	GER	NOR	FRA	FIN	SWI	JAP	DEN	SWE
21.8	22.1	22.4	22.5	22.7	23.1	23.1	23.1	23.1	23.2	23.2	23.3	23.4	23.5	23.5	23.6	24.0	24.3	24.6	25.0	25.1	26.1	27.6

HOW BIG IS THE AGE GAP?
Average age difference between spouses (years)

Greece	5.1	Spain	2.9	Norway	2.3
Germany	4.3	Switzerland	2.9	United Kingdom	2.3
Italy	3.9	Denmark	2.8	Australia	2.2
Japan	3.5	Finland	2.5	New Zealand	2.2
Austria	3.4	Belgium	2.4	Canada	2.1
Luxembourg	3.1	Sweden	2.4	France	2.1
Netherlands	3.0	Soviet Union	2.4	United States	1.9

FLEETING CHANCES

Men
30-year-olds who are unmarried (%)

Country	%
Sweden	47.1%
Denmark	35.5
United States	30.8
Finland	29.7
New Zealand	27.3
Norway	27.2
Switzerland	26.4
France	24.5
Germany	24.5
Austria	24.1
Netherlands	22.6
United Kingdom	22.2
Australia	19.4
Ireland	16.2
Spain	14.9
Italy	14.8
Japan	13.9

Women
30-year-olds who are unmarried (%)

Country	%
Sweden	60.0%
Denmark	48.5
Finland	39.2
Germany	37.5
Norway	37.2
United States	33.8
Switzerland	33.5
Austria	31.4
New Zealand	31.1
Netherlands	30.8
Japan	29.8
France	29.3
United Kingdom	28.7
Ireland	24.2
Australia	23.8
Greece	21.1
Italy	20.7

HOW MANY TIMES?
Percent of people who get married twice or more

SPA	IRE	ITA	POR	FRA	SWI	BEL	NET	JAP	GER	CAN	SWE	UK	USA
1.1	1.5	2.1	4.9	11.4	12.7	15.0	16.6	16.9	17.4	17.9	20.6	23.7	32.5%

MOST REMARRIAGES: THE U.S.

In family matters, Japan is the most conservative of the major industrial nations. Divorce is rare, single mothers still anomalous. Marriage remains an expectation of adult life. It is seen as a patriotic duty, important to the nation's moral and economic well-being. The Japanese believe that Western marriage is such a precarious proposition because it rests on the transitory state of passion and love. Indeed, Japanese does not contain the word *love*, merely *like* (*suki desu*) and *like a lot* (*dai suki desu*). Arranged marriage (*miai kekkon*) remains a common practice.

"A woman is expected to marry in her early or mid-twenties, have children and run the household. Around the age of 30, 'Miss' assumes a negative connotation."
—*Michiko Yamamoto,* Asahi Journal

Still, there has been a steady decline in the fertility rate, and women are marrying at an older age, causing Japanese politicians to despair of the younger generation.

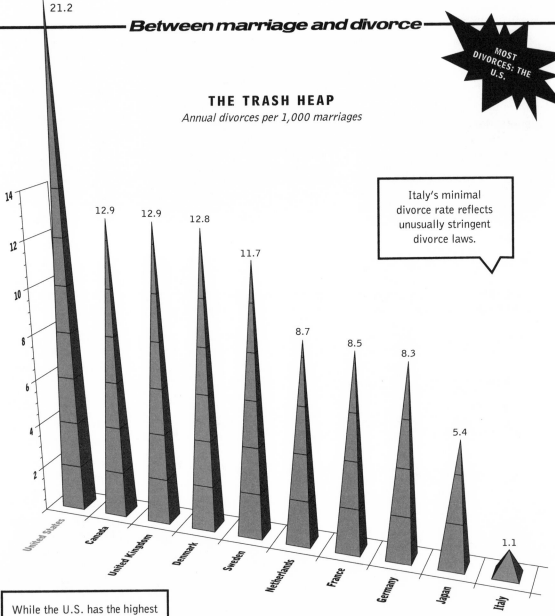

Between marriage and divorce

MOST DIVORCES: THE U.S.

THE TRASH HEAP
Annual divorces per 1,000 marriages

21.2 — United States
12.9 — Canada
12.9 — United Kingdom
12.8 — Denmark
11.7 — Sweden
8.7 — Netherlands
8.5 — France
8.3 — Germany
5.4 — Japan
1.1 — Italy

Italy's minimal divorce rate reflects unusually stringent divorce laws.

While the U.S. has the highest divorce rate in the world, it also has among the highest number of people who disapprove of divorce.

WHAT GOD HATH JOINED
Percent who say divorce is never justified

Belgium	28 %	Japan	21	United Kingdom	14
Spain	28	Italy	21	France	13
United States	22	Canada	19	West Germany	13
		Netherlands	19	Denmark	11

HOW MUCH LONGER?
Average length of a bad marriage (years)

Italy	9	Finland	4
New Zealand	7	France	4
Portugal	7	Greece	4
Belgium	6	United Kingdom	3
Germany	5	Sweden	3
Iceland	5	Switzerland	3
Norway	5	Austria	2
Australia	4	Netherlands	2
Denmark	4	United States	2

SEVEN-YEAR ITCH
Percent of divorces occurring within seven years

Japan	75%
United States	72
Austria	52
Iceland	50
Denmark	45
Greece	45
France	44
Luxembourg	40
Australia	39
United Kingdom	39
Germany	39
Sweden	39
Switzerland	38
Finland	37
Netherlands	37
Portugal	37
Norway	35
Belgium	34
New Zealand	31

Demographers argue that divorce rates, no matter how high, almost always understate levels of family breakup. Husband-and-wife separations aren't covered by divorce figures, nor are breakups of unmarried couples.

The divorce curve in America flattened out in the early 1980s and now may be starting a gentle descent. The first dip appeared in 1986. According to Arthur Norton of the U.S. Census Bureau, the oldest baby-boomers are now beyond the peak-divorce-rate age. They have made their mark on American history, though, as the generation with the highest number of marriage breakups. One-third of women between the ages of 35 and 39 have been divorced at least once. Even a turnaround would still leave the U.S. at the top of the world's divorce charts.

Myth:
Americans believe in marriage.

Reality:
They believe in short marriages.

233

Going it alone

The single fastest-growing demographic groups across the industrial nations are people living alone—men and women, young and old. And it is not just delays in marriage and longer and more independent widowhoods causing the growth in "aloneness." The most significant growth in single-person households is occurring among the middle-aged—the 45-to-64-year-old set.

Divorce is a significant factor, but so is the aging of the baby-boomers—young people who lived alone are now growing old. Demographers and planners speculate about a world society no longer based on the family unit. Who will care for the elderly? How will traditional family values be learned? And how will the population base be maintained? These are the looming issues for the West in the twenty-first century.

ONLY YOU

Percent of population living alone in 1960 (■) and in 1990 (■)

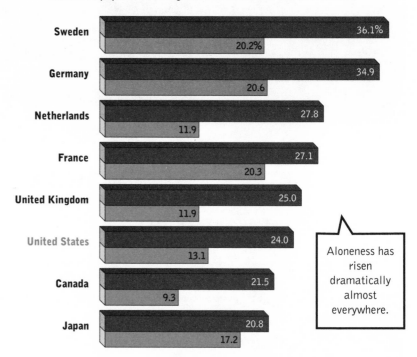

	1990	1960
Sweden	36.1%	20.2%
Germany	34.9	20.6
Netherlands	27.8	11.9
France	27.1	20.3
United Kingdom	25.0	11.9
United States	24.0	13.1
Canada	21.5	9.3
Japan	20.8	17.2

> Aloneness has risen dramatically almost everywhere.

SINGLED OUT

Percent of population over 18 and single

Sweden	53%		United States	43
Denmark	49		United Kingdom	43
Finland	49		Luxembourg	40
Austria	48		Spain	40
Iceland	47		Italy	39
Germany	46		Australia	38
Ireland	46		Belgium	38
France	45		Canada	38
Norway	45		New Zealand	38
Switzerland	45		Japan	37
Netherlands	43		Portugal	36
Soviet Union	43		Greece	34

POSTMODERN MATURITY

Percent of people 65 and older who live alone

In Japan, the extended family is still home to the older generation.

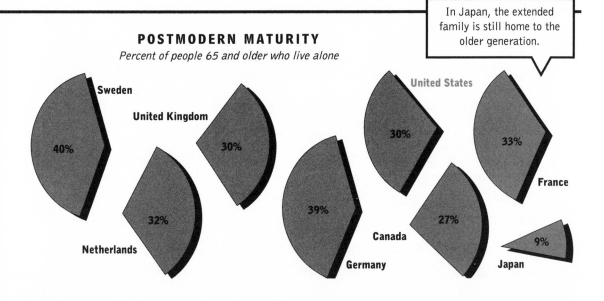

Sweden — 40%

United Kingdom — 30%

Netherlands — 32%

Germany — 39%

United States — 30%

Canada — 27%

France — 33%

Japan — 9%

ON MY OWN

Percent of women over 30 who have never married

13.3 % — United States

9.6 — Canada

9.1 — Japan

8.4 — Australia

8.0 — New Zealand

ALONE AGAIN

Percent of people who are widowed

Germany	8.8 %
Austria	8.8
Japan	7.7
Belgium	7.6
United Kingdom	7.3
France	7.0
Denmark	7.0
Italy	6.9
Sweden	6.8
Finland	6.8
Switzerland	6.1
Spain	5.9
United States	5.7
Netherlands	5.7
Australia	5.1
New Zealand	5.0
Canada	4.9
Ireland	3.7

235

The family

KIDS: 1960 VERSUS 1990
Average number of children per family in 1960 (■) and in 1990 (■)

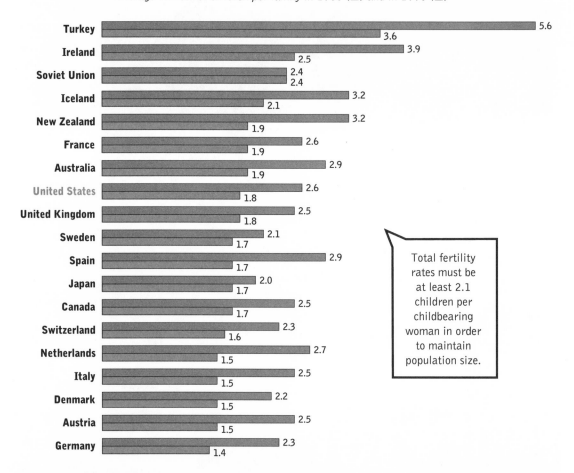

Country	1960	1990
Turkey	5.6	3.6
Ireland	3.9	2.5
Soviet Union	2.4	2.4
Iceland	3.2	2.1
New Zealand	3.2	1.9
France	2.6	1.9
Australia	2.9	1.9
United States	2.6	1.8
United Kingdom	2.5	1.8
Sweden	2.1	1.7
Spain	2.9	1.7
Japan	2.0	1.7
Canada	2.5	1.7
Switzerland	2.3	1.6
Netherlands	2.7	1.5
Italy	2.5	1.5
Denmark	2.2	1.5
Austria	2.5	1.5
Germany	2.3	1.4

> Total fertility rates must be at least 2.1 children per childbearing woman in order to maintain population size.

FULL HOUSE
Average number of people per household

Soviet Union	4.0	Portugal	2.9	United States	2.6
Ireland	3.7	Canada	2.8	Finland	2.6
Spain	3.5	Italy	2.8	Netherlands	2.5
Japan	3.1	Luxembourg	2.8	Switzerland	2.5
Greece	3.1	Austria	2.7	Denmark	2.3
Australia	3.0	France	2.6	Germany	2.3
New Zealand	2.9	United Kingdom	2.6	Sweden	2.2

MARRIED WITH KIDS

Households consisting of a married couple and children (%)

Japan	39.2 %
Netherlands	38.5
France	36.2
Canada	32.3
Germany	31.4
United Kingdom	28.0
United States	27.0
Sweden	21.7
Denmark	19.9

MARRIED WITHOUT KIDS

Households consisting of a married couple and no children (%)

United Kingdom	36.0 %
Sweden	33.1
Canada	32.2
United States	29.9
Japan	28.2
France	27.3
Germany	22.9
Netherlands	21.5
Denmark	21.1

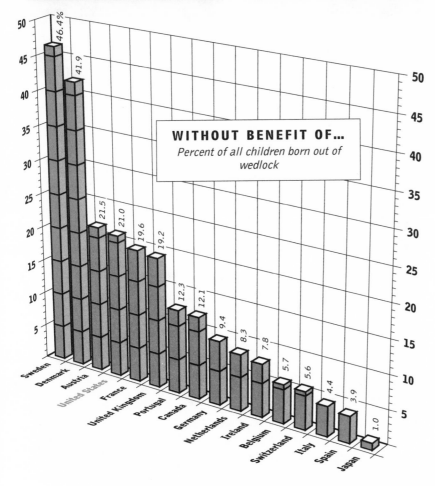

WITHOUT BENEFIT OF...

Percent of all children born out of wedlock

Sweden 46.4% • Denmark 41.9 • Austria 21.5 • United States 21.0 • France 19.6 • United Kingdom 19.2 • Portugal 12.3 • Canada 12.1 • Germany 9.4 • Netherlands 8.3 • Ireland 7.8 • Belgium 5.7 • Switzerland 5.6 • Italy 4.4 • Spain 3.9 • Japan 1.0

The family as it existed 50 years ago—multiple generations living in close proximity—no longer exists. The family as it existed twenty years ago—mother, father, two-plus children—is now merely one among numerous other living arrangements. Currently, the most common family unit in the U.S. is two adults living together, married or not, without children under the age of eighteen.

Unwed cohabitation is highest in Scandinavia. It is so prevalent that more and more cohabitants are included with married couples in official statistics. A recent survey showed that virtually all Swedes now live together before getting married.

That is, if they get married. Twenty-five percent of Swedish live-togethers never do. According to sociologist David Popenoe, "What has happened to the family in Sweden over the past few decades lends strong support to the proposition that as the welfare state advances, the family declines." Says Borje Dernulf of Sweden's Central Statistical Office, ➡

―――――――――――――― *The family* ――――――――――――――

*TOP SEXISTS:
THE FRENCH*

"We have so many couples living together that we have a problem defining what we mean by a family." There are now almost as many children born in Sweden to unmarried cohabitants as to married couples.

In 1988, Denmark became the first country to grant legal marital status to gay couples, conferring all rights and obligations it gives more traditional husbands and wives, including divorce and alimony.

The U.S. still has the highest number of single parents. This is not only because of its high divorce rates but also because of the striking prevalence of unmarried teenage mothers—a phenomenon that occurs nowhere else in the developed world.

Myth:
Europeans are socially liberated.

Reality:
Europeans still believe in traditional women's roles.

BAREFOOT AND PREGNANT
Percent who think women need children to be fullfilled

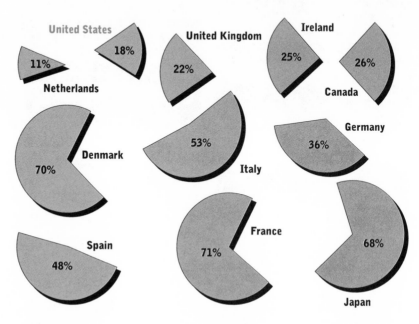

United States 11%
United States 18%
United Kingdom 22%
Ireland 25%
Canada 26%
Netherlands
Denmark 70%
Italy 53%
Germany 36%
Spain 48%
France 71%
Japan 68%

MAMA'S FAMILY
Percent of households headed by women

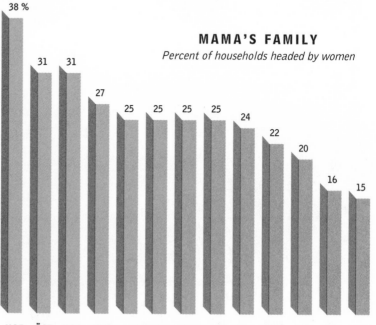

NOR	ÖST	USA	SWE	AUS	CAN	SWI	UK	NZL	FRA	ITA	SPA	JAP
38 %	31	31	27	25	25	25	25	24	22	20	16	15

CHILD SUPPORT
Percent of all families with only one parent

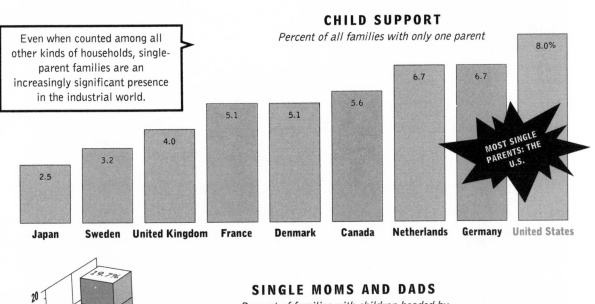

Even when counted among all other kinds of households, single-parent families are an increasingly significant presence in the industrial world.

8.0%

6.7   6.7

MOST SINGLE PARENTS: THE U.S.

5.6

5.1   5.1

4.0

3.2

2.5

Japan   Sweden   United Kingdom   France   Denmark   Canada   Netherlands   Germany   United States

SINGLE MOMS AND DADS
Percent of families with children headed by a single male, or by a single female

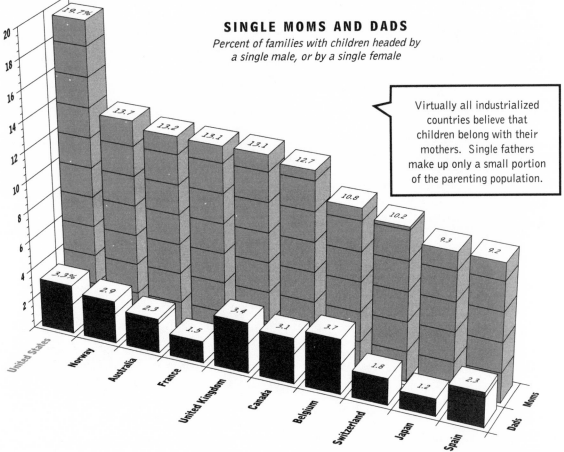

Virtually all industrialized countries believe that children belong with their mothers. Single fathers make up only a small portion of the parenting population.

19.7%

13.7   13.2   13.1   13.1   12.7   10.8   10.2   9.3   9.2

3.3%   2.9   2.3   1.5   3.4   3.1   3.7   1.8   1.2   2.3

United States   Norway   Australia   France   United Kingdom   Canada   Belgium   Switzerland   Japan   Spain

Dads   Moms

239

The family

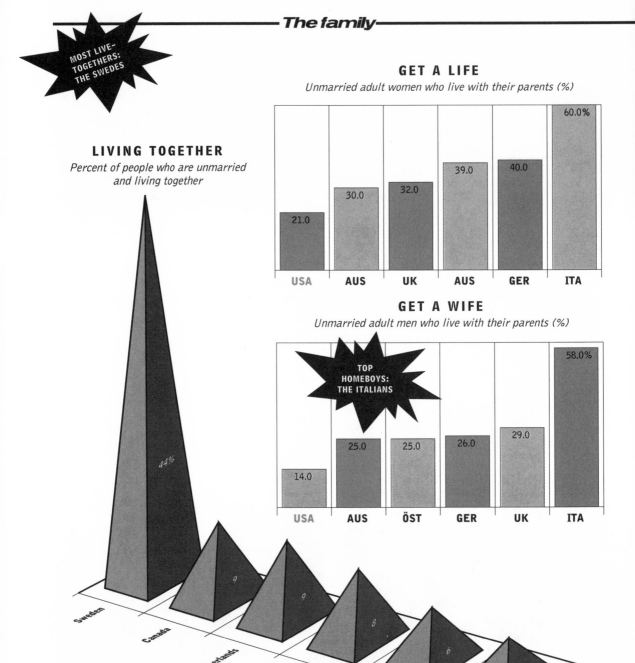

MOST LIVE-
TOGETHERS:
THE SWEDES

GET A LIFE
Unmarried adult women who live with their parents (%)

60.0%

40.0

39.0

32.0

30.0

21.0

USA | AUS | UK | AUS | GER | ITA

LIVING TOGETHER
*Percent of people who are unmarried
and living together*

GET A WIFE
Unmarried adult men who live with their parents (%)

TOP
HOMEBOYS:
THE ITALIANS

58.0%

29.0

26.0

25.0

25.0

14.0

USA | AUS | ÖST | GER | UK | ITA

44%

Sweden

Canada · 9

Netherlands · 9

France · 8

United Kingdom · 6

United States · 5

REAL MEN SAUTÉ

*Percent of married men who help
with the cooking*

United Kingdom	26%
Soviet Union	25
Australia	24
United States	22
East Germany	20
Canada	19
Finland	18
Netherlands	17
France	13
Norway	11
Belgium	6
Germany	6
Japan	4

A DAD WITH A FACE

*Percent of married men who help
with the kids*

Norway	30%
United States	28
East Germany	25
Soviet Union	25
Canada	24
United Kingdom	24
Finland	23
Australia	22
Netherlands	21
Belgium	19
Germany	16
France	15
Japan	6

EXTENDED FAMILIES

Households with grandmothers (■) and/or grandfathers (▨) living in (%)

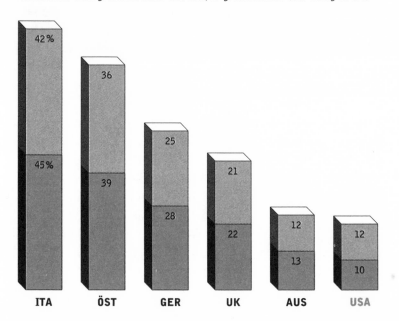

| ITA | ÖST | GER | UK | AUS | USA |

Detailed studies in Sweden, the country with the highest rate of cohabitating couples, show a breakup rate among live-togethers almost three times the rate for officially married couples. Such studies indicate that the real rate of family dissolution is probably twice as great as official divorce statistics say it is.

In a study on U.S. marriage trends, Arthur Norton and co-author Jane Moorman predict a continuing drop in the number of women who marry. In 1975, 87 percent of American women in their late twenties were married. Today, that number is 74 percent. In the near future, they say, lifetime marriage rates for women will not exceed 90 percent, five percentage points lower than the historic average.

Sex...who does what to whom?

It is difficult to appreciate that little more than a generation ago, the accepted standard in every industrial country was that only married people should have sex.

"Had we had more information about sexuality, we would have been able to intervene with AIDS in a much more rigorous and intelligent way," says WHO's Manuel Carballo, head of a global survey on human sexuality. While most of the traditionally puritanical regimes of the Third World have agreed to participate in the study, the U.S. has not. Secretary of Health and Human Services Louis Sullivan has problems with "the tone and contents of the questions." Among them: "Do you think your wife (or husband) has had sex with anyone else in the last 12 months?"

Myth:
The Dutch are a cold people.

Reality:
They're hot.

Whereas sexual repressiveness once defined an advanced society, over the past generation it is sexual freedom that has come to indicate wealthier and better-educated societies. Modern sexuality is one of the forces that has cast aside religious, cultural, nationalistic, and family constraints.

It would even appear that as one measure of progress, advanced societies have sex frequently and slowly, while poor societies, despite higher birth rates, do it less often and get less pleasure.

A recent study of sexuality in China found minimal foreplay—a possible result, the study speculated, of the fact that most Chinese keep their clothes on during sex. Only a third of urban women and 25 percent of rural women claimed to "very often" feel pleasure during intercourse. "We don't know how to estimate, but we think that female orgasm is very rare," said the study's author, Professor Liu Dalin.

Repression in the Soviet Union and East-bloc nations was not only political but sexual as well. "If you want to imagine the atmosphere in the Soviet Union, imagine a world before Kinsey—even before Freud," says Igor Kon, one of the few people in the former Soviet Union actually studying sex.

Sex has eclipsed morality and politics; it has now become a health issue. We are threatened not only by AIDS but also—at least in the U.S.—by the massive social, economic, and public-health repercussions of children having children.

Preferences and proclivities

WHO'S DOING IT?

Percent of men and women having premarital sex

Men

Finland	81%
United States	80
Germany	78
United Kingdom	77
France	77
Norway	75
Netherlands	71
Belgium	37
Japan	30

NOT DOING IT: THE JAPANESE

HOW OFTEN?

Times per month

Netherlands	8.5
Germany	6.9
Japan	4.9
United States	4.0
Finland	3.8

Women

Germany	83%
Finland	83
Netherlands	80
France	77
United Kingdom	76
Norway	67
United States	42
Belgium	39
Japan	14

Preferences and proclivities

Almost all epidemiologists—and certainly everyone involved in AIDS research—agree that there is an urgent need for more up-to-date information on sexual behavior. What little information there is often comes from too-small samplings, many conducted by popular magazines or other nonspecialists. The most definitive—or most widely cited, anyway—data is still that compiled in the late 1940s by Alfred Kinsey. While this was a breakthrough study, it was not based for the most part on accepted sampling methods. Most of the Kinsey respondents were white middle-class American men who had volunteered for the research—they were not a random sampling. And obviously Kinsey predated what has been the most dramatic era of sexual change—the era of the pill, the women's movement, the sexual revolution, and AIDS.

WITH HOW MANY?

Percent of people who have had two or more partners in the last twelve months

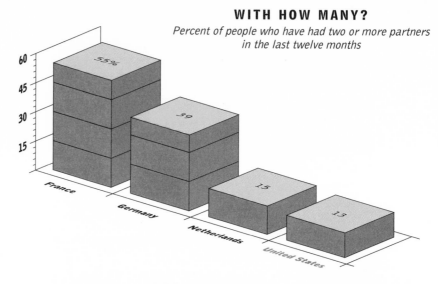

REALITY CHECK

Percent who approve of premarital sex

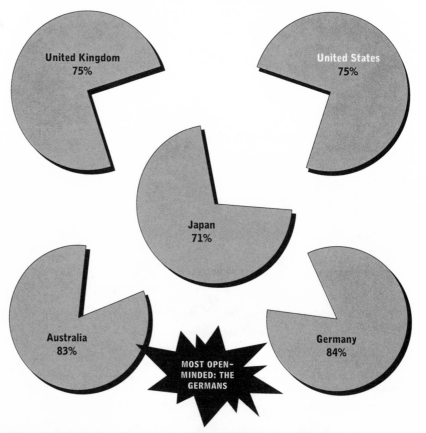

United Kingdom 75%

United States 75%

Japan 71%

Australia 83%

MOST OPEN-MINDED: THE GERMANS

Germany 84%

MOST ONANISTIC: JAPANESE MEN, GERMAN WOMEN

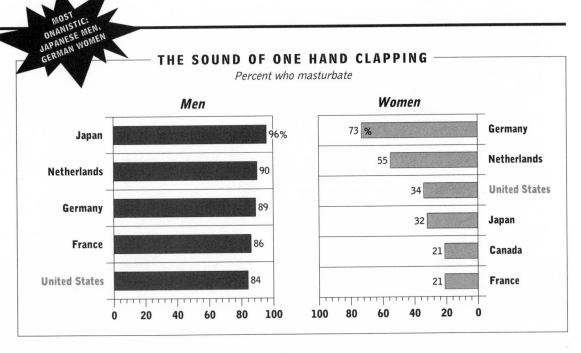

THE SOUND OF ONE HAND CLAPPING

Percent who masturbate

Men

Japan	96%
Netherlands	90
Germany	89
France	86
United States	84

Women

Germany	73%
Netherlands	55
United States	34
Japan	32
Canada	21
France	21

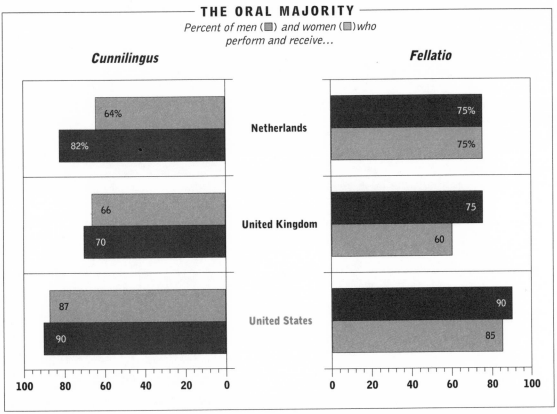

THE ORAL MAJORITY

Percent of men (■) and women (■) who perform and receive...

Cunnilingus

	Netherlands	
	64%	
	82%	

	United Kingdom	
	66	
	70	

	United States	
	87	
	90	

Fellatio

	Netherlands	
	75%	
	75%	

	United Kingdom	
	75	
	60	

	United States	
	90	
	85	

245

Preferences and proclivities

In 1988 in Georgia, James Moseley was sent to prison for five years for having consensual oral sex with his wife (he served 19 months).

Sodomy is prohibited in 25 states and in the District of Columbia.

In 1990, Donna E. Carrol accepted the state of Wisconsin's plea bargain of 40 hours of community service for her crime of adultery—which is still against the law in almost half of the 50 states.

In the U.K., Parliament passed a bill prohibiting the "promotion of homosexuality" by local governments.

In Poland, Lech Walesa has spoken of his wish to exclude all "moral undesirables" from Poland.

Myth:
America is at the forefront of gay pride.

Reality:
It leads the world in gay scorn.

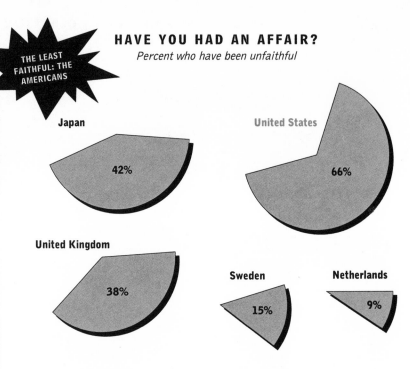

THE LEAST FAITHFUL: THE AMERICANS

HAVE YOU HAD AN AFFAIR?
Percent who have been unfaithful

Japan — 42%

United States — 66%

United Kingdom — 38%

Sweden — 15%

Netherlands — 9%

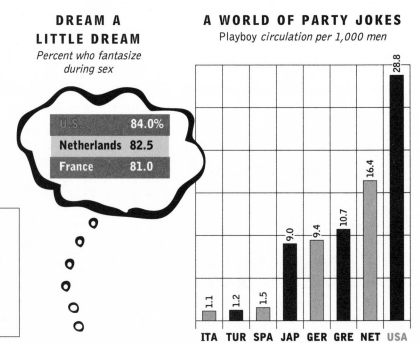

DREAM A LITTLE DREAM
Percent who fantasize during sex

U.S.	84.0%
Netherlands	82.5
France	81.0

A WORLD OF PARTY JOKES
Playboy *circulation per 1,000 men*

ITA	TUR	SPA	JAP	GER	GRE	NET	USA
1.1	1.2	1.5	9.0	9.4	10.7	16.4	28.8

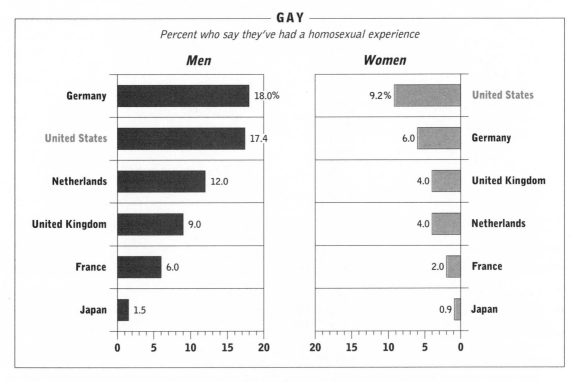

GAY

Percent who say they've had a homosexual experience

Men

Country	Percent
Germany	18.0%
United States	17.4
Netherlands	12.0
United Kingdom	9.0
France	6.0
Japan	1.5

Women

Country	Percent
United States	9.2%
Germany	6.0
United Kingdom	4.0
Netherlands	4.0
France	2.0
Japan	0.9

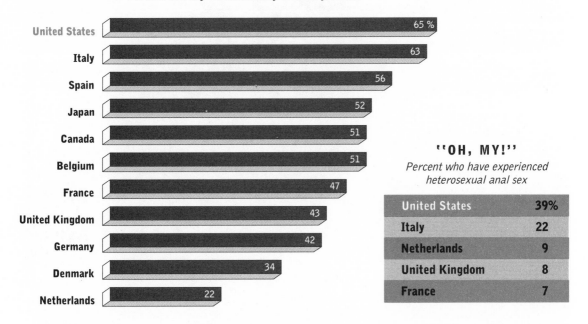

HATE-EROS

Percent who say homosexuality is never justified

Country	Percent
United States	65 %
Italy	63
Spain	56
Japan	52
Canada	51
Belgium	51
France	47
United Kingdom	43
Germany	42
Denmark	34
Netherlands	22

"OH, MY!"

Percent who have experienced heterosexual anal sex

Country	Percent
United States	39%
Italy	22
Netherlands	9
United Kingdom	8
France	7

Safe sex

Progress toward safer sexual practices depends on information and educational programs. While such information programs are widespread in the American gay community, they have barely reached the high-risk poor population in the U.S. In Europe and Japan, indications are that while information is widely available from saturation media campaigns, the general public has not yet been convinced that AIDS is an imminent threat, since infection rates are still relatively low.

Yet business in the famous bordellos of Hamburg's Reeperbahn is down 60 percent since 1985. The best-known spot, the 75-year-old Café-Hotel Lausen, sold its street window to McDonald's.

Myth:
AIDS has caused a radical change in sexual behavior.

Reality:
The change has just begun.

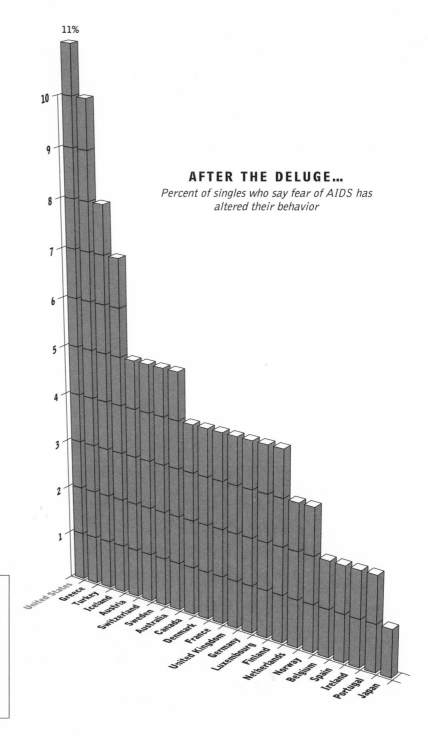

AFTER THE DELUGE...
Percent of singles who say fear of AIDS has altered their behavior

PRICIEST CONDOMS: ITALY

————THE LIFESAVER————

A month's supply
Price of 100 condoms ($)

Italy	$200	Denmark	65
Japan	125	Norway	64
United States	92	Greece	63
Switzerland	92	Netherlands	59
Spain	89	France	58
Canada	86	Portugal	57
Belgium	81	Sweden	51
Germany	76	Finland	50
New Zealand	75	United Kingdom	39
Austria	71	Turkey	36
Ireland	70	Australia	31

Enough to go around
Annual condom sales per adult male

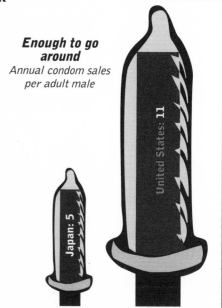

United States: 11

Japan: 5

DO YOU GET IT?
Percent who say AIDS is a concern

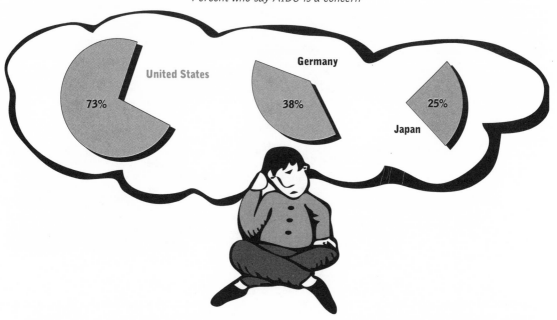

United States 73%

Germany 38%

Japan 25%

——————Teens—who's just saying no?——

A crucial distinction among nations is whether they regard teen sexuality as a health and educational issue or as a moral and political one. In the U.S., the latter point of view has resulted in strikingly higher rates of teen pregnancies, abortions, and maternity—along with the ensuing effects on educational and poverty levels. More even than AIDS, teen pregnancy may be America's most pervasive and threatening public-health problem.

A study by the Alan Guttmacher Institute of six countries—the U.S., Canada, England, France, the Netherlands, and Sweden—found that America's fundamentally different attitudes toward sex had implications for teen sexuality: "In the United States, sex tends to be treated as a special topic, set apart from normal life. At the same time, there is much ambivalence: sex is romantic but also sinful and dirty; it is flaunted but also something to be hidden. This ambivalence is less apparent in the ➤➤

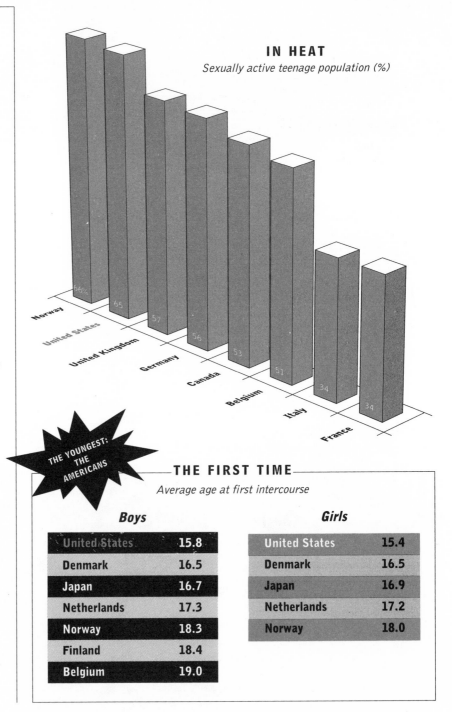

IN HEAT
Sexually active teenage population (%)

Norway 66%
United States 65
United Kingdom 57
Germany 56
Canada 53
Belgium 51
Italy 34
France 34

THE YOUNGEST: THE AMERICANS

THE FIRST TIME
Average age at first intercourse

Boys		*Girls*	
United States	15.8	United States	15.4
Denmark	16.5	Denmark	16.5
Japan	16.7	Japan	16.9
Netherlands	17.3	Netherlands	17.2
Norway	18.3	Norway	18.0
Finland	18.4		
Belgium	19.0		

MOST TRUTHFUL: THE DUTCH

WAS IT GOOD FOR YOU?

Percent who rate first coitus pleasurable

	Boys	Girls
Germany	83%	56%
France	74	50
United Kingdom	72	52
United States	68	59
Belgium	41	41
Netherlands	31	28

ABSTAINERS

Percent who by age 20 have not experienced intercourse

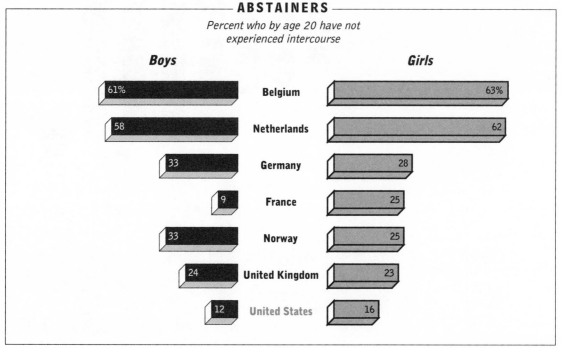

	Boys	Girls
Belgium	61%	63%
Netherlands	58	62
Germany	33	28
France	9	25
Norway	33	25
United Kingdom	24	23
United States	12	16

Teens—who's just saying no?

European countries, where matter-of-fact attitudes seem to be more prevalent....It stands to reason that where sexuality as a whole carries less emotional baggage, sex and pregnancy among teenagers are likely to be dealt with more realistically." The study concludes that "society's openness about sex may be an especially important factor influencing adolescent fertility and pregnancy."

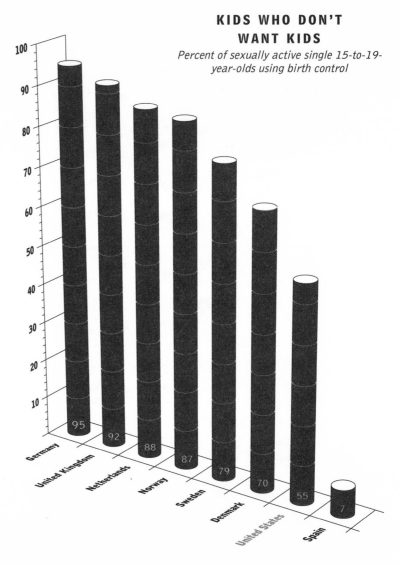

KIDS WHO DON'T WANT KIDS

Percent of sexually active single 15-to-19-year-olds using birth control

Germany 95
United Kingdom 92
Netherlands 88
Norway 87
Sweden 79
Denmark 70
United States 55
Spain 7

Myth:
No one says no anymore.

Reality:
The Japanese still do.

INTERNATIONAL PERIODS
Average age of menarche

Finland	13.3		United Kingdom	13
Norway	13.2		Japan	12.7
France	13		United States	12.5
Netherlands	13		Italy	12.1

PAPA DON'T PREACH

Teen pregnancies per 1,000 teenagers

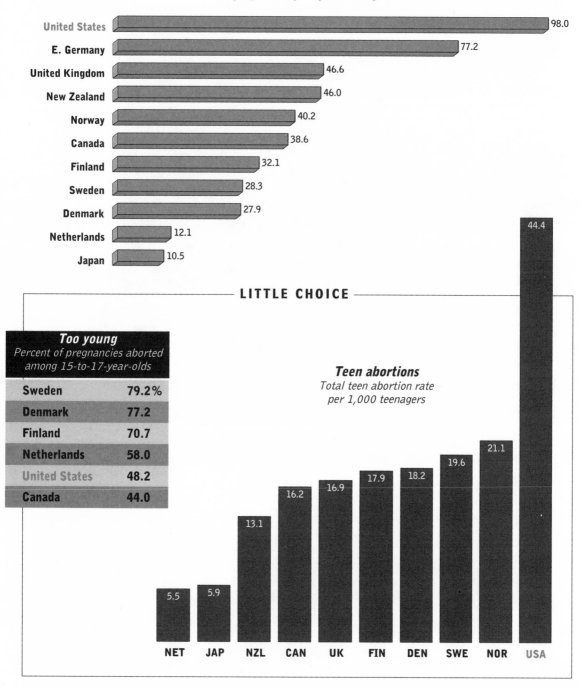

United States	98.0
E. Germany	77.2
United Kingdom	46.6
New Zealand	46.0
Norway	40.2
Canada	38.6
Finland	32.1
Sweden	28.3
Denmark	27.9
Netherlands	12.1
Japan	10.5

LITTLE CHOICE

Too young
Percent of pregnancies aborted among 15-to-17-year-olds

Sweden	79.2%
Denmark	77.2
Finland	70.7
Netherlands	58.0
United States	48.2
Canada	44.0

Teen abortions
Total teen abortion rate per 1,000 teenagers

NET	JAP	NZL	CAN	UK	FIN	DEN	SWE	NOR	USA
5.5	5.9	13.1	16.2	16.9	17.9	18.2	19.6	21.1	44.4

Teens—who's just saying no?

More than 33 percent of all children born outside of marriage are born to teenagers in the United States. In the overwhelming number of cases the father contributes no financial (or any other kind of parental) support. In Sweden, babies born to teenagers account for fewer than 6 percent of all out-of-wedlock births, and in France and Japan, fewer than 10 percent. In Sweden, in only 0.5 percent of all cases did a father not contribute support. More significantly, demographers say that teen birth in the U.S. appears to be less and less restricted to the lowest-income groups. Births to lower-middle-class white 15-to-17-year-olds climbed almost 10 percent between 1986 and 1988. "It's an information gap rather than purely an economic gap," says Stephanie Venture, a demographer at the National Center for Health Statistics.

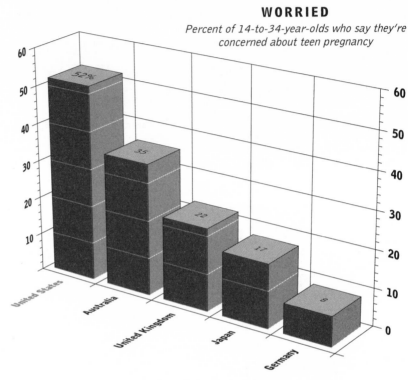

WORRIED
Percent of 14-to-34-year-olds who say they're concerned about teen pregnancy

United States — 52%
Australia — 35
United Kingdom — 22
Japan — 17
Germany — 6

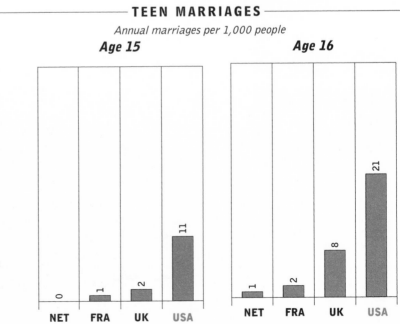

TEEN MARRIAGES
Annual marriages per 1,000 people

Age 15

NET	FRA	UK	USA
0	1	2	11

Age 16

NET	FRA	UK	USA
1	2	8	21

BABY LOVE
Teenage mothers per 1,000 teenagers

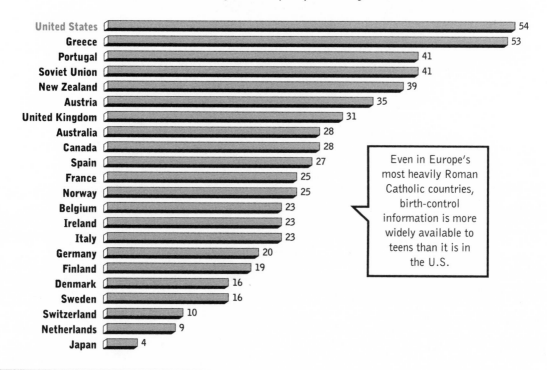

United States	54
Greece	53
Portugal	41
Soviet Union	41
New Zealand	39
Austria	35
United Kingdom	31
Australia	28
Canada	28
Spain	27
France	25
Norway	25
Belgium	23
Ireland	23
Italy	23
Germany	20
Finland	19
Denmark	16
Sweden	16
Switzerland	10
Netherlands	9
Japan	4

> Even in Europe's most heavily Roman Catholic countries, birth-control information is more widely available to teens than it is in the U.S.

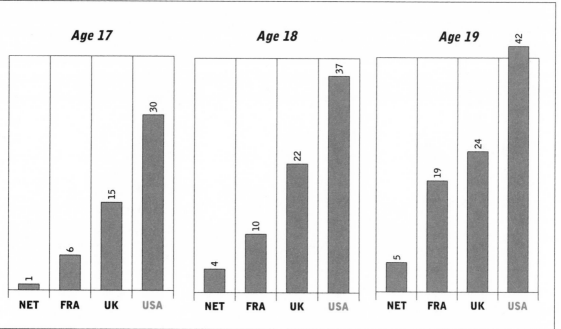

Age 17

NET	FRA	UK	USA
1	6	15	30

Age 18

NET	FRA	UK	USA
4	10	22	37

Age 19

NET	FRA	UK	USA
5	19	24	42

The fetal position

In many ways, the politics of reproduction is a traditional class issue. Reproductive health and knowledge—along with general sexual awareness and sophistication—bear a striking relationship to levels of wealth, age, and education.

The proportion of women of childbearing age who use no method of contraception is significantly higher in the U.S. than in any other major industrial nation. Notably, it was the U.S. that began the modern age of contraception, only to be overtaken and surpassed by the reproductive sophistication of virtually all other Western nations.

"Of...twenty Western countries [studied], the United States has a total fertility rate that falls somewhat above the middle. Its total abortion and pregnancy rates, however, are higher than those of most other Western countries. Because unplanned births as well as abortions are common in the United States, the unplanned pregnancy rate is also relatively high. Fully half of all conceptions are unintended."
—*The Alan Guttmacher Institute*

The higher you are on the socioeconomic ladder, the more likely you are to be knowledgeable about reproductive health and progressive in your thinking about reproductive issues.

It is not a coincidence that the U.S. has far more limited use of contraceptives than most other major industrial nations and that it has been the bloodiest battleground in the fight for reproductive rights. It boasts the largest poor population in the industrial world—people with limited access to birth-control methods and to information about reproduction. And it has two politically active religious groups: Roman Catholics and fundamentalist Protestants.

Europe, which has followed more secular trends in the modern era, has consistently been more tolerant. Indeed, with the development of RU-486, France has stepped to the technological forefront of reproductive health.

It takes only one dose of the drug during the first seven weeks of pregnancy to cause a miscarriage. The ultimate effect will be to make reproductive choice almost entirely a private affair: no hospital or clinic, no abortionist (and no chance of a botched procedure), no protestors. Almost inevitably, abortion will become little more complicated than a home pregnancy test.

Recently, though, anti-abortion groups have been more active in the U.K., Germany, France, Italy, and Spain. European women's groups argue that restrictions on American reproductive rights could fuel the anti-abortion movement in Europe.

The contraceptive societies

CONTRACEPTION

Percent of women who use some form of contraception

SPA	59
DEN	63
JAP	64
FRA	64
POR	66
USA	68
NZL	70
SWI	71
AUS	71
NET	72
CAN	73
SWE	78
ITA	78
GER	78
BEL	81
UK	83%

MISTAKES

Percent of pregnancies unwanted

France	11.3%
Finland	10.2
Denmark	8.6
Belgium	8.4
Canada	7.8
United States	7.4
Sweden	3.1
Spain	2.3

OB-GYN

Annual doctor visits for contraceptive consultations per 1,000 women

France	199
Germany	118
United States	12

The contraceptive societies

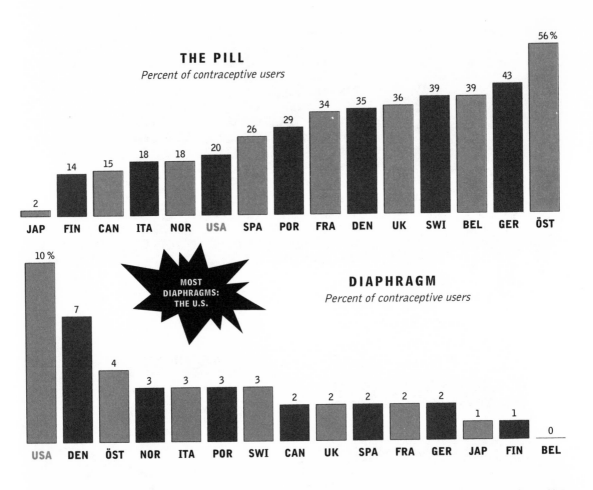

THE PILL
Percent of contraceptive users

JAP	FIN	CAN	ITA	NOR	USA	SPA	POR	FRA	DEN	UK	SWI	BEL	GER	ÖST
2	14	15	18	18	20	26	29	34	35	36	39	39	43	56%

MOST DIAPHRAGMS: THE U.S.

DIAPHRAGM
Percent of contraceptive users

USA	DEN	ÖST	NOR	ITA	POR	SWI	CAN	UK	SPA	FRA	GER	JAP	FIN	BEL
10%	7	4	3	3	3	3	2	2	2	2	2	1	1	0

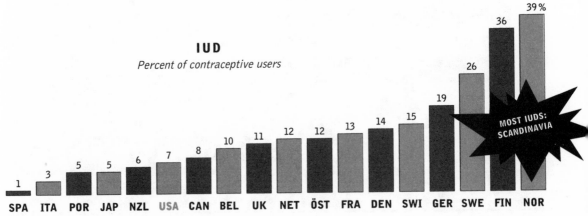

IUD
Percent of contraceptive users

MOST IUDS: SCANDINAVIA

SPA	ITA	POR	JAP	NZL	USA	CAN	BEL	UK	NET	ÖST	FRA	DEN	SWI	GER	SWE	FIN	NOR
1	3	5	5	6	7	8	10	11	12	12	13	14	15	19	26	36	39%

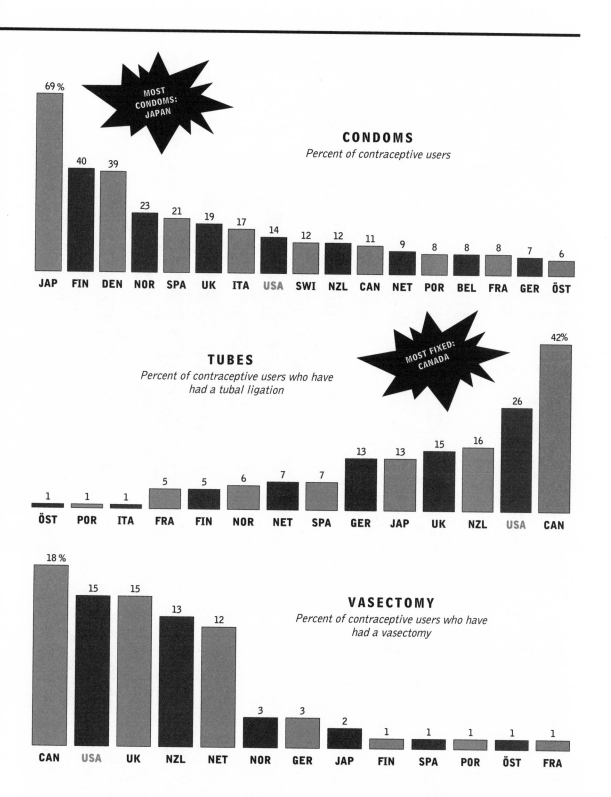

MOST CONDOMS: JAPAN

CONDOMS
Percent of contraceptive users

69 % JAP · 40 FIN · 39 DEN · 23 NOR · 21 SPA · 19 UK · 17 ITA · 14 USA · 12 SWI · 12 NZL · 11 CAN · 9 NET · 8 POR · 8 BEL · 8 FRA · 7 GER · 6 ÖST

TUBES
Percent of contraceptive users who have had a tubal ligation

MOST FIXED: CANADA

1 ÖST · 1 POR · 1 ITA · 5 FRA · 5 FIN · 6 NOR · 7 NET · 7 SPA · 13 GER · 13 JAP · 15 UK · 16 NZL · 26 USA · 42% CAN

VASECTOMY
Percent of contraceptive users who have had a vasectomy

18 % CAN · 15 USA · 15 UK · 13 NZL · 12 NET · 3 NOR · 3 GER · 2 JAP · 1 FIN · 1 SPA · 1 POR · 1 ÖST · 1 FRA

Birthing

In many countries, birth rates are still on the decline. There are few places in the industrialized world where enough babies are being born to replenish the population (on average, each woman needs to give birth to 2.1 children to keep the population stable). Italy's birth rate is near the lowest in the world. Japan's keeps falling, and so does Korea's. But in a few countries, some of them traditional trendsetters, babies are clearly back in style. Sweden now has one of the highest birth rates in Europe (just over 2.1, surpassed only by Iceland and Ireland). Denmark (up from 1.4 to 1.6), Norway (from 1.7 to 1.9), Germany (from 1.3 to 1.4), and the U.S. (almost 2) are all on the rise, with America at its highest point since the end of the baby-boom years. Demographers conjecture that the decline in under-30 mothers has reversed and that women are having babies in shorter intervals. In America, older mothers and young mothers are having babies.

HERE'S...BABY

Number of births per 1,000 people

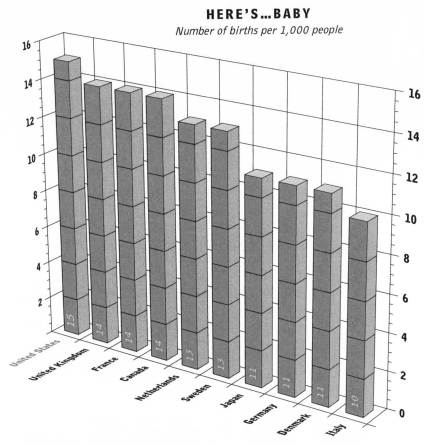

AGE OF CONCEPTION

Average age when a woman conceives

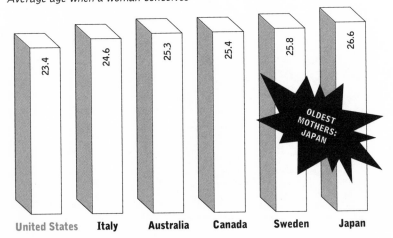

OLDEST MOTHERS: JAPAN

THIRTY–SOMETHING

Percent of women having their first child who are over 30

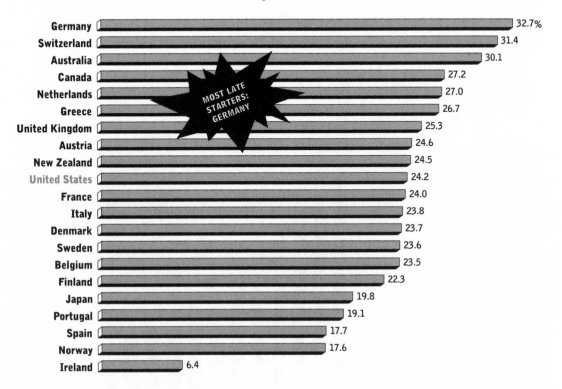

Country	Percent
Germany	32.7%
Switzerland	31.4
Australia	30.1
Canada	27.2
Netherlands	27.0
Greece	26.7
United Kingdom	25.3
Austria	24.6
New Zealand	24.5
United States	24.2
France	24.0
Italy	23.8
Denmark	23.7
Sweden	23.6
Belgium	23.5
Finland	22.3
Japan	19.8
Portugal	19.1
Spain	17.7
Norway	17.6
Ireland	6.4

MOST LATE STARTERS: GERMANY

FROZEN HERITAGE

Number of sperm banks

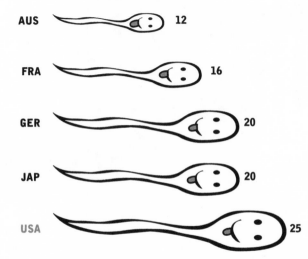

AUS	12
FRA	16
GER	20
JAP	20
USA	25

THE PETRIE DISH

Number of in-vitro-fertilization clinics

United States	200
France	100
Germany	60
United Kingdom	22
Canada	9
Netherlands	8
Sweden	4
Denmark	1

Birthing

Many older Japanese regard the nation's falling birth rate (now near 1.6 children per childbearing woman) as a national crisis.

"People feel so much pressure on the job that they work until nine, ten o'clock at night. Then they have another hour and a half home on the train, because most people can't afford a house anywhere near the office. You probably can't get a seat, and the train is full of drunks, singing and throwing up. After all that, who has the strength to get in bed and make a baby?"
—*Kunio Kitamura, Tokyo obstetrician*

Myth:
Cesarean sections cut infant mortality rates.

Reality:
The U.S. has the highest level of infant mortality and cesarean sections in the industrial world.

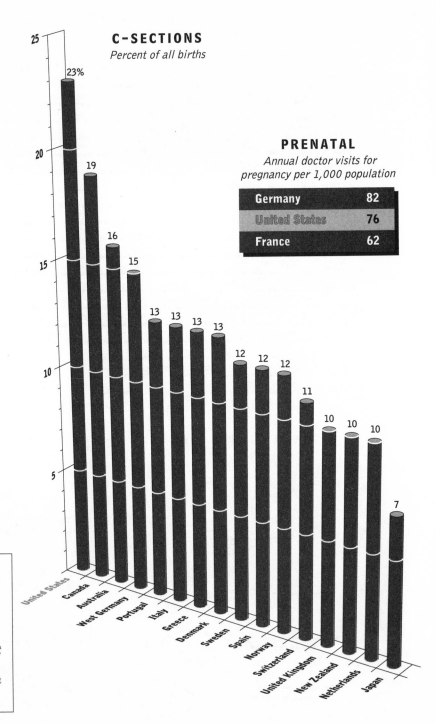

C-SECTIONS
Percent of all births

- United States — 23%
- Canada — 19
- Australia — 16
- West Germany — 15
- Portugal — 13
- Italy — 13
- Greece — 13
- Denmark — 13
- Sweden — 12
- Spain — 12
- Norway — 12
- Switzerland — 11
- United Kingdom — 10
- New Zealand — 10
- Netherlands — 10
- Japan — 7

PRENATAL
Annual doctor visits for pregnancy per 1,000 population

Germany	82
United States	76
France	62

THE REALLY NATURAL WAY
Babies born at home as a percent of all births

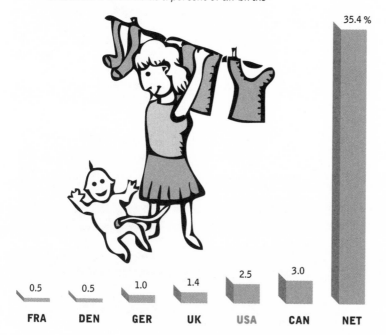

0.5	0.5	1.0	1.4	2.5	3.0	35.4 %
FRA	**DEN**	**GER**	**UK**	**USA**	**CAN**	**NET**

MATERNITY WARD
Average hospital stay for a normal delivery (days)

Switzerland	9.1
Germany	9.1
Netherlands	8.8
Japan	8.7
Norway	7.3
Austria	7.1
Finland	6.7
Australia	6.2
Sweden	5.9
Portugal	5.3
Denmark	5.3
Greece	5.0
Canada	4.8
Spain	4.0
United Kingdom	2.9
Turkey	2.7
United States	2.5

LOW-TECH DELIVERY
Number of practicing midwives

> Most births in the U.K. are attended by midwives.

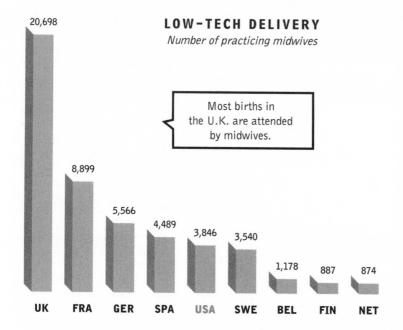

20,698	8,899	5,566	4,489	3,846	3,540	1,178	887	874
UK	**FRA**	**GER**	**SPA**	**USA**	**SWE**	**BEL**	**FIN**	**NET**

PREEMIES
Percent of all births

United States	7%
United Kingdom	7
Italy	7
Germany	6
Denmark	6
Canada	6
Austria	6
Switzerland	5
Japan	5
France	5
Sweden	4

MOST ABORTIONS: THE USSR

Flashpoint: abortion

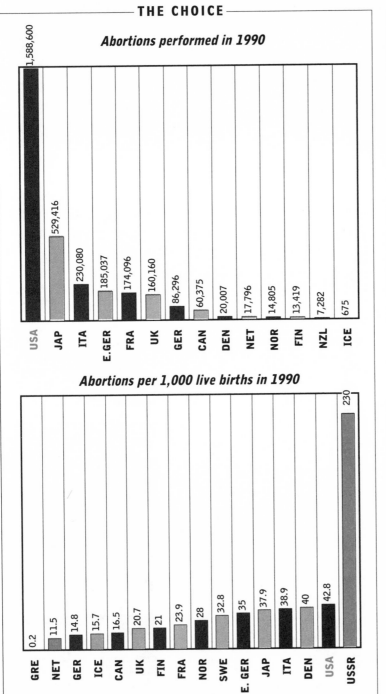

THE CHOICE

Abortions performed in 1990

USA	1,588,600
JAP	529,416
ITA	230,080
E.GER	185,037
FRA	174,096
UK	160,160
GER	86,296
CAN	60,375
DEN	20,007
NET	17,796
NOR	14,805
FIN	13,419
NZL	7,282
ICE	675

Abortions per 1,000 live births in 1990

GRE	0.2
NET	11.5
GER	14.8
ICE	15.7
CAN	16.5
UK	20.7
FIN	21
FRA	23.9
NOR	28
SWE	32.8
E. GER	35
JAP	37.9
ITA	38.9
DEN	40
USA	42.8
USSR	230

THE RATE
Percent of all pregnancies aborted

Soviet Union	54.9%
United States	29.7
Denmark	27.0
Japan	25.7
Sweden	24.9
Australia	20.4
United Kingdom	18.6
Finland	18.0
Canada	16.6
Iceland	14.0
New Zealand	13.6
Belgium	12.2
Netherlands	9.0

THE RIGHT
Number of years abortion has been legal

Japan	43
Canada	22
Australia	22
Finland	21
Denmark	21
United States	18
Sweden	16
Germany	15
Norway	15
New Zealand	14
Portugal	13
Netherlands	10

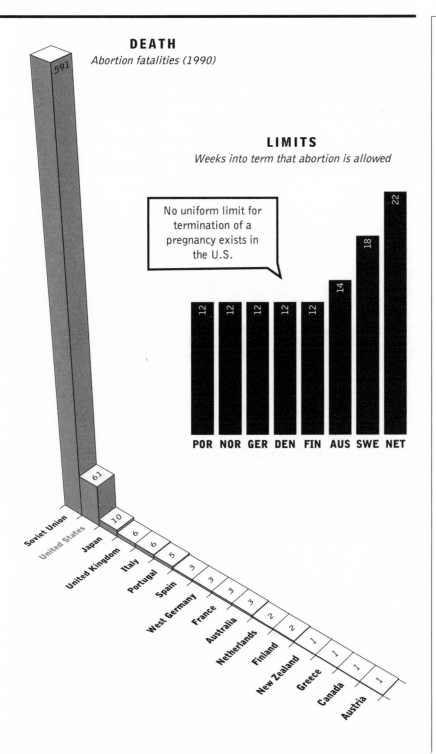

DEATH
Abortion fatalities (1990)

LIMITS
Weeks into term that abortion is allowed

No uniform limit for termination of a pregnancy exists in the U.S.

591

POR NOR GER DEN FIN AUS SWE NET
12 12 12 12 12 14 18 22

61

Soviet Union
United States
Japan 10
United Kingdom 6
Italy 6
Portugal 5
Spain 3
West Germany 3
France 3
Australia 3
Netherlands 2
Finland 2
New Zealand 1
Greece 1
Canada 1
Austria 1

The abortion debate pits modern life—its values, its demands, its culture, its technology—against a fading life in which families existed in different forms, in which women behaved in different social and economic ways, in which sexual relationships were more uniformly prescribed, and in which technology was not a central part of reproduction. It is ironic that the U.S., the nation that swept all other nations into the modern vortex— cultural, technological, and economic—is the one still so clearly at war with its past.

The French manufacturer of the abortion pill, RU-486, has so far refused to bring the product to the U.S. because of threats of protests by the right-to-life movement. The New Hampshire Legislature, usually a conservative bastion, has offered the state as a testing site to speed the drug's approval by the Food and Drug Administration.

And the winner is...

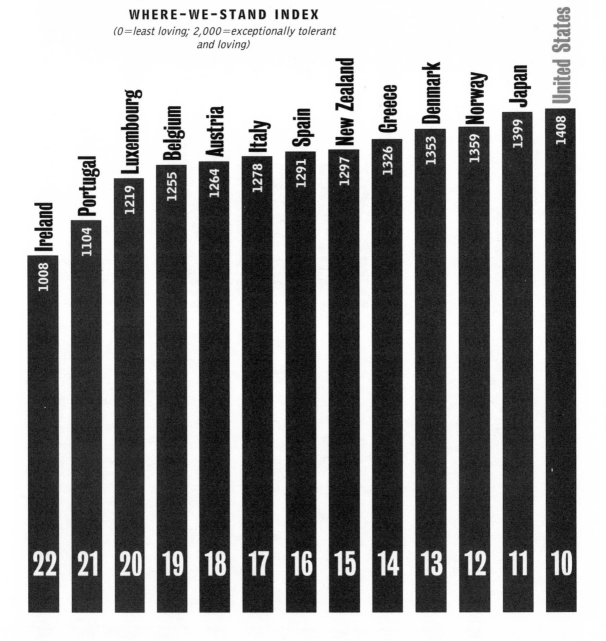

WHERE–WE–STAND INDEX
*(0=least loving; 2,000=exceptionally tolerant
and loving)*

Ireland	Portugal	Luxembourg	Belgium	Austria	Italy	Spain	New Zealand	Greece	Denmark	Norway	Japan	United States
1008	1104	1219	1255	1264	1278	1291	1297	1326	1353	1359	1399	1408
22	21	20	19	18	17	16	15	14	13	12	11	10

The Netherlands

Canada — 1423
9

Switzerland — 1439
8

France — 1450
7

Sweden — 1462
6

United Kingdom — 1485
5

Finland — 1496
4

Australia — 1512
3

Germany — 1522
2

1571
1

The Dutch have the most sex with the least amount of negative repercussions. There are fewer reported extra marital affairs in the Netherlands, fewer teen pregnancies and teen abortions than in any other industrial country, and the Dutch abortion rate is among the lowest. Even with some of the most liberal matrimony laws, the Netherlands has among the lowest divorce rates. What's more, a biological liberalism has resulted in probably the most enlightened approach to birthing: there are ten times more home births in the Netherlands than in any other industrial nation. With the most tolerance for sexual orientation, the Netherlands has pioneered an open and safe society.

THE BEST HOME

Clean space

Our filth unites us. Politically, the world remains divided into nation-states; ecologically, we are one. It all floats downstream. One nation's exhaust kills another's rivers; one nation's industrialization nullifies another's cleanup; one nation's rise from poverty is another's hole in the ozone.

Four out of five people in Europe, the U.S., and Japan live in urban areas. But "downtown" for most practical purposes doesn't exist anymore; sprawling, continuing populated areas do. In 1900, Los Angeles, Tokyo, and Amsterdam existed as concentrations of people surrounded by what surely seemed like limitless countryside. L.A., of course, has no center whatsoever now, but stretches 60 miles north, south, and east. Tokyo, with a population of 11.8 million, sits in the middle of the Kanto plain, among another 25 million people. Were it not for government-mandated green spaces, Amsterdam would now be united with Rotterdam, Utrecht, and The Hague to create one continuous national sprawl.

The earth is losing its forests, its topsoil, and its stratospheric ozone, while its deserts grow, its greenhouse gases expand, its acid rain increases, and its air pollution chokes cities around the globe.

Many businessmen, economists, and politicians believe that technology will save us—that human history is the story of man's gradual conquest of nature, and man will master this problem, too. Indeed, they expect the global cleanup to be an important source of jobs and economic growth.

Ecologists have a starker view: Nothing short of fundamental changes in human behavior and national economic systems can save the earth.

The clash between these two points of view may very well define global conflicts into the next century, replacing anticommunism as the organizing theme of world politics.

Already eco-politics is one of the fastest-growing political movements in Western Europe. Virtually all political groups from the center leftward have rushed to court the eco-vote and establish an eco-identity. Benito Craxi, head of Italy's Socialist Party, assured followers that although the party's symbol, a rose, is red, its stem is green.

In America, environmental issues still carry little weight in national elections, biting most sharply on the local level, in neighborhoods and towns. But America is still the world's premier polluter.

City life

METROPOLITAN MAN
Percent of population that is urbanized

UK 92%
NET 88
GER 86
ÖST 86
SWE 83
JAP 77
CAN 76
SPA 76
USA 74
FRA 73
NOR 73
ITA 67
SWI 58
IRE 57

City life

CLUSTERING
Urban growth: 1960-1990 (%)

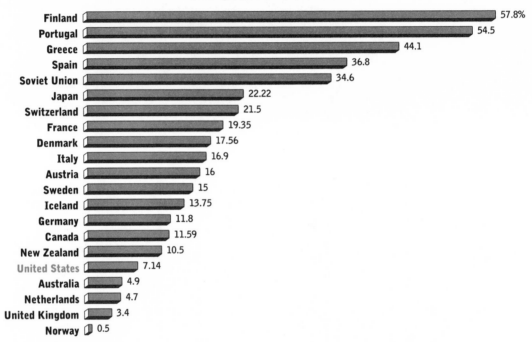

Finland	57.8%
Portugal	54.5
Greece	44.1
Spain	36.8
Soviet Union	34.6
Japan	22.22
Switzerland	21.5
France	19.35
Denmark	17.56
Italy	16.9
Austria	16
Sweden	15
Iceland	13.75
Germany	11.8
Canada	11.59
New Zealand	10.5
United States	7.14
Australia	4.9
Netherlands	4.7
United Kingdom	3.4
Norway	0.5

THIS OLD HOUSE
Housing built before World War II (%)

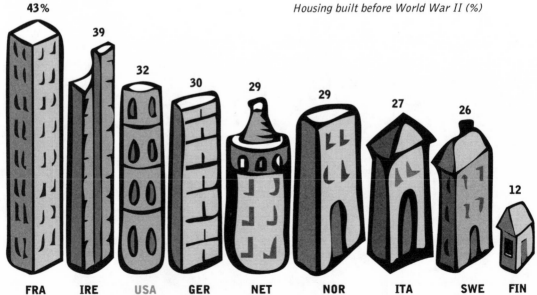

FRA	IRE	USA	GER	NET	NOR	ITA	SWE	FIN
43%	39	32	30	29	29	27	26	12

YOUR PICNIC AREA
Urban green space per person (square yards)

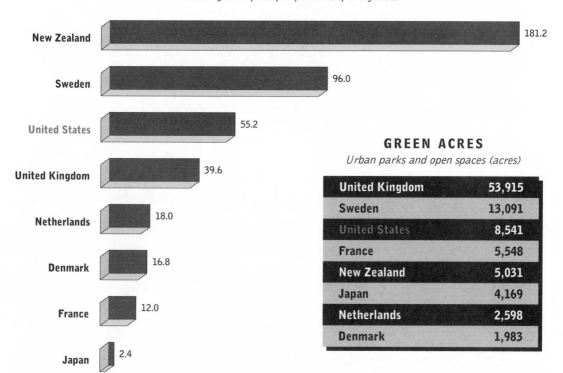

New Zealand	181.2
Sweden	96.0
United States	55.2
United Kingdom	39.6
Netherlands	18.0
Denmark	16.8
France	12.0
Japan	2.4

GREEN ACRES
Urban parks and open spaces (acres)

United Kingdom	53,915
Sweden	13,091
United States	8,541
France	5,548
New Zealand	5,031
Japan	4,169
Netherlands	2,598
Denmark	1,983

CONDO NATIONS
Housing built after World War II (%)

FIN	SWE	ITA	NET	GER	USA	NOR	IRE	FRA
88%	74	73	71	70	68	64	61	57

Getting there

THEY PAVED PARADISE
Miles of road per square mile of land area

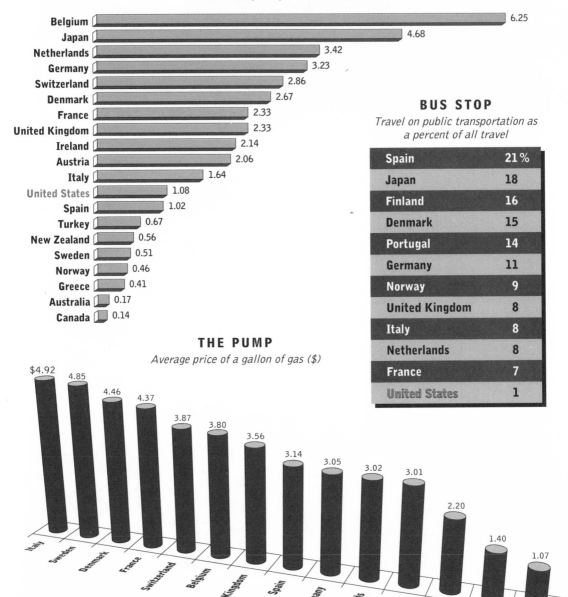

Belgium	6.25
Japan	4.68
Netherlands	3.42
Germany	3.23
Switzerland	2.86
Denmark	2.67
France	2.33
United Kingdom	2.33
Ireland	2.14
Austria	2.06
Italy	1.64
United States	1.08
Spain	1.02
Turkey	0.67
New Zealand	0.56
Sweden	0.51
Norway	0.46
Greece	0.41
Australia	0.17
Canada	0.14

BUS STOP
Travel on public transportation as a percent of all travel

Spain	21%
Japan	18
Finland	16
Denmark	15
Portugal	14
Germany	11
Norway	9
United Kingdom	8
Italy	8
Netherlands	8
France	7
United States	1

THE PUMP
Average price of a gallon of gas ($)

Italy	$4.92
Sweden	4.85
Denmark	4.46
France	4.37
Switzerland	3.87
Belgium	3.80
United Kingdom	3.56
Spain	3.14
Germany	3.05
Netherlands	3.02
Japan	3.01
Australia	2.20
Canada	1.40
United States	1.07

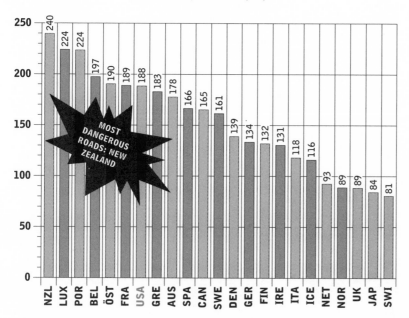

ROAD KILL
Auto deaths per million people

MOST DANGEROUS ROADS: NEW ZEALAND

NZL 240, LUX 224, POR 224, BEL 197, ÖST 190, FRA 189, USA 188, GRE 183, AUS 178, SPA 166, CAN 165, SWE 161, DEN 139, GER 134, FIN 132, IRE 131, ITA 118, ICE 116, NET 93, NOR 89, UK 89, JAP 84, SWI 81

FREQUENT FLIERS
Annual air miles per person

NZL 2,023, USA 1,698, AUS 1,513, SWI 1,350, CAN 1,105, NET 1,014, UK 902, NOR 829, IRE 625, SWE 575, FRA 530, FIN 506, DEN 476, GRE 466, JAP 425, BEL 410, SPA 354, GER 344, LUX 251, ITA 207, ÖST 166

In the U.S., it's gridlock. In Germany, *Verkehrsinfarkt* (traffic infarction). Indeed, some of the world's worst traffic jams are in the land of Mercedes, BMW, Audi, and Porsche. The pure driving pleasure of Hitler's legendary Autobahn (German highways have no speed limits; efforts to impose one meet the kind of resistance that stymies gun-control initiatives in the U.S.) has come face-to-face with the highest automobile density in the world. The German Social Democrats have proposed an ecological tax on gasoline that would raise the cost of a gallon from $3.05 to $5.00. The Ecological Research Institute in Heidelberg says that for cars to pay the true cost of the damage they inflict on the nation's environment, the price of gas should be $12 a gallon.

The countryside

Europeans, Japanese, and Americans have all eagerly left the land. Likewise, they all seem to want to go back to it somehow—mostly on weekends. Kent, Sussex, and Surrey, in southern England, are known as the Stockbroker Belt. Real-estate prices in parts of Tuscany have quintupled over the last decade; in the Hamptons, they've increased tenfold. This year's ultra-chic rustic retreat is Montana. One of the biggest growth areas in travel in the 1990s is expected to be agri-tourism, wherein a vacationer pays to do hard farm chores. At the same time, one school of environmentalists is calling for the radical depopulation of rural areas. A recommendation for restoring the American Great Plains, in a report that has come to be called the Buffalo Commons plan: "The wisest thing the [U.S.] federal government can do, is start buying back great chunks of the Plains, replant the [prairie] grass, reintroduce the bison—and turn out the lights."

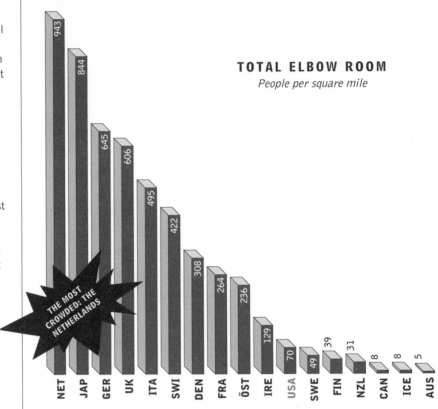

TOTAL ELBOW ROOM
People per square mile

THE MOST CROWDED: THE NETHERLANDS

NET 943 | JAP 844 | GER 645 | UK 606 | ITA 495 | SWI 422 | DEN 308 | FRA 264 | ÖST 236 | IRE 129 | USA 70 | SWE 49 | FIN 39 | NZL 31 | CAN 8 | ICE 8 | AUS 5

FARM COUNTRY
Percent of land devoted to agriculture

Denmark	61.6%	United States	20.7
Italy	41.4	Austria	18.3
Spain	40.9	Japan	12.6
Portugal	38.8	Ireland	11.2
Turkey	35.7	Switzerland	10.4
France	35.5	Finland	7.9
Germany	30.6	Sweden	7.3
Greece	30.1	Australia	6.4
United Kingdom	29.1	Canada	5.0
Netherlands	26.7	Norway	2.8
Belgium	24.5	New Zealand	1.9

DIRT ROADS

Unpaved roads as a percent of all public roads

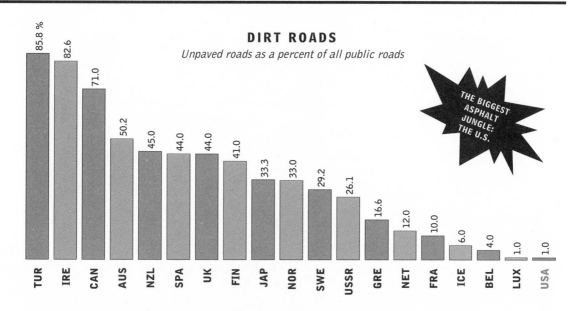

THE BIGGEST ASPHALT JUNGLE: THE U.S.

TUR	85.8 %
IRE	82.6
CAN	71.0
AUS	50.2
NZL	45.0
SPA	44.0
UK	44.0
FIN	41.0
JAP	33.3
NOR	33.0
SWE	29.2
USSR	26.1
GRE	16.6
NET	12.0
FRA	10.0
ICE	6.0
BEL	4.0
LUX	1.0
USA	1.0

THIS LAND IS YOUR LAND

Protected land as a percent of total land area

Once considered wasteland, much of the world's protected lands are now under development pressure from mining, logging, and farming interests.

TUR	0.3
IRE	0.4
USSR	0.9
BEL	2.6
FIN	2.6
SWI	3.0
CAN	3.7
SWE	4.1
GRE	4.1
ITA	4.3
NET	4.4
AUS	4.8
SPA	5.1
JAP	6.4
DEN	6.7
POR	6.8
ICE	7.9
FRA	8.2
USA	8.6
NZL	10.5
UK	10.6
GER	11.3
NOR	15.5
ÖST	19.3
LUX	25.1 %

INTERNATIONAL HARVESTERS

Tractors per 1,000 people

Finland	58	Canada	35	New Zealand	24	Switzerland	17
Iceland	54	France	30	Italy	23	Belgium	13
Austria	47	Sweden	27	United States	22	Netherlands	12
Ireland	47	Germany	27	EC	22	Turkey	12
Norway	41	Japan	25	Greece	19	United Kingdom	10
Denmark	40	Australia	24	Spain	18	Portugal	8

Eco-crisis

A U.N. summit convened in Nairobi in 1991 to hammer out an agreement to reduce carbon dioxide—the principal man-made gas responsible for the greenhouse effect—by the year 2000. The EC and Japan have campaigned strongly for the adoption of a timetable to curtail the growth of CO_2 emissions, with the goal of holding emissions in the year 2000 to 1990 levels. The U.S. is the world's largest total emitter of carbon dioxide and second only to the former East Germany in per capita emissions (air pollution is 50 times higher in East Germany than in West Germany). But Washington refuses to endorse any policy of mandatory cuts.

Myth:
The U.S. has cleaned up its act.

Reality:
It's still the world's biggest polluter.

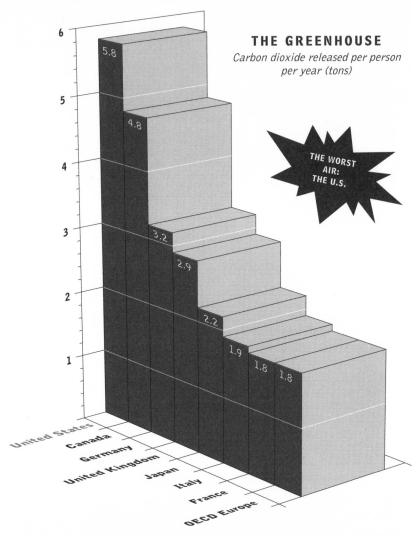

THE GREENHOUSE
Carbon dioxide released per person per year (tons)

THE WORST AIR: THE U.S.

United States 5.8
Canada 4.8
Germany 3.2
United Kingdom 2.9
Japan 2.2
Italy 1.9
France 1.8
OECD Europe 1.8

SMOG
Total carbon monoxide annually emitted (tons)

United States	60,900		Sweden	1,754
Canada	10,100		Netherlands	1,229
Germany	8,926		Austria	1,084
France	6,198		Norway	649
Italy	5,571		Switzerland	621
United Kingdom	5,264		Ireland	456
Spain	3,780		Portugal	267

ACID RAIN
pH value of rainwater

On the pH scale, the lower the number, the greater the acidity.

POR	BEL	ICE	IRE	UK	NET	FIN	FRA	GER	DEN	ÖST	NOR	CAN	USA	SWE	JAP
6.0	5.8	5.3	5.1	5.1	4.9	4.5	4.5	4.5	4.5	4.4	4.4	4.3	4.3	4.1	3.9

NOISE POLLUTION
Percent of population regularly exposed to more than 60 decibels of street noise at home

USA	NET	GER	DEN	SWE	UK	NOR	SWI	GRE	FRA	ÖST	BEL	POR	JAP
18.0	20.0	20.2	21.0	23.2	25.0	26.0	28.0	30.0	33.1	35.0	39.0	50.0	58.0%

THE NOISIEST PLACE: JAPAN

TONS OF GUNK YOU BREATHE
Debris inhaled per person per year (pounds)

CAN	SPA	USA	IRE	BEL	FIN	SWE	AUS	POR	EUR	NET	GER	DEN	FRA	ÖST	ITA	NZL	NOR	UK	GRE	SWI	TUR	JAP
173	90	81	61	59	44	44	40	29	26	24	24	20	20	15	15	15	15	11	9	9	7	2

279

Eco-crisis

In the highly industrialized upper Silesia area of Poland, children have up to five times as much lead in their blood as the children of Western Europe. One source for lead: vegetables. A current joke in Poland asks, What do you get when you boil down a ton of cabbage? Answer: a cannonball.

At 1,637 pounds per person, the U.S. produces twice the garbage that Europe and Japan do. With the advent of disposable sheets, gowns, and syringes, every hospital patient in the U.S. generates 15 pounds of waste a day—some of it too toxic for conventional dump sites. America will have used up 80 percent of its landfill areas by 2010. Japan will reach maximum capacity by 2005. The Netherlands has already reached its limits.

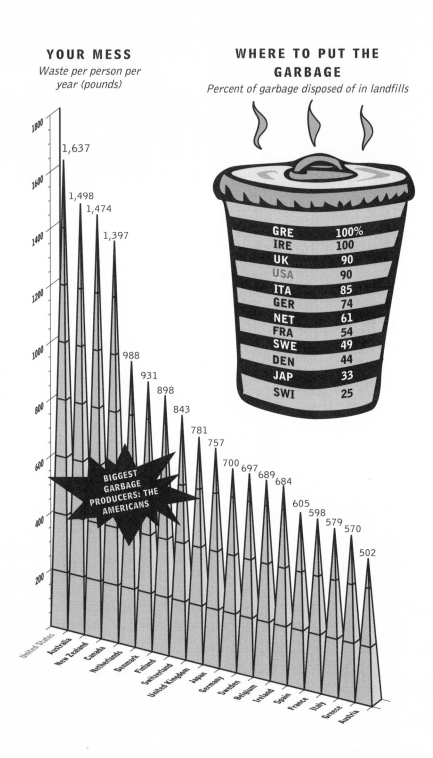

YOUR MESS
Waste per person per year (pounds)

1,637 — United States
1,498 — Australia
1,474 — New Zealand
1,397 — Canada
988 — Netherlands
931 — Denmark
898 — Finland
843 — Switzerland
781 — United Kingdom
757 — Japan
700 — Germany
697 — Sweden
689 — Belgium
684 — Ireland
605 — Spain
598 — France
579 — Italy
570 — Greece
502 — Austria

BIGGEST GARBAGE PRODUCERS: THE AMERICANS

WHERE TO PUT THE GARBAGE
Percent of garbage disposed of in landfills

GRE	100%
IRE	100
UK	90
USA	90
ITA	85
GER	74
NET	61
FRA	54
SWE	49
DEN	44
JAP	33
SWI	25

HOT RODS
Nuclear waste generated per energy unit (tons)

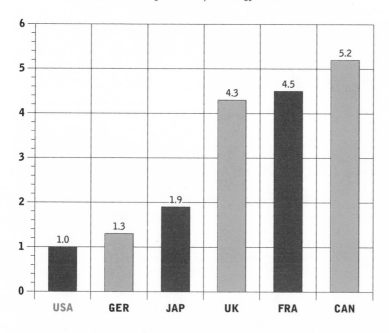

	USA	GER	JAP	UK	FRA	CAN
	1.0	1.3	1.9	4.3	4.5	5.2

WHAT'S BUGGING YOU?
Pesticides per square mile (tons)

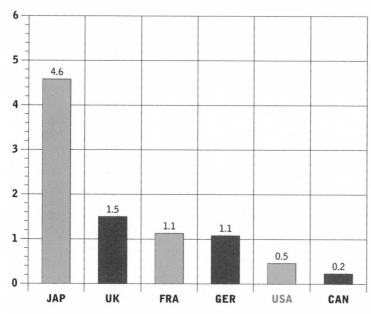

	JAP	UK	FRA	GER	USA	CAN
	4.6	1.5	1.1	1.1	0.5	0.2

GREETINGS FROM LOVE CANAL
Total chemical and biological waste generated each year (thousands of tons)

United States	265,000
Germany	5,000
Greece	3,904
United Kingdom	3,900
Canada	3,290
Italy	3,000
France	2,000
Spain	1,708
Netherlands	1,500
Belgium	915
Japan	666
Sweden	500
Australia	300
Austria	200
Denmark	125
Finland	124
Norway	120
Switzerland	120
Ireland	20
Luxembourg	4

Eco-crisis

SLICKS
Number of major oil spills (1976–1989)

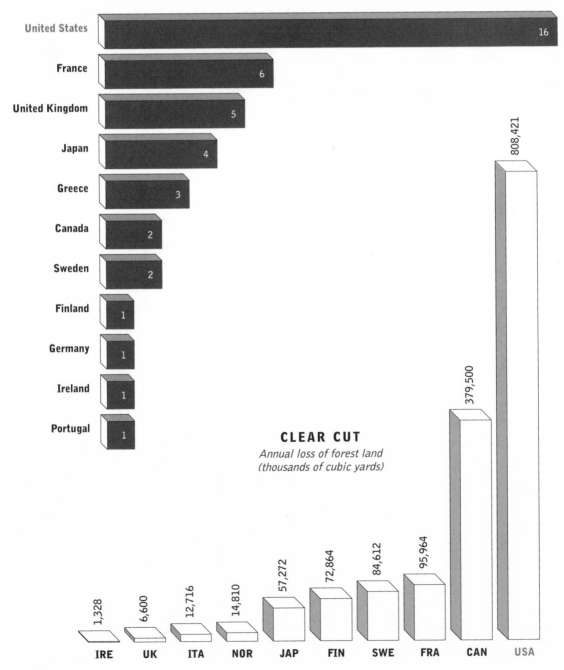

United States	16
France	6
United Kingdom	5
Japan	4
Greece	3
Canada	2
Sweden	2
Finland	1
Germany	1
Ireland	1
Portugal	1

CLEAR CUT
*Annual loss of forest land
(thousands of cubic yards)*

IRE	UK	ITA	NOR	JAP	FIN	SWE	FRA	CAN	USA
1,328	6,600	12,716	14,810	57,272	72,864	84,612	95,964	379,500	808,421

The pollution machine

BIGGEST OIL GUZZLERS: THE U.S.

OIL GUZZLERS
Energy units of oil burned annually

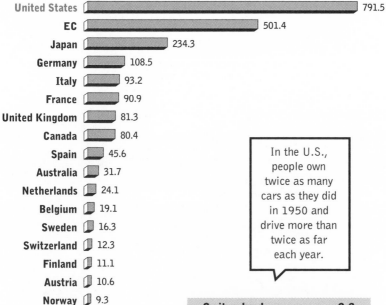

United States	791.5
EC	501.4
Japan	234.3
Germany	108.5
Italy	93.2
France	90.9
United Kingdom	81.3
Canada	80.4
Spain	45.6
Australia	31.7
Netherlands	24.1
Belgium	19.1
Sweden	16.3
Switzerland	12.3
Finland	11.1
Austria	10.6
Norway	9.3
Denmark	9.0
New Zealand	4.1
Ireland	4.0
Iceland	0.7

> In the U.S., people own twice as many cars as they did in 1950 and drive more than twice as far each year.

It would be fairly easy to boost the average mileage of American cars from 26.5 mpg to 45 mpg, notes *Time* magazine, but President Bush has refused to raise the federally mandated average above 27.5 mpg.

"Long before all the world's people could achieve the American dream...the planet would be laid waste."
—*Alan Durning,* State of the World 1991

"Americans did not fight and win the wars of the 20th century to make the world safe for green vegetables."
—*Richard Darman, director of the U.S. Office of Management and Budget*

THE CAR POOL
People per car

United States	1.8
Iceland	1.9
Canada	2.1
Germany	2.1
Australia	2.2
Luxembourg	2.2
New Zealand	2.2
Switzerland	2.3
Italy	2.4
Sweden	2.4
France	2.5
Norway	2.6
United Kingdom	2.7
Finland	2.8
Netherlands	2.8
Austria	3.7
Spain	3.7
Belgium	3.8
Japan	4.0
Denmark	4.3
Ireland	5.0
Greece	6.7
Portugal	7.6

Myth:
America needs a four-door car.

Reality:
It really needs only two doors.

The pollution machine

COAL COUNTRY
Energy units of coal generated annually

America and Eastern Europe have something in common: They burn most of the world's coal—the cheapest energy and the dirtiest.

OZONE BUSTERS
Total chlorofluorocarbons emitted per year (millions of tons)

World	1,300		Belgium	12
OECD	901		Greece	12
United States	332		Portugal	12
Japan	95		Switzerland	10
Germany	71		Austria	9
Italy	67		Turkey	9
United Kingdom	67		Denmark	6
France	65		Finland	6
Spain	45		Sweden	6
Canada	34		Ireland	4
Australia	20		New Zealand	3
Netherlands	17		Norway	1

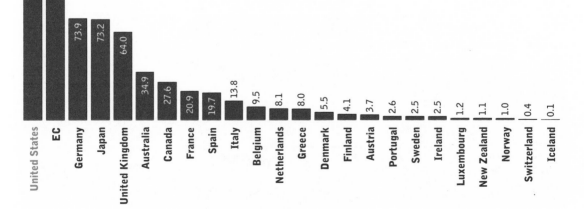

United States	458.0
EC	229.0
Germany	73.9
Japan	73.2
United Kingdom	64.0
Australia	34.9
Canada	27.6
France	20.9
Spain	19.7
Italy	13.8
Belgium	9.5
Netherlands	8.1
Greece	8.0
Denmark	5.5
Finland	4.1
Austria	3.7
Portugal	2.6
Sweden	2.5
Ireland	2.5
Luxembourg	1.2
New Zealand	1.1
Norway	1.0
Switzerland	0.4
Iceland	0.1

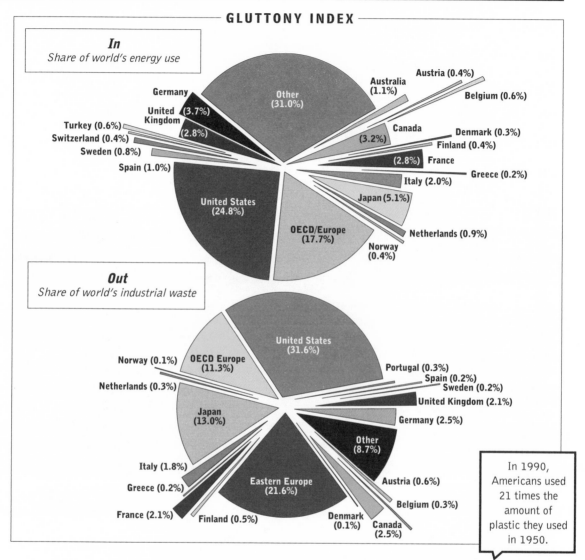

GLUTTONY INDEX

In
Share of world's energy use

Germany (3.7%)
United Kingdom (2.8%)
Turkey (0.6%)
Switzerland (0.4%)
Sweden (0.8%)
Spain (1.0%)
United States (24.8%)
OECD/Europe (17.7%)
Norway (0.4%)
Japan (5.1%)
Italy (2.0%)
France (2.8%)
Greece (0.2%)
Finland (0.4%)
Denmark (0.3%)
Canada (3.2%)
Netherlands (0.9%)
Belgium (0.6%)
Austria (0.4%)
Australia (1.1%)
Other (31.0%)

Out
Share of world's industrial waste

Norway (0.1%)
Netherlands (0.3%)
OECD Europe (11.3%)
United States (31.6%)
Japan (13.0%)
Italy (1.8%)
Greece (0.2%)
France (2.1%)
Finland (0.5%)
Eastern Europe (21.6%)
Denmark (0.1%)
Canada (2.5%)
Austria (0.6%)
Belgium (0.3%)
Other (8.7%)
Germany (2.5%)
United Kingdom (2.1%)
Sweden (0.2%)
Spain (0.2%)
Portugal (0.3%)

> In 1990, Americans used 21 times the amount of plastic they used in 1950.

A-PLANTS
Energy units of nuclear power produced annually

EC	163.3		United Kingdom	18.7
United States	146.2		Sweden	17.2
France	79.2		Spain	14.6
Japan	47.7		Belgium	10.7
Germany	38.9		Switzerland	6.0
Canada	20.8		Finland	5.0

PLASTIC PEOPLE
Annual plastic consumption (tons)

EC	163.3
United States	146.2
France	79.2
Japan	47.7
Germany	38.9
Canada	20.8

──What's being done?──

"We treat nature like we treated workers a hundred years ago. We included then no cost for the health and social security of workers in our calculations, and today we include no cost for the health and security of nature."
—Bjorn Stigson, chief executive of AB Flakt, a Swedish engineering firm

"The great engineering projects of the next century will be not the civil engineering of dams or bridges, but the bio-engineering of sewage works and waste tips. The star scientists will be those who find cheaper ways to dispose of plastics or to clean up contaminated soil. For far-sighted companies, the environment may turn out to be the biggest opportunity for enterprise and invention the industrial world has seen."
—The Economist

"The wealthier industrial countries— especially the dozen that have stabilized their population ➻➙

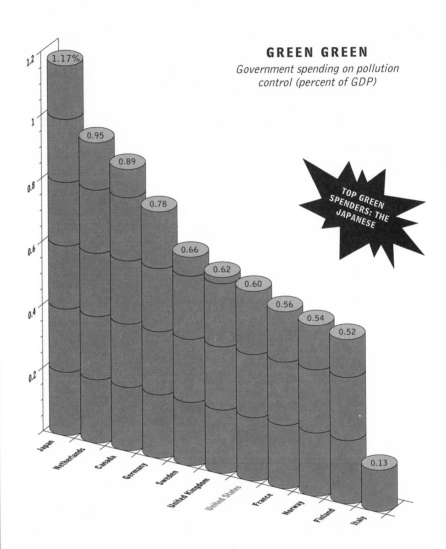

GREEN GREEN
Government spending on pollution control (percent of GDP)

TOP GREEN SPENDERS: THE JAPANESE

Japan	1.17%
Netherlands	0.95
Canada	0.89
Germany	0.78
Sweden	0.66
United Kingdom	0.62
United States	0.60
France	0.56
Norway	0.54
Finland	0.52
Italy	0.13

AGAINST THE WIND
Energy units of alternative energy generated annually

United States	103.1	Finland	6.2	Ireland	1.5
Canada	34.0	Austria	5.4	Denmark	1.1
EC	26.1	Australia	5.4	Greece	0.7
Sweden	11.7	New Zealand	3.8	Iceland	0.6
Norway	10.9	Germany	3.5	United Kingdom	0.4
Japan	8.9	Switzerland	3.4	Belgium	0.2
France	8.0	Spain	2.1	Netherlands	0.2
Italy	6.8	Portugal	1.7	Luxembourg	0.0

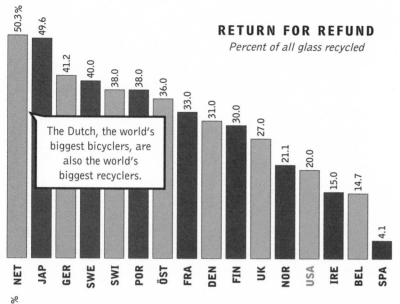

RETURN FOR REFUND
Percent of all glass recycled

> The Dutch, the world's biggest bicyclers, are also the world's biggest recyclers.

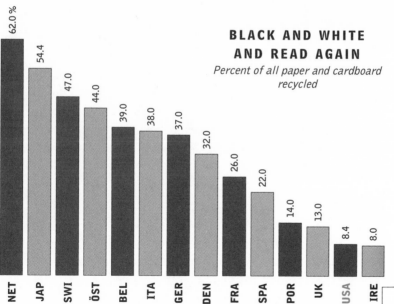

BLACK AND WHITE AND READ AGAIN
Percent of all paper and cardboard recycled

WHO'S LOOKING AHEAD?
Percent of government R&D spent on environment

Germany	3.4%		France	0.7
Canada	2.2		United States	0.5
Italy	1.9		Japan	0.4
United Kingdom	1.3			

size, including Austria, Germany, Italy, Norway, Sweden, and Switzerland—are in the best position to begin satisfying their needs with no net degradation of the natural resource base. These countries could be the first to benefit from realizing that some growth costs more than it is worth, and that an economy's optimum size is not its maximum size."
—*Sandra Postel and Christopher Flavin,* State of the World 1991

President Bush has pledged to plant a billion trees by the end of the century.

Myth: *The U.S. has a recycling program.*

Reality: *Its efforts trail far behind those of all other major industrial countries.*

Safe streets

Nothing separates the U.S. from the other advanced nations of the world more than the amount and the horror of its violent crime. It is the smoking gun—the glaring evidence of what happens when you mix social failure with too many firearms.

When seventeen-year-old Junko Furuta, riding her bike home from work, was kidnapped in Tokyo by a group of teenage boys who took her home, kept her prisoner for 40 days, raped, beat, tortured, burned, and starved her, and finally stuffed her into an oil drum and covered her with concrete, it set off a national debate about whether or not the "American disease" was inevitably in Japan's future. "The Devil-Children of the Comics and Video Age ...U.S. Style Violence, Will It Take Over Japan?" asked a weekly magazine.

"You can see the society collapsing," pronounced Susumu Oda, one of Japan's best-known child psychiatrists. "Sooner or later what is happening in America will happen here." There were 23,000 murders in America last year; Japan—which had 1,441—still has a long way to go.

The reasons for U.S. crime illustrate the differences between the U.S. and its competitor nations: its shrinking middle class and rising extremes of wealth and poverty, the lack of social-welfare policies, the deficient educational system, the frontier mythology, the drugs, the guns.

Crime has been on a steady rise throughout Europe and in Japan since the early 1950s, and many criminologists have expected it to "break out" in those countries in a way similar to what has happened in the U.S. A rise in crime is often thought to go hand in hand with rising affluence; as the gulf between rich and poor widens, the have-nots turn to illegal means to get their share. Affluence also creates a larger drug market. Throughout much of Europe, street crime—thievery and vandalism—is on the rise, but it is nowhere near the problem it is in the U.S.

Until recently, most European nations looked on drug use as more an illness than a crime. With a rise in both drug use and crime rates, however, that attitude is changing.

In Japan, the penetration of organized crime—the Yakuza—into legitimate businesses has grown at a relentless pace. Indeed, Japanese mobsters hired the president's brother, Prescott Bush, for advice on an investment.

In the area of violent crime—murder, rape, and armed robbery—the U.S. remains unique. Experts have begun to employ the kind of mass psychological profiles of the type used to understand German and Japanese behavior during World War II to explain how and why Americans differ so profoundly, and so horrifyingly, from other, more peaceful human beings.

Police blotter

MURDERS
Per 100,000 people

United States	8.40
Canada	5.45
Denmark	5.17
France	4.60
Portugal	4.50
Australia	4.48
Germany	4.20
Belgium	2.80
Spain	2.28
Switzerland	2.25
Italy	2.18
Norway	1.99
United Kingdom	1.97
Austria	1.80
Greece	1.76
Sweden	1.73
Turkey	1.45
Japan	1.20
Ireland	0.96
Finland	0.70

RAPES
Per 100,000 people

United States	37.20
Sweden	15.70
Denmark	11.23
Germany	8.60
Norway	7.87
United Kingdom	7.26
Finland	7.20
France	6.77
Switzerland	6.15
Luxembourg	5.00
Spain	4.43
Austria	4.40
Belgium	4.00
Greece	2.40
Ireland	1.72
Japan	1.40
Portugal	1.20
Turkey	0.40

Police blotter

ARMED ROBBERY
Per 100,000 people

SPA	USA	CAN	FRA	BEL	UK	AUS	ITA	SWE	GER	IRE	DEN	FIN	SWI	NOR	GRE	JAP
265	221	94	90	66	63	52	50	49	47	46	44	38	23	22	7	1

AUTO THEFT
Per 100,000 people

TUR	JAP	IRE	GRE	GER	BEL	FIN	CAN	SPA	ITA	FRA	USA	UK	NOR	DEN	SWE	AUS
8	28	30	58	114	201	247	344	356	364	420	583	624	665	700	714	771

WHITE-COLLAR CRIMES
Per 100,000 people

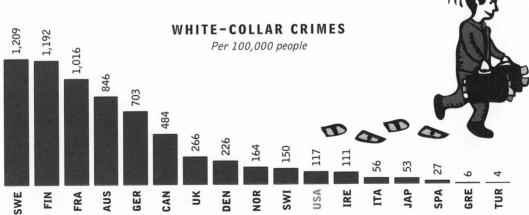

SWE	FIN	FRA	AUS	GER	CAN	UK	DEN	NOR	SWI	USA	IRE	ITA	JAP	SPA	GRE	TUR
1,209	1,192	1,016	846	703	484	266	226	164	150	117	111	56	53	27	6	4

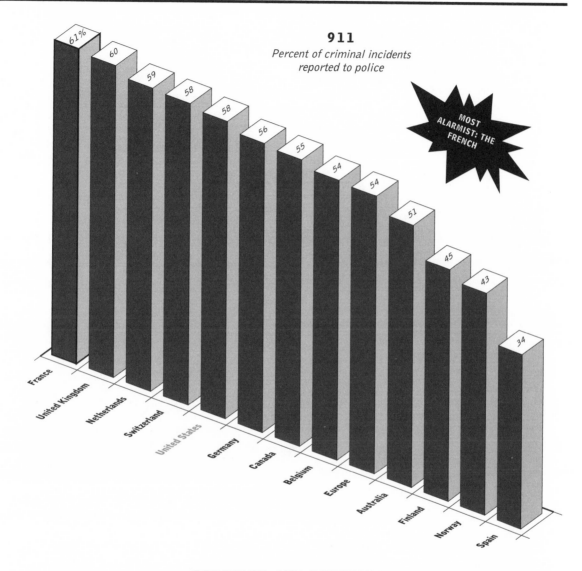

911
*Percent of criminal incidents
reported to police*

MOST
ALARMIST: THE
FRENCH

France 61%
United Kingdom 60
Netherlands 59
Switzerland 58
United States 58
Germany 56
Canada 55
Belgium 54
Europe 54
Australia 51
Finland 45
Norway 43
Spain 34

BREAKING AND ENTERING
Incidents per 100,000 people

Denmark	2,412	United States	1,309	Ireland	855
Australia	1,962	Spain	1,232	France	674
Germany	1,918	Finland	1,008	Belgium	623
United Kingdom	1,627	Luxembourg	984	Greece	257
Sweden	1,555	Switzerland	976	Japan	211
Canada	1,386	Austria	910	Norway	93

Criminal element

Japan's Yakuza, or Boryokudan ("the violent ones"), grossed more than $10 billion last year by some estimates, one-third of that take coming from their dealings in methamphetamine—speed. The FBI says Japan's organized crime controls 90 percent of the drug traffic to Hawaii. According to the FBI, the Yakuza's interests also include gun-running, corporate extortion and protection rackets, prostitution, pornography, and loan-sharking. While their Mafia counterparts in America have been systematically decimated over the past decade by federal prosecutions, the Yakuza, along with other Asian crime organizations, continues to grow in membership, influence, and profitability.

Myth:
America is the land of James Dean.

Reality:
Ducktails, hot rods, and juvenile delinquents have moved to Japan.

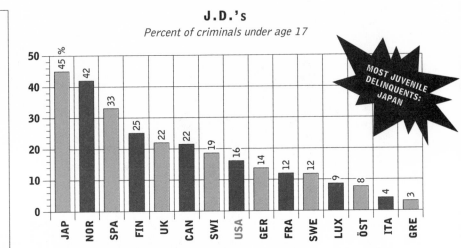

J.D.'s
Percent of criminals under age 17

MOST JUVENILE DELINQUENTS: JAPAN

JAP	NOR	SPA	FIN	UK	CAN	SWI	USA	GER	FRA	SWE	LUX	ÖST	ITA	GRE
45%	42	33	25	22	22	19	16	14	12	12	9	8	4	3

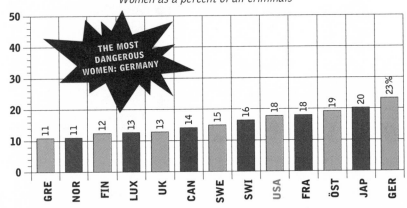

THELMA, LOUISE, ET AL.
Women as a percent of all criminals

THE MOST DANGEROUS WOMEN: GERMANY

GRE	NOR	FIN	LUX	UK	CAN	SWE	SWI	USA	FRA	ÖST	JAP	GER
11	11	12	13	13	14	15	16	18	18	19	20	23%

OUR THING
Estimated number of organized-crime-group members

84,000 — **Japan**

19,000 — **Italy**

11,000 — **United States**

Police

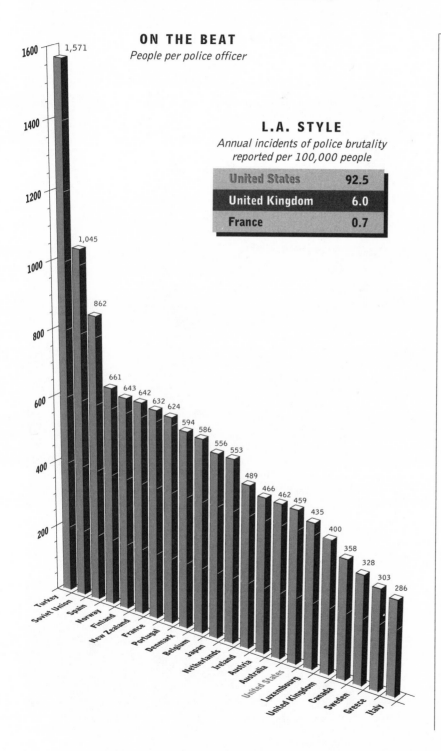

ON THE BEAT
People per police officer

Turkey — 1,571
Soviet Union — 1,045
Spain — 862
Norway — 661
Finland — 643
New Zealand — 642
France — 632
Portugal — 624
Denmark — 594
Belgium — 586
Japan — 556
Netherlands — 553
Ireland — 489
Austria — 466
Australia — 462
United States — 459
Luxembourg — 435
United Kingdom — 400
Canada — 358
Sweden — 328
Greece — 303
Italy — 286

L.A. STYLE
*Annual incidents of police brutality
reported per 100,000 people*

United States	92.5
United Kingdom	6.0
France	0.7

The Los Angeles Police Department became the scourge of international human-rights watchdogs when a group of its officers—in full view of a passerby's camcorder—pummeled, kicked, beat, and used a stun gun on Rodney King, a black man who had been stopped for a traffic violation.

Japan, too, in a kind of unmasking of its social harmony and consensus, has experienced an increasing antagonism between citizens and police. The 1990 riots in Airin, a slum neighborhood in Osaka, pitting 2,500 policemen against an onslaught of rock throwers, were provoked by alleged police harassment and corruption. "The police treat us like garbage," said Masaru Kikuchi, a construction worker in the neighborhood.

Guns

The 200 million privately owned firearms in the U.S. could arm almost every man, woman and child in the country. Nearly 70 million of those weapons are handguns. Every day, on average, a child under fourteen is shot dead with one of those handguns, 25 adults are murdered, 33 women raped, 575 people robbed, and 1,116 threatened or assaulted.

In contrast to the 8,915 handgun murders in the U.S. in 1988, 7 people were murdered in the U.K. with handguns, 19 in Sweden, 53 in Switzerland, and 8 in Canada.

And yet there is virtually no chance that U.S. politicians will defy the gun lobby and enact meaningful gun control—even of automatic weapons that have no usefulness outside the drug trade and Teflon bullets that are meant for one purpose only: penetrating the bulletproof vest of a policeman.

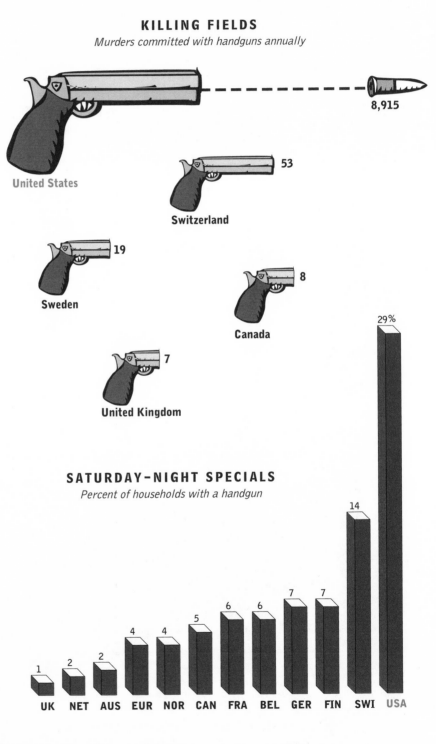

KILLING FIELDS
Murders committed with handguns annually

8,915

United States

53

Switzerland

19

Sweden

8

Canada

7

United Kingdom

SATURDAY-NIGHT SPECIALS
Percent of households with a handgun

29%

14

7   7

6   6

5

4   4

1   2   2

UK   NET   AUS   EUR   NOR   CAN   FRA   BEL   GER   FIN   SWI   USA

Drugs

WHITE OUT
Pounds of cocaine confiscated per year

SWE	4
GRE	4
IRE	7
JAP	29
OST	31
LUX	46
DEN	119
BEL	196
SWI	675
ITA	1,471
POR	1,749
FRA	2,068
CAN	2,906
GER	3,098
NET	3,142
SPA	4,048
USA	224,712

Experts believe the American drug market is near the saturation point, and while the fight for market share might well become more lethal, the industry's real growth will be in Europe and Japan. As imports rise, costs drop and the customer base increases.

European law-enforcement groups have quadrupled their spending on antidrug measures in the last five years. The Europeans are determined, however, not to repeat the mistakes the U.S. made by emphasizing prohibition to the virtual exclusion of all other policies and approaches. As much of an establishment voice as *The Economist* recently declared that prohibition was a proven failure and called for a policy of drug legalization and control. Europe, however, has yet to demonstrate any effective alternatives.

THE TRAFFIC
Annual drug-related crimes per 100,000 people

Sweden	362	Norway	148	Finland	39
Switzerland	283	Germany	139	Portugal	14
New Zealand	276	France	86	Greece	16
Denmark	253	Austria	65	U.K.	16
Luxembourg	253	Belgium	63	Japan	2
United States	234	Spain	61	Turkey	1
Canada	233	Italy	54	Ireland	1

BUSTED
Annual drug arrests as a percent of all arrests

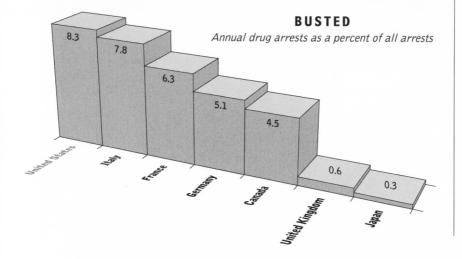

United States 8.3 · Italy 7.8 · France 6.3 · Germany 5.1 · Canada 4.5 · United Kingdom 0.6 · Japan 0.3

Punishment

UP THE RIVER
Total prison population

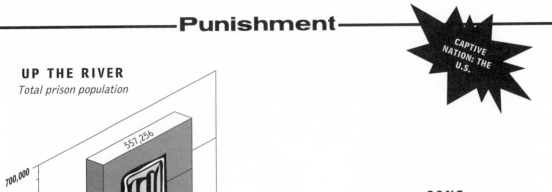

557,256

700,000

600,000

500,000

400,000

300,000

200,000

100,000

55,457
54,204
52,076
46,423
34,675
29,344
6,450
5,862
5,827
4,716
4,679
3,469

United States
United Kingdom
Japan
Germany
France
Italy
Spain
Belgium
Austria
Netherlands
Sweden
Switzerland
Denmark

CONS
Prisoners per 1,000 people

United States	4.2
United Kingdom	1.0
Germany	0.8
France	0.8
Austria	0.8
Spain	0.8
Switzerland	0.7
Denmark	0.7
Belgium	0.7
Italy	0.6
Sweden	0.6
Japan	0.4
Netherlands	0.4

EXECUTIONS
(1984–1988)

> The death penalty has been abolished in every industrial country except the U.S. and Japan.

93

DEATH ROW
Inmates with capital sentences

2,124

10

38

| **Japan** | United States | | **Japan** | United States |

THE LAST ONE TO GO
Year of the most recent execution

Iceland	1830		Denmark	1950
Portugal	1849		Belgium	1950
Sweden	1910		Netherlands	1952
Finland	1944		Ireland	1954
Switzerland	1944		New Zealand	1957
Italy	1947		Canada	1962
Norway	1948		United Kingdom	1964
Germany	1949		Australia	1967
Luxembourg	1949		Spain	1975
Austria	1950		France	1977

The U.S. imprisons more people than any other country, surpassing even the most repressive police states. At 426 inmates per 100,000 residents, the U.S. is rivaled only by South Africa, at 333 prisoners per 100,000. Even in its totalitarian heyday, the Soviet Union jailed nearly 40 percent fewer of its citizens. Beyond the issue of expense—$16 billion annually, with the yearly cost per prisoner approximating the tuition for a year at a top private college—imprisonment breeds repeated imprisonment.

Prison reform has become the "Willie Horton Dilemma": Having terrified the electorate, as George Bush did in 1988, with tales of raping and rampaging prisoners on their liberal-politician-supported prison furloughs, politicians can hardly now tell voters, *Overall, we'll get a better result if we let everyone go.*

The most extreme and ineffective preventative of all, of course, is the death penalty. It too thrives not so much as a crime-prevention tool but as a piety and shibboleth.

297

The pursuit of happiness

The word *weekend* is understood in every language. Among America's contributions to the world, leisure time is nearly on a par with political freedom.

> "We are at a point in history where...the value of time is reaching parity with the value of money."
> —*John Robinson, director of the Use of Time Project, University of Maryland*

Yoka, the Japanese word for free time, means "time left," a kind of lesser order of time, not equal in value to time that is otherwise occupied.

> "What we are observing is the increasing leisure hours of people moving increasingly towards entertainment. What they are doing with their time is consuming entertainment— American entertainment—all over the industrialized world."
> —*Federal Reserve Board chairman Alan Greenspan*

Not only has the right to leisure time revolutionized the workplace and the notion of basic human needs, it has also spawned the world's biggest and fastest-growing industries: travel and entertainment. "The most important megatrend of the century is the availability of free time," says Gianni De Michelis, Italy's foreign minister. It is a revolution that has just begun. In the coming years, it will become a virtual currency in itself, with workers eagerly accepting lower pay and less responsibility in exchange for shorter hours. An increasing number of employee benefit plans are even allowing workers to "purchase" extra vacation time.

While the concept is American, the real talent has been European, with Americans asking, How do Europeans live so well? How do they manage to have so much free time? How do they all get such long vacations? Such early, and lucrative, retirements? The answers tend to involve words that make Americans shudder: *welfare, taxes, unions*.

Leisure, on the other hand, has been a nearly foreign concept in Japan. The only time a salaryman lets his hair down is for an occasional drink with office colleagues. To many Japanese, the very reason for their country's awesome economic success is that they have been willing to forgo leisure in favor of relentless toil—leading France's prime minister, Edith Cresson, to call the Japanese "economic animals."

But that is about to change. The mighty MITI has declared that the Japanese people must relax in the 1990s.

Free time

MAGAZINES, BOOKS, NEWSPAPERS, AND CEREAL BOXES
Hours per week spent reading

Netherlands	5.5
Finland	5.0
Japan	4.3
Switzerland	4.2
Norway	4.0
United States	3.7
Canada	3.5
France	3.4
Austria	2.7
United Kingdom	2.6

TOP BOOKWORMS: THE DUTCH

VEGGING OUT
Hours per week spent in front of the TV

Japan	24
United States	16
Netherlands	13
Canada	13
Austria	11
France	10
United Kingdom	10
Finland	9
Switzerland	9
Norway	7

Free time

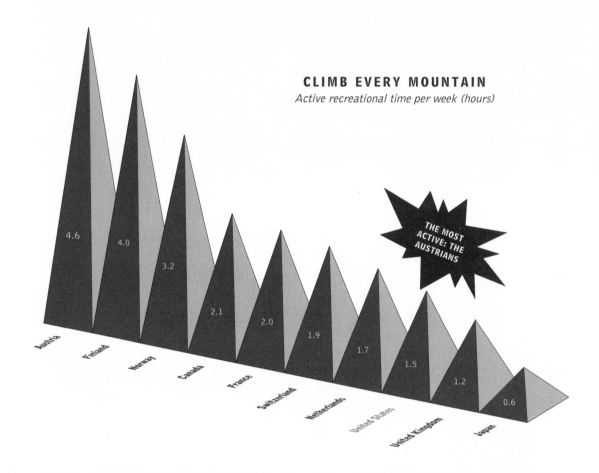

CLIMB EVERY MOUNTAIN
Active recreational time per week (hours)

THE MOST ACTIVE: THE AUSTRIANS

Austria 4.6
Finland 4.0
Norway 3.2
Canada 2.1
France 2.0
Switzerland 1.9
Netherlands 1.7
United States 1.5
United Kingdom 1.2
Japan 0.6

PARTY TIME
Hours spent socializing per week

Norway	13
Canada	11
Netherlands	10
Austria	9
Finland	9
France	8
United States	8
Switzerland	7
Japan	3

BUSY TIME
Hours spent on organizational tasks per week

Japan	2.0
Netherlands	1.6
United States	1.1
Finland	1.0
Norway	0.7
Canada	0.6
United Kingdom	0.5
Austria	0.4
France	0.2

Time off

WISH YOU WERE HERE

*Legal minimum number of vacation days
(average for U.S.)*

USA	10
JAP	10
CAN	10
GER	18
SWI	20
FIN	20
BEL	20
AUS	20
UK	22
SPA	22
NET	24
FRA	25
ITA	28
SWE	30
DEN	30
ÖST	30

The Japanese government would like people to work no more than 1,800 hours a year. But the Japanese now work 2,088 hours and aren't showing much interest in slowing down. In the U.S., the average work year is 1,957 hours; in France, 1,646 hours.

To promote leisure time, MITI has been adding new holidays to the Japanese work schedule. Says MITI director Tetuso Matsufuji: "I know Americans are very skeptical of our changing work habits. We have to convince our people to accept more leisure."

THE LONGEST WEEKEND

Public holidays

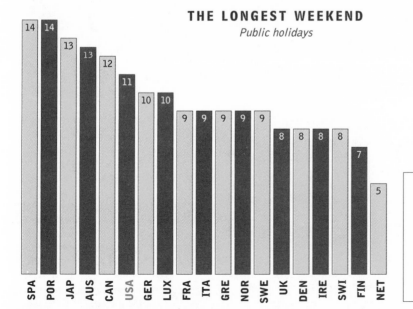

SPA	POR	JAP	AUS	CAN	USA	GER	LUX	FRA	ITA	GRE	NOR	SWE	UK	DEN	IRE	SWI	FIN	NET
14	14	13	13	12	11	10	10	9	9	9	9	9	8	8	8	8	7	5

Myth:
Wealth brings leisure.

Reality:
The wealthiest nations have the least amount of vacation time.

Travel

Travel, once almost the exclusive province of the ugly American, is now one of the main entitlements of the affluent everywhere, making it the world's largest and fastest-growing industry, with total expenditures expected to reach $200 billion by the end of the century.

Virtually all Europeans get at least four weeks of vacation a year, many get six, and eight is common for longtime employees. An average holiday abroad lasts three to five weeks.

Five million foreign tourists visited the U.S. in 1990. With the fall of the dollar, the world's expanding economies, cheaper airfares, and the ever-growing urge to travel, the United States Travel and Tourism Agency estimates that 100 million foreign tourists will visit the U.S. in the year 2000.

TRAVELERS' CHECKS
International travel spending ($ billions)

Germany	$23.1
United States	15.2
United Kingdom	13.9
Japan	10.2
France	5.8
Canada	5.4
Switzerland	4.3
Sweden	4.2
Netherlands	3.9
Italy	3.8
Austria	3.3
Belgium	2.9
Norway	2.4
Denmark	2.2
Spain	2.0
Australia	1.7

MAGIC KINGDOM
Annual visits per person to a theme park

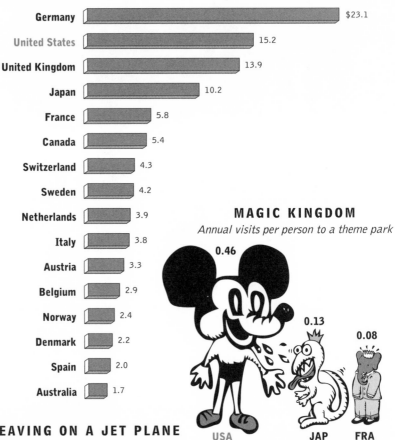

0.46 USA
0.13 JAP
0.08 FRA

LEAVING ON A JET PLANE
Total trips abroad in a year (thousands)

United States	6,912
Europe	5,650
Japan	3,295
United Kingdom	1,800
Germany	1,115
France	625
Italy	370
Switzerland	285
Netherlands	225

"I'M A-GOIN' HOME"
Average length of a trip abroad (days)

United Kingdom	27.9
Germany	26.6
France	25.7
Italy	25.0
United States	20.6

Sports

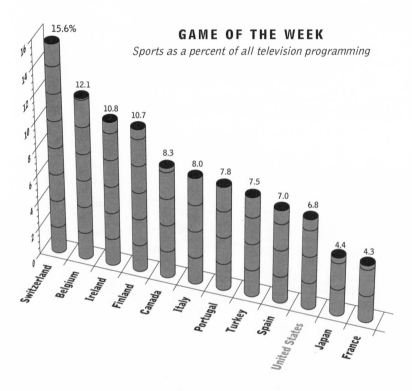

GAME OF THE WEEK
Sports as a percent of all television programming

- Switzerland 15.6%
- Belgium 12.1
- Ireland 10.8
- Finland 10.7
- Canada 8.3
- Italy 8.0
- Portugal 7.8
- Turkey 7.5
- Spain 7.0
- United States 6.8
- Japan 4.4
- France 4.3

Buoyed by cable and satellite television, athletic-wear marketers, and the global popularity of American culture, sports have joined the list of U.S. entertainment exports. Basketball, a generation ago an exclusively American pastime, is now among the world's biggest sports.

THE GOLD
Total Olympic winners

United States	795	Switzerland	64
Soviet Union	474	Netherlands	56
Germany	376	Canada	53
East Germany	203	Austria	46
United Kingdom	178	Belgium	36
France	168	Denmark	33
Sweden	167	New Zealand	25
Italy	162	Turkey	24
Finland	130	Greece	22
Norway	96	Ireland	5
Japan	88	Spain	5
Australia	73	Portugal	2

Myth:
American men are always stretched out on the couch watching the game.

Reality:
The Europeans are.

And the winner is...

WHERE-WE-STAND INDEX

(0=least habitable; 2,000=the most habitable)

New Zealand	Spain	Australia	Netherlands	Belgium	United States	France	Denmark	Canada	Luxembourg	United Kingdom	Germany	Portugal
713	920	923	1021	1042	1067	1082	1104	1111	1115	1124	1126	1174
22	21	20	19	18	17	16	15	14	13	12	11	10

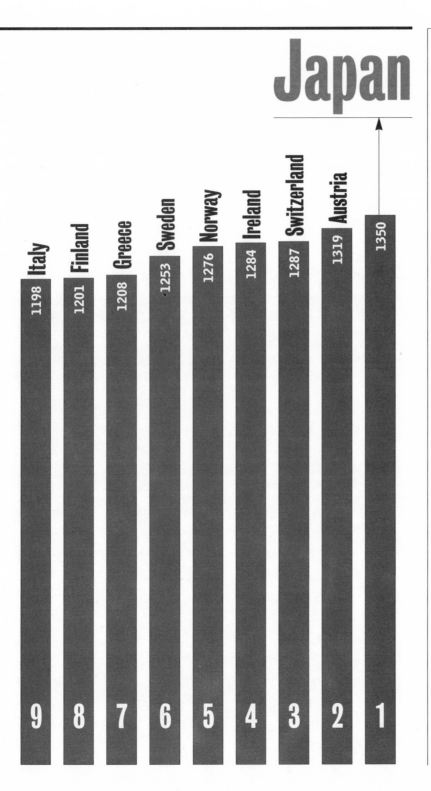

Japan

Its stellar environmental record and striking lack of crime put Japan on top of the list of the best place to live. Even with its densely populated areas, Japan has some of the industrial world's cleanest air and water and some of its safest streets. Ironically for the nation that makes the largest portion of the world's cars, Japan is the least auto-fixated culture. Eighteen times more people use public transportation in Japan than in the U.S. As for crime, it is the least violent of the industrial nations. Murder, rape, and assault, virtual commonplaces in the U.S., are wholly aberrant occurrences in Japan.

Appendices

Sources

The Wealthiest | CHAPTER 1: *Where has the affluent society gone?*

MEMBERS OF THE COUNTRY CLUB: *The New York Times; Statistical Abstract of the United States; Economic Outlook 1960–89* (Organization for Economic Cooperation and Development); *Statistics on the Member Countries* (OECD); *USA Today* **WHO GETS THE BIGGEST PAYCHECK?:** *Prices and Earnings Around the Globe* (Union Bank of Switzerland); *Statistical Abstract of the United States;* Eurostat; *Demographic Yearbook* (United Nations); Luxembourg Income Study data base; *The New York Times* **WHAT PRICE GLORY?:** *The Economist; Prices and Earnings Around the Globe* (UBS); *World Motor Vehicle Data* (Motor Vehicle Manufacturers Association); *Eurodata* (Reader's Digest Association); *International Marketing Data and Statistics* (Euromonitor); *The Wall Street Journal* **DO YOU OWN YOUR OWN HOME? (IS THAT THE REAL TEST?):** *Eurodata* (RDA); *International Marketing Data and Statistics* (Euromonitor); Arthur Andersen Real Estate Services Group; *Business Month* **WHO'S WORTH THE MOST?:** International Savings Bank Institute; *Economic Outlook: Historical Savings of the Member Countries 1960–88* (OECD) **WHO OWES THE MOST?:** *American Banker; Credit Card Management; The Wall Street Journal* **WHO PAYS THE MOST TAXES?:** *Revenue Statistics of the Member Countries 1965–90* (OECD); *National Tax Journal; Statistics on the Member Countries* (OECD); *The Tax/Benefit Position of Production Workers 1985–89* (OECD); *Government Finance Statistics Yearbook* (International Monetary Fund); *World Development Report* (International Bank for Reconstruction and Development); *Vital Speeches of the Day* **WHERE ARE THE FILTHY RICH?:** *Fortune; The Economist; Japan Economic Almanac; Automotive News; Civil Aviation 1989: Statistics of the World* **WHO'S BEEN LEFT BEHIND?:** *The State of Working America,* Lawrence Mishel and David M. Frankel, eds.; *World Development Report* (The World Bank)

The Wealthiest | CHAPTER 2: *The balance sheet*

THE BIG MACRO: *The European; Statistical Abstract of the United States; Economic Outlook* (OECD) **HEY, BIG SPENDER:** *International Financial Statistics Yearbook* (IMF); *Government Finance Statistics Yearbook* (IMF); *Economic Report of the President* (U.S. Departments of Commerce and the Treasury) **HOW BAD IS OUR DEBT, REALLY?:** *Government Finance Statistics* (IMF); *International Financial Statistics* (IMF); *Economic Outlook* (OECD); *Statistics on the Member Countries* (OECD) **A PRECARIOUS BALANCING ACT:** *International Financial Statistics Yearbook* (IMF); *The Wall Street Journal* **PANIC IN THE STREETS! INFLATION:** *Statistics on the Member Countries* (OECD); *The Economist* **BIG BUSINESS:** *Fortune; World Motor Vehicle Data* (MVMA); *Electronics in the World* (Electronic International Corporation); *World Press Review; Industry Week* **THE MARKET:** *Financial Times; Fortune* **CREDIT REPORT:** *Institutional Investor; The Economist*

The Smartest | CHAPTER 1: *The best schools*

CAN YOU BUY QUALITY?: *Digest of Education Statistics* **WHERE DOES IT ALL GO?:** *Education in OECD Countries 1990* (OECD); *Prices and Earnings Around the Globe* (UBS); *Fortune; The New York*

Times **WHAT ARE YOU GETTING?:** *Digest of Education Statistics; Education in OECD Countries* (OECD); *The Atlantic Monthly; World Education Encyclopedia,* George Thomas Kurian; *Statistical Yearbook* (UNESCO); *Education Week* **WHO STUDIES HARDEST?:** *Fortune; World Education Encyclopedia,* George Thomas Kurian; *Issues in Science Education: Science Competence in a Social and Ecological Context,* Torsten Husén and John P. Keeves, eds.; *The Atlantic Monthly; U.S. News and World Report* **WHAT THE TESTS SHOW:** *Digest of Education Statistics;* National Endowment for the Humanities **HOW MUCH IS ENOUGH?:** *Human Development Report* (United Nations Development Programme); *Education in OECD Countries* (OECD); **WHO'S BEEN LEFT BEHIND?:** *Through a Glass, Darkly,* Jean-Pierre Vélis (UNESCO); *Statistics on the Member Countries* (OECD)

The Smartest | CHAPTER 2: *Stepping into the knowledge society*

BRAINPOWER: *Statistical Yearbook* (UNESCO); Cambridge International Reference on Current Affairs **INVENTING THE NEW WORLD:** *Statistics on the Member Countries* (OECD); *The New York Times* **COMPUTERS:** *Computer Industry Almanac: International Statistics; Eurodata* (RDA); *Statistical Abstract of the United States;* Cray Research; *Business Week; Asian Business; PC Week; Harvard Business Review* **TELECOMMUNICATIONS:** *The Observer* (OECD); Japan Ministry of Finance; Japan Ministry of International Trade and Industry; *Eurodata* (RDA); *Fortune; Telephony; The National Telecommunications and Information Administration Infrastructure Report: Telecommunications in the Age of Information* (U.S. Department of Commerce); *The Wall Street Journal; Financial Times; International Telecommunications Statistics* (Siemens); *Executive Speeches*

The Smartest | CHAPTER 3: *Culture—high and low*

AUDIOVISUAL IMPERIALISM: *Newsweek; The New York Times; International Marketing Data and Statistics* (Euromonitor); *Eurodata* (RDA); *Statistical Yearbook* (UNESCO); *Business Week; Statistical Yearbook of the Netherlands; World Communications Report* (UNESCO); *Japan Statistical Yearbook; Fortune; European Marketing Data and Statistics* (Euromonitor); *The New York Times; Time* **THE WORD:** *Statistical Yearbook* (UNESCO); *Eurodata* (RDA); *European Marketing Data and Statistics* (Euromonitor); *Statistical Abstract of the United States; Statistics on the Member Countries* (OECD) **ARTS FOR ART'S SAKE:** *Japan Statistical Yearbook;* American Council for the Arts; *Statistics on the Member Countries* (OECD); *Statistical Abstract of the United States*

The Healthiest | CHAPTER 1: *What kills you?*

WHAT ARE YOUR CHANCES?: *Nature; The Economist; World Health Statistics Annual* (World Health Organization) **THE HEART OF THE MATTER:** *World Health Statistics Annual* (WHO); *World Health Statistics Quarterly* (WHO); Center for Demographic Studies; *The Economist* **THE GEOGRAPHY OF CANCER:** International Union Against Cancer; *Europe; Time* **AIDS TOLL:** *HIV/AIDS Surveillance* (U.S. Department of Health and Human Services); Federal Centre for AIDS, Canada; Infectious Disease Control Division, Japan; *Aids Surveillance in Europe* (European Centre for the Epidemiological Monitoring of Aids); Current Science Ltd. **FINAL EXIT:** *World Health Statistics Annual* (WHO); *Acta Psychiatricia Scandaneviza* **WHO'S WASTED?:** *Report on the World Social Situation* (UN Economic and Social Council); *World Health Statistics Quarterly* (WHO); *International Narcotics Control Board Annual* (UN); *The Economist; U.S. News and World Report* **WHO'S SMOKING:** *World Health Statistics Quarterly* (WHO); *American Journal of*

Public Health; *World Health Statistics Annual* (WHO) **WHO'S DRINKING?:** *British Journal of Addiction*; *Alcohol Related Problems in High Risk Groups* (WHO); *The Los Angeles Times*; *Journal of the American Medical Association*; *Economic Commission for Europe Annual* (UN); *Statistical Yearbook of the Netherlands*; *Statistical Abstract of the United States*; *United Kingdom Annual Abstract of Statistics* **WHAT'S COOKING?:** *Food and Agricultural Organization*; *Consumer Markets Abroad*; *Statistical Abstract of the United States*; *European Marketing Data and Statistics* (Euromonitor); *The New York Times*; *International Statistical Yearbook* (The Brewer's Society); *Public Health Implications of Alcohol Production and Trade* (WHO); *World Health Statistics Annual* (WHO); *International Herald Tribune*, *Consumer Markets Abroad* **KILLER SKYLINE:** *World Health Statistics Annual* (WHO); *World Health Statistics Quarterly*

The Healthiest | CHAPTER 2: *What health-care system works?*

RATING THE SYSTEMS: *Journal of the American Medical Association*; *Health Affairs*; *Health Care Systems in Transition* (OECD) **WHO LIVES?:** *World Health Statistics Annual* (WHO); *World Health Statistics Quarterly* (WHO); OECD; *Newsweek* **WHO DIES?:** *World Health Statistics Annual* (WHO); *The Wall Street Journal* **WHO WILL TAKE CARE OF YOU?:** *World Development Report* (World Bank); *Human Development Report* (UNDP); *World Health Statistics Annual* (WHO); *Mental Health Services in Europe* (WHO); *Statistical Abstract of the United States*; *Health Care Systems in Transition* (OECD); *Women in the World*, Joni Seager; *Euro Reports Studies* (WHO); *Comparative International Vital and Health Statistics Report* (U.S. Department of HHS); *International Marketing Data and Statistics* (Euromonitor); *The Economist*; *The New York Times*; *Nature*, *Vital Speeches of the Day* **HOW MUCH DOES YOUR CARE COST?:** *Health Care Systems in Transition* (OECD); *The New York Times*; *Financing and Delivering Health Care* (OECD); *U.S. News and World Report*; *The Economist*; *Business Insurance*, *Health Care Financing Review*, *The Wall Street Journal* **THE DRUGGIEST**: *International Narcotics Control Board Annual* (UN); *Psychoactive Drugs: Improving Prescribing Practices* (WHO); U.S. Senate Special Committee on Aging; *Human Development Report* (UNDP); *A Competitive Assessment of the U.S. Pharmaceutical Industry* (U.S. Department of Commerce) **THE CUTTING EDGE:** *Health Care Systems in Transition* (OECD); *Measuring Health Care 1960–83* (OECD); *No Circ Newsletter* (National Organization of Circumcision Information Resource Centers); *The Circumcision Decision*, Edward Wallerstein **SCREWUPS:** *Law, Medicine & Health Care*, *Dealing With Medical Malpractice*, Marilynn M. Rosenthal **AND WHO PAYS?:** *Social Security Programs Throughout the World* (U.S. Department of HHS); *Health Care Financing Review*, *Health Care Systems in Transition* (OECD)

The Busiest | CHAPTER 1: *Is labor working?*

MAKING IT!: *Industry Week*; *The Brookings Review*, *International Journal of Technology Management*; *The Machine That Changed The World*, James P. Womack, Daniel T. Jones, and Daniel Roos; *The Washington Post* **THE FAITHFUL AND DILIGENT:** *Statistics on the Member Countries* (OECD); U.S. Department of Labor; *European Economic Review*, *The World Competitiveness Report 1991* (The World Economic Forum and IMD) **THE SUITS:** *Statistics on the Member Countries* (OECD); *Journal of International Business Studies*; *The Service Industries Journal*; *Employment Outlook* (OECD); *The Making of Managers*, Charles Handy; *Agenda for Civil Justice Reform in America* (President's Council on Competitiveness); Hay Group; *Chief Executive*, *The State of Working America*, Lawrence Mishel and David M. Frankel, eds.; *Vital Speeches of the Day*; *The New York Times*; *U.S. News and World Report*, *Industry Week* **THE OLD BLUE COLLAR:** *Handbook of*

International Trade and Development Statistics (UN); *Labor Force Statistics* (OECD); *Historical Statistics* (OECD); *The Economist* **THE NEW BLUE COLLAR:** *Statistics on the Member Countries* (OECD); *Journal of International Business Studies; Financial Times* **AND WHO'S STILL DOWN ON THE FARM?:** *Statistics on the Member Countries* (OECD); *Labour Force Statistics 1969–89* (OECD) *Yearbook of Labour Statistics Retrospective Edition 1945–89* (International Labour Organisation); *Handbook of International Trade and Development Statistics* (UN); *The Wall Street Journal* **ON THE JOB OR ON THE DOLE:** *Statistics on the Member Countries* (OECD); *Yearbook of Labour Statistics* (ILO) **MALCONTENTS:** *Statistics on the Member Countries* (OECD); *European Economic Review;* Institut der Deutschen Wirtschaft

The Busiest | CHAPTER 2: *The universal office*

WHY THEY CALL IT "TRAVAIL": International Survey Research Corporation; **OFFICE TECH:** Xerox Corporation; *Yearbook of Advanced Technology* (Elsevier Advanced Technology); *Computer Industry Almanac* **OFFICE POLITICS:** *Observer* (OECD); U.S. Department of Labor; *Consumer Markets Abroad; Business Week; Quarterly Journal of Economics; Financial Times; The Economist*

The Freest | CHAPTER 1: *The political life*

BY THE PEOPLE: *The Economist; The Almanac of Transatlantic Politics,* Matthew Cossolotto; *The MTV/Yankelovich World Monitor* (Music Television); *Democracies: Patterns of Majoritarian and Consensus Government in Twenty-One Countries,* Arend Lijphart; *The World's Women 1970–1990* (UN); *World Political Almanac,* Chris Cook, ed.; *European Politics Reconsidered,* Guy B. Peters; *The New Yorker* **WHO'S IN CHARGE?:** *Western Europe 1989: A Political and Economic Survey* (Europa Publications); *European Politics Reconsidered,* Guy B. Peters; *Democracies: Patterns of Majoritarian and Consensus Government in Twenty-One Countries,* Arend Lijphart; Officials of the U.K., Italian, German, and Japanese embassies in the U.S.; White House Press Office; *Parliamentary Affairs; The New York Times; The Los Angeles Times; The Enigma of Japanese Power,* Karel van Wolferen **MONARCHS, DICTATORS, AND SCANDALS:** *Western Europe 1989: A Political and Economic Survey* (Europa); *World Political Almanac,* Chris Cook, ed.; *The Economist; Political Scandals and Causes Célèbres Since 1945: An International Reference Compendium* **HOW THE CENTER HOLDS:** *Democracies: Patterns of Majoritarian and Consensus Government in Twenty-One Countries,* Arend Lijphart; *World Encyclopedia of Political Systems and Parties,* George F. Delury, ed; *Revolutionary and Dissident Movements,* Henry W. Degenhardt, ed., *Political Parties of the World,* Alan J. Day, ed.; *Yearbook on International Communist Affairs 1990,* Richard F. Staar, ed.; *The Economist; The Social Context of Politics* **PARLIAMENT OF WHORES?:** *World Political Almanac,* Chris Cook, ed.; Officials of the U.K., Italian, German, and Japanese embassies in the U.S.; White House Press Office; *The Economist; The World's Women 1970–1990* (UN); *Yearbook of Australia; The Almanac of Transatlatic Politics,* Matthew Cossolotto; *Japan Statistical Yearbook; New Zealand Official Yearbook; Financial Times; Statistical Abstract of the United States; European Politics Reconsidered,* Guy B. Peters; *United States of Ambition,* Alan Ehrenhalt; *Scholastic Update; Washingtonian* **WHAT MAKES JOHNNY RUN?:** *The Economist; Financing the 1988 Election,* Herbert E. Alexander; *Parliamentary Affairs; Comparative Political Finance in the 1980s,* Herbert E. Alexander; *Advertising Age; The Europa World Book 1990; Yearbook Australia; The New York Times; The Economist; Time* **PERMANENT GOVERNMENT:** *Statistics on the Member Countries* (OECD); *Human Settlements* (UN); *Democracies: Patterns of Majoritarian and Consensus Government in*

Twenty-one Countries, Arend Lijphart **ORDER OR DISORDER:** *World Handbook of Political and Social Indicators,* Charles L. Taylor; *International Terrorism in the 1980s: A Chronology of Events,* Edward F. Micholus, Todd M. Sandler, and Jean M. Murdoch; *Insight; Newsweek; Time*

The Freest | CHAPTER 2: *Freedom's just another word*

RIGHTS: *The New York Times; Human Development Report* (UNDP) **RELIGION:** *The Economist World Atlas and Almanac; The World Almanac and Book of Facts,* Mark S. Hoffman, ed.; *Zionist World Handbook* (Jewish Information Center); *Statistical Abstract of the United States; World Christian Encyclopedia,* David Barrett; *The War Against the Jews 1933–1945,* Lucy S. Dawidowicz; *The MTV/Yankelovich World Monitor* (MTV); **ETHNICITY:** *The Economist World Atlas and Almanac; The World Almanac and Book of Facts,* Mark S. Hoffman, ed.; *Demographic Yearbook* (UN); *American Sociological Review, The New York Times; The New Yorker, The Economist* **SEXUAL EQUALITY:** United Nations; *Journal of Economic Literature; The World's Women 1970–1990* (UN); *Politics and Sexual Equality: The Comparative Position of Women in Western Democracies,* Pippa Norris; *Statistical Record of Women Worldwide,* Linda Schmittroth, ed.; *Women in the World,* Joni Seager; *The Economist*

The Freest | CHAPTER 3: *Defense—safe or sorry?*

WHAT HAS IT COST?: *The Rise and Fall of the Great Powers,* Paul Kennedy ; *Statistics of the Member Countries* (OECD); *World Military and Social Expenditures,* R. L. Sivard; *The Military Balance* (International Institute for Strategic Studies); *The Economist; Financial Times* **BODY COUNT:** *World Military and Social Expenditures,* R. L. Sivard; *The Military Balance* (IISS); *Western Europe 1989: A Political and Economic Survey* (Europa Publications); *The MTV/Yankelovich World Monitor* (MTV) **ENGAGEMENTS:** *The Military Balance* (IISS) **NUKES:** *The SIPRI Yearbook* (Stockholm International Public Research Institute); *The Military Balance* (IISS); **ARMS SALES:** *The SIPRI Yearbook* (SIPRI); *The Washington Post* **OTHER METHODS:** *Statistics on the Member Countries* (OECD); *Annual Report to the Congress* (National Advisory Council on International Monetary and Financial Policies)

The Best Lovers | CHAPTER 1: *Who lives with whom?*

BETWEEN MARRIAGE AND DIVORCE: *Monthly Labor Review, The World's Women 1970–1990* (UN); *Demographic Yearbook* (UN); *Report on the World Social Situation* (UN Economic and Social Council); *American Journal of Physical Anthropology; Psychologia; Asahi Journal; Public Interest* **GOING IT ALONE:** *Monthly Labor Review, The World's Women 1970–1990* (UN); *Demographic Yearbook* (UN); *Below-Replacement Fertility in Industrial Societies,* Kingsley Davis, Mikhail S. Bernstam, and Rita Ricardo-Campbell, eds.; *The Wall Street Journal;* **THE FAMILY:** *Demographic Yearbook* (UN); *The World's Women 1970–1990* (UN); *Monthly Labor Review, Report on the World Social Situation* (UN Economic and Social Council); *World Population at the Turn of the Century* (UN); *Culture Shift in Advanced Industrialized Countries,* Ronald Inglehart; *Statistical Abstract of the United States; Japan Statistical Yearbook; British Social Attitudes,* Rojer Jowell, Sharon Witherspoon, and Lindsay Brook (Social and Community Planning Research); The Alan Guttmacher Institute; *The State of Families,* Ray Marshall; *Public Interest; Newsweek; The Economist; U.S. News and World Report; The New York Times*

The Best Lovers | CHAPTER 2: *Sex: who does what to whom?*

PREFERENCES AND PROCLIVITIES: *Science, Time, The New York Times; Medical Sexology,* Romano Forleo and Willy Pasini, eds.; *Archives of Sexual Behavior, The Kinsey Institute New Report on Sex,* June M. Reinsisch; *Seksualiteit in Nederland,* Gertjan Van Zessen and Theo Sandfort, eds.; *Sex Education and Adolescence in Europe,* Mikolaj Kozakiewicz (International Planned Parenthood Federation); *Index of International Public Opinion; Masters and Johnson on Sex and Human Loving,* William H. Masters, Virginia E. Johnson, and Robert C. Kolodny; *Studies in Family Planning; Journal of the American Medical Association; The MTV/Yankelovich World Monitor* (MTV); *Sex and Morality in the U.S.,* Albert D. Klassen, Colin J.Williams, and Eugene E. Levitt; *Journal of Sex Research; Nature; Culture Shift in Advanced Industrialized Countries,* Ronald Inglehart; *Publishers Weekly; Playboy; Ms.* **SAFE SEX:** *Index of International Public Opinion; The MTV/Yankelovich World Monitor* (MTV); United Nations Populations Council; *What Counts: The Complete Harper's Index,* Charis Conn and Ilena Silverman; Family Health Institute; *The New York Times* **TEENS—WHO'S JUST SAYING NO:** *Adolescent Reproductive Behavior* (UN Department of International Economic and Social Affairs); *USA Today; Seksualiteit in Nederland,* Gertjan Van Zessen and Theo Sandfort, eds.; *Social Science Medicine; Pregnancy, Contraception and Family Planning Services in Industrialized Countries,* Elise F. Jones et al.(Alan Guttmacher Institute); *Sex Education and Adolescence in Europe,* Mikolaj Kozakiewicz (IPPF); *Sex and Morality in the U.S.,* Albert D. Klassen, Colin J. Williams, and Eugene E. Levitt; *Adolescent Reproductive Behavior* (UN Department of IESA); *Teenage Pregnancy in Industrialized Countries,* Elise F. Jones et al. (Alan Guttmacher Institute); *The MTV/Yankelovich World Monitor* (MTV); *Business Week*

The Best Lovers | CHAPTER 3: *The fetal position*

THE CONTRACEPTIVE SOCIETIES: Alan Guttmacher Institute; *The World's Women 1970–1990* (UN); *Pregnancy, Contraception and Family Planning Services in Industrialized Countries,* Elise F. Jones et al. (Alan Guttmacher Institute); *Levels and Trends of Contraceptive Use* (UN); *Comparative International Vital Health Statistics Report* (U.S. Department of Health and Human Services) **BIRTHING:** *The State of the World's Children* (United Nations Children's Fund); *Demographic Yearbook* (UN); U.S. Department of Commerce; *Made to Order: The Myth of Reproductive and Genetic Progress,* Patricia Spallone and Deborah Lynn Steinberg; *Journal of the American Medical Association; American Journal of Public Health; Having a Baby in Europe* (WHO); *Comparative International Vital Health Statistics Report* (U.S. Department of HHS); *Health Care Financing Review* (U.S. Department of HHS); *Health Care Systems in Transition* (OECD); *World Health Statistics Annual* (WHO); *World Development Report* (World Bank); *American Demographics; The Washington Post* **FLASHPOINT: ABORTION:** *Statistical Abstract of the United States; Monthly Bulletin of Statistics* (UN); *Statistical Yearbook* (UN); United Nations Population Council; *Family Planning Perspectives; International Handbook on Abortion,* Paul Sachdev, ed.; *World Health Statistics Annual* (WHO); *The Economist*

The Best Home | CHAPTER 1: *Clean space*

CITY LIFE: *World Development Report* (World Bank); *Human Development Report* (UNDP); *Urban Policies in Japan* (OECD); *Statistical Abstract of the United States;* Eurostat; *Norway Statistical Yearbook; Statistical Yearbook of Finland; Statistical Abstract of Sweden* **GETTING THERE:** *World Road*

Statistics (World Road Federation); *American Planning Association Journal*; *Prices and Earnings Around the Globe* (UBS); *The Economist; World Monitor* **THE COUNTRYSIDE:** *Statistics on the Member Countries* (OECD); *Environmental Data Compendium* (OECD); *World Resources* (World Resources Institute); *World Road Statistics* (WRF); *The New York Times Magazine* **ECO-CRISIS:** *Statistics on the Member Countries* (OECD); *Environmental Data Compendium* (OECD); *The New York Times State of the World* (Worldwatch Institute); *Business Week* ; *Facing America's Trash: What Next for Municipal Solid Waste* (U.S. Office of Technology Assessment); *The Economist;* **THE POLLUTION MACHINE:** *World Motor Vehicle Data* (MVMA); *Statistics on the Member Countries* (OECD); *Environmental Indicators* (OECD); *Environmenal Data Compendium* (OECD); *State of the Environment* (OECD); *Time* **WHAT'S BEING DONE?:** *Statistics on the Member Countries* (OECD); *State of the Environment* (OECD); *Statistical Abstract of the United States; International Marketing Data and Statistics* (Euromonitor); *European Community Annual; The Economist; State of the World* (Worldwatch Institute); *Time*

The Best Home | CHAPTER 2: *Safe streets*

POLICE BLOTTER: *The Wall Street Journal; Business Week; International Crime Statistics* (International Criminal Police Organization); *Statistical Abstract of the United States; Experiences of Crime Across the World*, Jan J.M. van Dijk, Pat Mayhew, and Martin Killias **CRIMINAL ELEMENT:** *International Crime Statistics* (Interpol); *The Economist; The New York Times; The Wall Street Journal; Business Week; Vital Speeches of the Day; The Chicago Tribune, Atlanta Constitution* **POLICE:** *World Encyclopedia of Police Forces and Penal Systems*, George Thomas Kurian; *Police Studies* **GUNS:** *Experiences of Crime Across the World* (Van Dijk);*The New York Times; The New York Times Magazine* **DRUGS:** *Human Development Report* (UNDP); *International Crime Statistics* (Interpol); International Narcotics Control Board; *MTV/Yankelovich World Monitor* (MTV); *The Economist; The Wall Street Journal* **PUNISHMENT:** *The Economist; Japan Statistical Yearbook; International Crime Statistics* (Interpol); *Report of the Secretary General* (UN Economic and Social Council); The Sentencing Project; *The Los Angeles Times; The Washington Post; Time*

The Best Home | CHAPTER 3: *The pursuit of happiness*

FREE TIME: *The Christian Science Monitor; The Economist; Time; Living Conditions in OECD Countries* (OECD); *The MTV/Yankelovich World Monitor* (MTV) **TIME OFF:** *Money; Consumer Markets Abroad* **TRAVEL:** *Travel and Leisure's World Travel Overview*, U.S. Departments of Transportation and Commerce; *Time; The Los Angeles Times; America;* World Tourism Organization; U.S. Travel and Tourism Administration **SPORTS:** *Japan Statistical Yearbook; Statistical Yearbook* (UNESCO); *The World Almanac and Book of Facts; The Complete Book of the Olympics*, David Wallechinsky; *Forbes; Business Week*

Glossary & abbreviations

AUS Australia

BEL Belgium

CAN Canada

CAP Common Agriculture Policy of the European Community, a system of subsidies and price supports.

CURRENT ACCOUNT BALANCE Trade measurement that adds "invisible" trade to the merchandise, or "visible" trade balance. Invisible trade includes payment and income in services, such as banking, tourism, insurance, and consulting; dividend and interest payments; development assistance provided by governments to the United Nations and similar international organizations; and remittances from working abroad.

DEN Denmark

EC European Community of nations. The twelve current members are Belgium, Denmark, France, Germany, Greece, Ireland, Italy, Luxembourg, the Netherlands, Portugal, Spain, and the United Kingdom.

EEA European Economic Area, a free-trade zone comprising the member countries of the European Community and the European Free Trade Association.

EFTA European Free Trade Association.

The members are Austria, Finland, Iceland, Norway, Sweden, and Switzerland.

E.GER Former East Germany

EUR OECD Europe

FIN Finland

FRA France

GDP Gross domestic product, the total value of goods and services produced by a country. **GDP PER CAPITA**, or the value of goods and services per person, is often called **STANDARD OF LIVING**.

GER Germany

GNP Gross national product, the total income of a country. GNP measures both domestic product and income earned overseas.

GRE Greece

GROUP OF SEVEN The seven democratic industrial nations with the largest economies: Canada, France, Germany, Italy, Japan, the United Kingdom, and the United States. Sometimes called the **G7** or the **MAJOR INDUSTRIAL NATIONS**, the seven attempt to coordinate their individual economic and political policies through regular contacts and an annual summit of the heads of government.

ICE Iceland

IEA International Association for the Assessment of Educational Achievement, which develops tests to compare student achievement among different countries.

IMF International Monetary Fund, a United Nations–associated agency that lends money and development assistance to developing countries.

INDEXES Scales that measure more than one piece of information. For example, the Drug Price Index examines average prices of several different drugs and adjusts for both currency fluctuations and cost-of-living differences, then assigns each country a score on a scale where 100 equals the lowest cost.

IRE Ireland

ITA Italy

JAP Japan

LUX Luxembourg

MEDIAN The middle figure in a group of numbers or values arranged according to size, either lowest to highest or vice versa.

MIPS Millions of instructions per second, a measurement of computer power.

MITI Japan's Ministry of International Trade and Industry. MITI plans national economic policies and selects potentional export industries for government assistance.

MTOE Millions of tons of oil equivalent, a measure of energy used to compare different types of fuel, specifically the amount of energy produced by burning 1 million tons of oil.

NET Netherlands

NIES Newly industrialized economies,

nations that generally have developed large manufacturing industries for exported goods but do not have standards of living equivalent to those of the developed world.

NOR Norway

NZL New Zealand

OECD Organization for Economic Cooperation and Development, a Paris-based organization comprising the democratic, industrialized, free-market nations with the highest standards of living. The membership includes the G7, the non-G7 members of the EC and EFTA, plus Australia, New Zealand, and Turkey. The former Yugoslavia held observer status with the OECD but was not a member.

OECD EUROPE The European members of the OECD

ÖST Austria

PER CAPITA Per person—used, for example, in the phrase *income per capita.*

POR Portugal

S.KOR South Korea

SPA Spain

SWE Sweden

SWI Switzerland

TUR Turkey

TWN Taiwan

UK United Kingdom

USA United States of America

USSR Former Union of Soviet Socialist Republics

WHO World Health Organization, a United Nations–associated agency that coordinates worldwide health programs.

Index

E

M

V